DATE DUE

NO 14 '01		
JY 17 '02		
AP 6 '04		
NO 18 '04		

DEMCO 38-296

THE
HOLY WAR IDEA
IN
WESTERN
AND
ISLAMIC TRADITIONS

JAMES TURNER JOHNSON

THE
HOLY WAR IDEA
IN
WESTERN
AND
ISLAMIC
TRADITIONS

The Pennsylvania State University Press
University Park, Pennsylvania

Library of Congress Cataloging-in-Publication Data

Johnson, James Turner.
    The holy war idea in western and Islamic traditions / James Turner
Johnson.

        p.   cm.
    Includes bibliographical references (p.   ) and index.
    ISBN 0-271-01632-9 (cloth : alk. paper)
    ISBN 0-271-01633-7 (pbk. : alk. paper)
    1. War—Religious aspects—Christianity.   2. War—Religious
aspects—Islam.   3. Jihad.   I. Title.
BT736.2.J64   1997
297'.7—dc20   96-25660
                                                                    CIP

It is the policy of The Pennsylvania State University Press to use acid-free paper for
the first printing of all clothbound books. Publications on uncoated stock satisfy the
minimum requirements of American National Standard for Information Sciences—
Permanence of Paper for Printed Library Materials, ANSI Z39.48-1992.

CONTENTS

PREFACE   vii

1. TWO CULTURES, TWO TRADITIONS: OPENING A DIALOGUE   1

2. THE IDEA OF HOLY WAR   29

3. HOLY WAR AND THE QUESTION OF JUSTIFICATION   47

4. AUTHORITY TO MAKE HOLY WAR   77

5. THE CONDUCT OF HOLY WAR   101

6. HOLY WAR AND THE PRACTICE OF STATECRAFT   129

   CONCLUSION   169

   NOTES   173

   WORKS CITED   177

   INDEX   183

PREFACE

No issue focuses the differences between the Christian West and Islam more deeply or with more relevance than the idea of holy war. For the West today, war for religion is a phenomenon that belongs properly to the past, to a time less advanced and less rational than our own. When we of the contemporary West think of holy war in connection with Islam, we are likely to identify it with religious fanaticism, with unremitting hostility to Western and pro-Western governments, and with acts of terrorism such as car-bombings, kidnapings, and assassinations.

By contrast, within the framework of Islam war for religion is associated with continuous striving in the path of faith by heart, tongue, and hands. The Arabic word for this striving is *jihad*. Indeed, holy war as such, or "striving by the sword," is the "lesser" jihad, and many Muslims, like many in the West, are troubled by the use of appeals to jihad to justify acts of terror and political violence. At the same time, the Islamic conception of war for religion reflects a deeply rooted understanding of religion as properly integral to the political order and its needs, a conception radically at odds with modern Western culture's separation of church and state and its institution of secular society as the norm for political life. The differences between these two cultures on war for religion thus point to a more fundamental difference in how religion is understood in relation to the political community, that community's norms, and the conduct of its affairs.

Building on the substantial base of earlier historical and thematic scholarship, I attempt in this book to compare how the two cultures have historically defined the interrelationship of religion, statecraft, and war. I try to show how these traditions have helped shape the cultures that have produced them.

While the weight of this study is primarily on the roots and historical development of the two cultural traditions, my intent throughout this inquiry is to shed light on attitudes, ideals, and behavior in the present, especially as they bear on real problems that affect relations between the West and Islam in the contemporary world. Even so, just as this is not centrally a book of history but of reflection on the meaning of history, its chief focus is not these contemporary problems or relationships in themselves but the deeper substrate of the normative traditions underlying and influencing them. In this inquiry I aim to engage the increasing number of people who recognize the important role that religion has played and continues to play in the political life of these two cultures. Among these potential readers are members of the policy community, academics and students in several fields, and portions of the general public—persons who have either themselves studied or debated over the role of religion relative to politics and the political community or who have followed these studies and debates as interested observers.

My purpose in this book is to facilitate a constructive dialogue between the two cultures on the nature of war for religion and the relation of religion to statecraft. I draw on my own and other earlier work on the Western cultural traditions of holy war and "just" war. For the religion and culture of Islam I have had to construct a parallel base of understanding from existing, more specialized, scholarship, examining Islamic tradition thematically and longitudinally to identify empirical and theoretical aspects of warfare for the faith.

To understand the historical and thematic shape of the Islamic tradition of jihad and to explore possible comparisons with the Western tradition of the just war, John Kelsay of Florida State University and I organized in 1988–89 a series of five seminars that brought a number of scholars of the religion and culture of Islam together with a like number of scholars knowledgeable in aspects of the "just war" tradition. The two books of essays that resulted from those seminars (Johnson and Kelsay 1990 and Kelsay and Johnson 1991) began the task of a systematic comparative understanding of these two traditions on war. We defined this project, in broad terms, by the major criteria of the just war *jus ad bellum* and *jus in bello*. We took care to introduce topics such as terrorism and the immunity of noncombatants to ensure a relevance to contemporary issues.

This book represents an effort to continue and extend the conversation between traditions begun in this earlier collaboration. Here I seek to delve more deeply into the particular subject of war in the name of religion, to understand the relevant Islamic normative tradition on its own terms, and to identify and explore commonalities and differences between Western and Islamic culture on this subject.

In my work on this topic I have benefited greatly from interaction with the participants in the seminars mentioned above, my students in the departments of religion and political science at Rutgers University, and the members of various audiences to which I have given presentations on aspects of subjects treated in this book over the last several years. These last include especially the Ethics Section of the American Academy of Religion and the project on War and Culture of the Rutgers Center for Historical Analysis.

My particular thanks go to John Kelsay, Bruce Lawrence, and William V. O'Brien, all of whom read the typescript in various stages and made valuable suggestions, which I have attempted to honor. I also greatly appreciate the advice and assistance of Peter Potter of Penn State Press, who shepherded this book through the review and publication process with great diligence and care.

My research for this study was carried out in the Alexander Library at Rutgers and the Firestone Library at Princeton. That research was completed and most of the first draft of the typescript written during a year of leave supported by a Fellowship for College Teachers from the National Endowment for the Humanities. Work on the book was finished during a further semester of academic leave funded by Rutgers University. I am deeply grateful for this support, without which this study would not have been possible.

1

Two Cultures,
Two Traditions:
Opening a Dialogue

Debating the Relevance of Religion
for the Conduct of Statecraft

Are religions and religious traditions relevant for the conduct of statecraft? The concept of the holy war brings this question into stark focus. In modern Western thought, as one of the legacies of the Enlightenment, the answer to this question has long been a definite no. Politics and religion belong to two distinct spheres, not to be mingled. Each sphere has its own separate and distinctive institutions. In politics, the principal institution is the state, defined ideally as a universal construct appropriate for all political communities regardless of their cultural context. Religion, however, has no principal institution, but rather expresses itself through various characteristic institutional forms shaped by local culture and historic background. Each sphere also has its own appropriate concerns. In politics, the interests of the political community predominate, while in religion, the focus is on the spiritual and ethical life of the individual.

Wars for religion confound this notion of separate spheres at its very core by mingling religion and politics. They deny the idea of the state as a universal institution that transcends local culture and history. Similarly, they deny the concept that the political interests of a particular community can be separated from its religious and other ideals. Thus from the standard Enlightenment perspective wars for religion are anachronisms and have no place in the modern world. There is, however, another possibility: perhaps the Enlightenment concept of distinct spheres is wrong.

Three current debates challenge this Enlightenment legacy on the relation of religion to the political. Each, in its own way, draws attention to the question of the importance of cultural norms and traditions for human communities and the prospects for relations among these communities. The first of these debates is over the adequacy of the political realist paradigm, a challenge newly invigorated after the end of the cold war by the increase in conflicts fueled by ethnic, religious, and other cultural differences. The second debate, largely focused by Samuel P. Huntington's idea of a coming clash of civilizations, is over the importance of civilizations or cultures relative to the makeup of the state and to international relations. The third debate, stemming particularly from the work of the philosopher Alasdair MacIntyre, asks whether ethical concepts are rooted in particular historical traditions (as MacIntyre argues) or in universal rational ideas (as the main lines of Enlightenment thought maintain).

These three debates have involved different but overlapping groups of participants, and different but overlapping approaches to the relationship between religion and politics. At the same time, they have in common a conviction that the established conventions of Western thought are inadequate for a comprehensive understanding of the political community and the nature of statecraft.

The Two Challenges to the Realist Paradigm

The challenge to political realism takes two forms. The first challenge to the realist paradigm is the argument that U.S. policymakers should take into account values and value traditions that are central to this country's nature and history. These values, this argument goes, should be factored into the calculation of what counts as U.S. interests.

In foreign policy those values most often mentioned are economic capitalism, democratic forms of government, and human rights, as well as conceptions of international order incorporating such values. Belonging to this last category are my own arguments in earlier work (e.g., Johnson 1981, 357–66; 1984) applying value concepts from the Western cultural tradition of just war to contemporary issues in U.S. military policy. In the domestic arena, liberals and conservatives differ sharply over the importance of values in the political sphere. Both sides agree that values are relevant for politics; however, they differ over which values to incorporate in policy.

Here I join those critics of the realist paradigm who argue that an understanding of religiously rooted values and concepts is essential to understanding politics. Rather than taking religion and politics as distinct spheres that should not be intermingled—as the realists do—I begin with the fact that in the idea and practice of holy war the two are inextricably intertwined. My focus, then, is on understanding this interrelation. How has the tradition of the holy war taken shape in the two cultures examined here? How has it influenced statecraft historically within these two cultures? How is it relevant for contemporary statecraft?

The second challenge to the realist paradigm is the accusation that U.S. analysts and policymakers have failed to recognize the simple fact that politics in some countries cannot be understood without reference to religion. This line of attack is stated sharply in a recent book with a provocative title: *Religion: The Missing Dimension in Statecraft* (Johnston and Sampson 1994). In that book Barry Rubin, in an essay sharply critical of U.S. analysis and policy toward countries in whose politics religion has been a significant factor, links the American separation of religion from politics to three errors deriving from realist thought: first, the definition of religion in the West "as a theological set of issues rather than as a profoundly political influence"; second, the expectation that the role of religion will "inevitably decline" as a result of the process of modernization; and third, a reading of Marx's characterization of religion as the "opiate of the masses" to mean that religion is "a distraction from the important things of life" (Johnston and Sampson 1994, 20–21). For Rubin these misconceptions all derive from the political realist paradigm dominant for the last half-century. He contends that this paradigm is inadequate and deceptive and leads to bad foreign policy (33).

Elsewhere in the same volume Edward Luttwak takes the assault on the idea that religion has no relevance to politics much deeper. Luttwak finds the roots of this idea in the Enlightenment's prejudice against religion as, in Voltaire's terms, "a worthless collection of orations and miracles" (Johnston and Sampson 1994, 9). This "Enlightenment prejudice" against religion, Luttwak continues, has led to a "widespread refusal to extend recognition to the entire religious dimension of politics and conflict" (9–10), with disastrous results in numerous recent and contemporary cases, including conflicts involving several Muslim societies (Iran, Lebanon, Sudan) and movements (the Intifadah).

Reality, indeed, has never been as rational as the Enlightenment would have it, and its notion of the marks of progress in human history is far from being accepted across all human cultures. Religion, rather than being a declining presence in history, has emerged as a vibrant element in many cultures and a focal influence on politics in a considerable number of them. Religious traditions, rather than withering into irrelevance, have in these cases been actively engaged as sources of normative wisdom. While individual states have remained the focal actors in the political sphere, broader groupings of states have coalesced around shared cultures, calling into question the idea of the state as an institution that inherently transcends cultures.

My argument intersects this form of the debate over realism in different ways for the two cultures I examine. I acknowledge the parallel between the realist paradigm rooted in the Enlightenment and the explicit rejection of holy war in the West throughout the modern period and focus here on the value concerns that led to this rejection and to the structuring of modern Western political thought around the separation of religion from politics. On the other hand, I take seriously the importance of an integral connection between religion and politics throughout Islamic tradition and the continuing relevance of concepts related to war for religion in that culture. For both cultural traditions my aim is to moderate the extreme elements in both approaches to understanding the relation of religion and politics in order to build a bridge across the divisions between them.

The Debate over the Importance of Civilizations for Politics

The approach taken in this book also intersects importantly with another recent debate, one principally focused by Samuel P. Huntington's *Foreign Affairs* article of 1993, "The Clash of Civilizations?" (Huntington 1993). Huntington argues that "a crucial, indeed a central, aspect of what global politics is likely to be in the coming years" is conflict engendered by differences between and among civilizations, in contrast to earlier historical stages in which conflicts were characteristically among princes (the century and a half following the Peace of Westphalia), nation states (beginning with the wars of the French Revolution), and ideologies (epitomized by the struggles among fascism, communism, and liberal democracy) (22–23). A civilization, for Huntington, is "the highest cultural grouping of people and the broadest level of cultural identity people have short of that which distinguishes humans from other species" (24). "Civilizations are differentiated from each other," he continues, "by history, language, culture, tradition and, most important, religion. The people of different civilizations have different views on the relations between God and man, the individual and the group, the citizen and the state, parents and children, husband and wife, as well as differing views of the relative importance of rights and responsibilities, liberty and authority, equality and hierarchy" (25). He concludes, "Differences do not necessarily mean conflict, and conflict does not necessarily mean violence. Over the centuries, however, differences among civilizations have generated the most prolonged and the most violent conflicts" (25).

In a response to Huntington's essay Albert L. Weeks noted that his analysis resurrects "an old controversy in the study of international affairs: the relationship between 'microcosmic' and 'macrocosmic' forces" or, in plainer language, the controversy between advocates of the idea of the nation state as the basic unit of world politics and advocates of the idea that what matters in world affairs is found at the level of the civilizations to which nation states belong. Among the partisans of the former position Weeks lists Hans Morgenthau, John H. Herz, and Raymond Aron; among those of the latter he lists Huntington with Oswald Spengler, Arnold Toynbee, Quincy Wright, and F. N. Parkinson (Weeks 1993, 24).

One may, of course, as I do, accept the fundamental perspective of this latter school of thought, that state behavior is influenced by the overall cultural frame ("civilization," in the term favored by Huntington and Weeks) without buying into the details of any particular statement of this point of view. In an earlier book (Johnson 1981, 41–44) I drew on Wright to argue for the importance of fundamental values present in a culture in defining effective restraints on the resort to war and the conduct of war, and to argue that in wars across major cultural boundaries one should expect such restraints generally to be much less effective. At the same time, I criticized Wright's distinction between a civilization's international and domestic uses of ethical, religious, or philosophical claims as overdone and misleading when applied to modern international law, a system of agreements, principles, and rules that is somewhere between a domestic system of laws and an ethical code. Values and claims rooted in one culture can, I contend, be translated into forms that transcend that culture to permit agreement and the making of common cause between cultures.

Similarly, I share with Huntington's critics certain reservations and disagreements over particulars of the analysis in "The Clash of Civilizations." (Huntington's essay and a number of immediate responses to it are collected in Huntington et al. 1993.) Yet at the same time, I agree with Huntington's contention that civilizations in fact matter, that history, religion, and other cultural factors are relevant within the politics of states (see Huntington 1993, 48). Indeed, one of my explicit purposes in writing this book was to do exactly what Huntington calls for in his final paragraph, where he argues that the implications of taking civilizational differences and potential conflicts seriously "require the West to develop a more profound understanding of the basic religious and philosophical assumptions underlying other civilizations and the ways in which people in those civilizations see their interests. It will require an effort to identify elements of commonality between Western and other civilizations" (49).

Thus by comparing Western and Islamic traditions on war for religion, I have engaged the debate launched by Huntington's essay at the level of the next step called for by Huntington: an effort to increase understanding across civilizational boundaries and identification of common elements across civilizations. Like Huntington, I here anticipate no universal civilization "for the relevant future," but rather "a world of different civilizations, each of which will have to learn to coexist with the others" (49).

The Communitarian-Liberal Dispute over the Basis of Ethics

While the debate launched by Huntington has had its primary effect within the policy community and among political scientists, political and cultural historians, and associated students and members of the general public, a related debate has engaged principally the academic fields of religious and philosophical ethics. This is the debate over the so-called communitarian understanding of ethics developed in the writings of Alasdair MacIntyre and others, as opposed to various "liberal" models of ethics, which in various ways trace back to the Enlightenment embrace of the concept of a non-culture-bound rationality as the source of all ethical value. This latter view has provided the norm for modern Western philosophical ethics and those versions of religious ethical reflection which aim to identify common ethical values and conceptions of right behavior across the world's religions.

MacIntyre argues, by contrast, that ethical conceptions are rooted in particular cultural experience over history. His position is consonant with forms of religious ethics that emphasize the particularity of a faith's own history and beliefs but at odds with conceptions of ethics as rooted in universal rational ideals abstracted from such traditions of history and beliefs. "Man without culture," he writes, "is a myth" (MacIntyre 1981,

151). Though his argument is focused on variant traditions within Western cultural history, it carries clear implications for the larger traditions defined by different cultures or, in Huntington's preferred term, civilizations. In *Whose Justice? Which Rationality?* a book exploring several contrasting ethical traditions, MacIntyre states the central issue this way: "What the Enlightenment for the most part made us blind to and what we now need to recover is . . . a conception of rational enquiry as embodied in a tradition, a conception according to which the standards of rational justification themselves emerge from and are part of a history in which they are vindicated" (MacIntyre 1988, 7).

Only a bit later he connects this general statement of perspective, which had been the focus of his earlier book, *After Virtue* (MacIntyre 1981), to the project of examining particular traditions: "It is critical that the concept of tradition-constituted and tradition-constitutive rational enquiry cannot be elucidated apart from its exemplifications" (MacIntyre 1988, 10). If MacIntyre is correct, and I believe he is, then the concept of war for religion, together with its penumbra of integrated value concepts and institutional structures in the West and in the Islamic world provides a fundamentally important exemplification of rational inquiry about the relation between religion and the political community, and in particular the conduct of statecraft in accord with normative cultural assumptions.

The debate MacIntyre has been central in launching and carrying forward is not only about how to conceive rational enquiry about ethics, but also about the implications of doing so. Does rooting such enquiry in traditions imply that there are no universals, no ways of carrying on conversations and finding commonalities across the borders of different traditions? If this a problem among the variant ethical traditions of the West, the cases on which MacIntyre focuses, then it is a far greater difficulty when the traditions concerned are those of different major cultures or civilizations. Such an argument is between two extreme forms of universal claim: the first being the Enlightenment belief in a common human rationality, nowhere fully expressed but in principle accessible to all humanity; the second being the perspective of particular value traditions which understand their own ethical norms to apply to all humanity and may read this claim to universal applicability as justifying hegemonic domination of other cultures.

Each type of claim has its own strengths and weaknesses. Enlightenment approaches seek to create a common discourse that rises above particular differences to a higher level of shared understanding. MacIntyre's criticism is that in serving this aim such discourses end up being about nothing in particular and thus do not serve well the connections to historical communities that are necessary for humanity. Discourse constituted by and constituting traditions, on the other hand, serves the particulars of human existence well but at the expense of tending toward a conception of the world as discretely compartmentalized, with only superficial communication possible across the borders between compartments—a conception similar to Huntington's description of competing civilizations, though with a good many more fault lines. In *Whose Justice? Which Rationality?* MacIntyre draws attention to the importance of the dissonances in how different communities understand ethics and highlights the potential for conflict this dissonance breeds. Yet he is convinced that conversation and mutual understanding is nonetheless possible across differing traditions.

> What . . . an individual has to learn is how to test dialectically the theses proposed to him or her by each competing tradition, while also drawing upon these same theses in order to test dialectically those convictions and responses which he or she has brought to the encounter. Such a person has to become involved in the conversation between traditions, learning to use the idiom of each in order to describe and evaluate the other or others by means of it. So each individual will be able to turn his or her own initial incoherences to argumentative advantage by requiring of each tradition that it supply an account of how these incoherences are best to be characterized, explained, and translated. (MacIntyre 1988, 398)

A "conversation between traditions" is what this book is about, and later in this chapter I have more to say about the particular problems of identifying and overcoming the dissonances between the two traditions I examine here. In the present context, though, it is important to reiterate the importance of the communitarian-liberal debate for the other two debates the present study intersects.

Most fundamentally, the debates over the adequacy of political realism and over the idea of the "clash of civilizations" instantiate and exemplify for statecraft and political analysis the argument advanced by MacIntyre between the perspectives of Enlightenment-based liberalism and of communitarianism or traditionalism. The modern conception of the state, as well as the conception that states exist properly to serve interests and not ideals (the former conceived as rationally objective and the latter as inherently particularist), are examples of ways of thinking that deny the importance of historical experience and tradition for defining political communities and influencing their behavior. On this question I stand with MacIntyre, Huntington, and the critics of the adequacy of the realist paradigm in holding that traditions matter, and that while conflict between traditions is to be expected, the most complete way to overcome such friction is to take traditions seriously enough to bring them into conversation with each other.

The theoretical analysis of the Western and Islamic traditions on war for religion I undertake in this book thus stands within a context of broad contemporary debate about the role of religion and religiously informed historical traditions in statecraft. This study has implications both for policy analysis and for policy formulation and action. It responds directly to the call to correct realism by taking seriously the role of religion and religiously based values in the politics of states, to Huntington's argument for the importance of civilizations in global politics and his call to identify "elements of commonality" between the West and other civilizations, and MacIntyre's statement of the importance of traditions of value for normative conceptions and his urging of a "conversation between traditions" as the way to reach agreements on values and behavior.

War for religion as an element in statecraft is a particularly important and useful focus for an inquiry intersecting and expressing these concerns.

War for Religion and Cultural Experience

The subject of war for religion is one on which the cultures of Islam and the West are deeply divided. While for common opinion in the West such warfare is a phenomenon belonging to less advanced stages of civilization, for many in the contemporary Islamic world the idea of warfare for religion represents a dynamic force for causes ranging from spiritual renewal to violent struggle in the name of Islam. The roots of this cultural divide run deep. The different contemporary perspectives of these cultures have been shaped by their different historical experiences and particularly by the influence of their respective normative traditions on religion, war, and statecraft. In the context of Western culture its normative tradition provides the fundamental understanding of war for religion and the conceptual language for placing it relative to religion itself, on the one hand, and the government of the political community, on the other. Within the context of Islamic culture its normative tradition defines the scope and nature of the religio-political community that is the ideal world of Islam. Each of these cultures tends to view the other in terms of its normative understanding of itself. The goal of this study is to understand these two traditions and develop a basis for conversation between them.

Approaching War for Religion in Western Cultural Context

I originally became interested in the problem of war for religion or holy war when writing *Ideology, Reason, and the Limitation of War* (Johnson 1975) two decades ago. In that book war for religion formed a moving focus for understanding the development of Western moral attitudes toward war from the medieval to the modern period. One focal concern was the relation between the ideas and practices of holy war and the broader tradition of just war as it developed from the Middle Ages up through the Catholic-Protestant wars of religion during the Reformation era. A second interest was the resounding rejection of the concept of holy war by Western culture in the aftermath of the Reformation. The issue of holy war lies near the core of the relation between church and state during a critical formative period in Western culture, while the idea of just war reveals a great deal not only about how the West thinks about itself but also about how it is able to view other cultures. Thus to begin the present comparative study it is useful to identify why early modern Western culture first accepted war for religion and then rejected it, exactly what was rejected, and the implications of this cultural decision for subsequent normative conceptions of the justification and conduct of war in Western tradition.

Perhaps the fundamental point is that the idea of holy war never enjoyed a secure place in Western moral doctrine on war and statecraft for a variety of reasons, of which three are the most important. First, the idea of holy war in Western culture had not one but several often competing substantive forms. Rationales for such warfare, and particularly conceptions of justification, authorization, and conduct, have accordingly been discontinuous and sometimes conflicting. Second, the relation of the Christian religion to the state has been ambivalent from the beginning, so that the idea of holy war is not at the core of Christian self-understanding but is rather an idea associated with particular historical periods and forms of religio-political relationships. And, third, the major normative tradition on war and statecraft in the West is not that of holy war but that of the just war, a broad cultural consensus shaped by temporal as well as religious influences. The idea of the holy war developed as an element within the broader and more continuous tradition of the just war, but always in some tension with the content and direction of the broader tradition. As the just war consensus coalesced more and more firmly over a period from the twelfth to the fourteenth centuries, the rationale for holy war—that is, for religious justification and authorization for war—diminished to an element within the normative rationale governing temporal warfare. As a part of this development, in the context of the close relations between church and state characteristic of medieval Christendom there remained a place for princes to undertake war for religious reasons, but there was no longer an understanding of holy war as "the just war of the Church." War for religion thus became a somewhat tainted concept, one which could equally well underwrite religious persecution using the powers of the temporal authorities or provide a religious cover for fundamentally political conflicts.

All these latent difficulties with the idea of war for religion in Western culture decisively came together and reached a critical stage in the sixteenth and seventeenth centuries, when this culture came face to face with two challenges. First, as the result of the discovery of the New World, it had to confront the problem of whether and how military force might be used in dealing with the non-Christian inhabitants of that world. A particular problem was whether military means might be used to support or coerce conversion, that is, whether war might be fought for the purpose of advancing Christian religion. Second, as a result of the Reformation, Europe had to face the same sort of question at home, with the result a century of internecine warfare in the name of religion. In both cases the final resolution was to reject the concept of war to propagate or enforce religious beliefs, but reaching this resolution was a long and bloody process both in Europe and abroad.

The Western rejection of holy war at the beginning of the modern period was, as a result of these historical experiences, not simply intellectual but also deeply emotional and political. First, against often impassioned arguments to the contrary, normative theological opinion coalesced around the idea that only defense of religion, not its propagation, could justify use of military force. "Difference of religion is not a cause of just war," wrote the magisterial just war theorist Franciscus de Victoria[1] in the middle of the sixteenth century (Victoria, *De Jure Belli*, sec. 10, in Victoria 1917). His immediate context was what the Spanish might rightly do in dealing with the pagan Native Americans, but the effect of his judgment was to reject the core justification for offensive war of religion in any context. Victoria went still further, establishing the pattern for other major theological just war theorists of his time, by limiting the justifying causes of war to those knowable through natural reason. By thus defining justified war in terms accessible in principle to all persons regardless of religion, Victoria removed the possibility of a separate category of religiously defined war, able to be invoked only by those of the true faith. (See further Johnson 1981, 96–98.) Removing the theological justification for offensive holy war was an essential first step.

Nonetheless, a full cultural rejection of war for religion had to await the experience of fratricidal religious warfare which followed on the Protestant Reformation. This experience gave birth to a second element in the Western cultural rejection of holy war, one not intellectual but emotional and psychological: a sense of revulsion at the brutality of war for religion. "Who will beleeve that your cause is just when your behaviours are so unjust?" a peasant challenges a soldier in a work from the 1580s protesting the ravages of the French wars of religion (La Noue, 1587). This sense of revulsion magnified as religious wars continued to rend Christendom, culminating in the horrors of the Thirty Years War, a bitterly fought conflict that devastated much of northern Europe.

A third theme in the rejection of war for religion was political: the inversion and redefinition of the relation between church and state; the character and rule of the state was no longer subject to right religion, rather, the character of right religion for a given domain was determined by the state. Under the old concept of the relation between church and state, the church claimed the right of judging and disciplining even the highest of temporal rulers for violations of the laws of the church. A well-known example is the papal excommunication of Henry VIII of England for violating church rules on divorce and remarriage: Henry was not a proper Christian, hence the Holy See declared him unfit to rule. In the religious wars following the Reformation Catholic denial of the right of Protestant princes to rule generated numerous excommunications and numerous demands that Catholic temporal authorities enforce such ecclesiastical judgments.

The new concept, that the church is subject to governance by the state, not only took away the religious pretense to supremacy over temporal affairs but granted temporal authorities supremacy in religious affairs. This change is exemplified by the formula "Cuius regio, eius religio" that ended the first series of wars for religion in Germany in 1555. This formula gave the prince of each of the affected German states the right to determine whether his territory would be Protestant or Catholic. Slow to spread and hotly fought over, this idea did not become universal in Europe until toward the end of the Thirty Years War almost a century later. In the short run, it fomented as much religiously inspired violence as it prevented. Over the long run, though, this development reduced religion from a supreme principle to only one element of the ongoing historical experience of each individual political community.

This change in the relative relationship of religion and the state made the protection of religion a matter internal to each state, not something to be fought for between states. The temporal cause of religion within each state was thus relativized alongside other concerns that were the responsibility of the state but subordinate to fundamental interests without which the state could not exist and function, such as the protection of the state's territory and its sovereignty relative to other states. Both in theory and in the practice of states the legitimate causes for war were redefined in terms of the state's natural and historical rights—in particular, the rights of sovereignty and territoriality. Defense of religion was still permitted, but only as a function of these core rights; offensive war for the sake of religion was consensually erased from the picture.

The normative concept of war in Western culture thus developed in correlation with the theological, psychological, and political rejection of war for religion early in the modern period. This normative concept provided an essential part of the modern concept of the state by assigning the right to make war to states and limiting the justifications of war to reasons of state. In the relations among states this normative concept of war underlay efforts to control the conduct of war by an increasingly specific body of moral and legal rules defining proper targets, specifying the proper treatment of combatants and noncombatants, and distinguishing legitimate from illegitimate means of war.

Grotius's *The Law of War and Peace (De Jure Belli ac Pacis)*, first published in 1625 and subsequently republished and translated many times over, is a landmark in the development of this new conception. Written during the Thirty Years War, this work embodied the growing rejection of war for religion and sought to define relations among states in both war and peace on a basis in nature and historical experience. While the fundamental normative understanding of war remained, for Grotius and for Western culture generally, in the form of the just war tradition, he shaped and focused this inherited tradition in new ways by his analysis, deemphasizing some elements and emphasizing others. Within the *jus ad bellum*, the inherited tradition on when it is just to make war, Grotius stressed the right of "defense of persons and property" (bk. 2, sec. 1) while denying claims to authority and justification of offensive war, naming specifically those claims advanced on behalf of the church and the Holy Roman Emperor (bk. 2, sec. 22).

While thus emphasizing the restrictedness of the *jus ad bellum* Grotius paid much attention (the whole of book 3) to the analysis of rules by which war should be fought, building on the *jus in bello* of the inherited tradition and developing it in detail. Grotius distanced these restrictions on the waging of war from the argument put forward by holy war apologists of the period that rights over others in war derive from religious belief. By contrast, his analysis traced some *in bello* restrictions to natural law and others to the common historical experience of nations in fighting war. Into this latter category he placed rules and customs based in the specific Christian heritage of European societies, developing these rules and customs as limits on the practices of war, not as the basis of a rationale for unlimited war against those of different religious beliefs.

The importance of this refocusing of the traditional just war categories is seen vividly from the perspective of later developments in Western normative conceptions of war, including the emergence of positive international law. After Grotius the authority to make war came to be specified as a *compétence de guerre* possessed only by sovereign states, a concept still effectively the core of the contemporary international order. In the twentieth century such agreements as the League of Nations Covenant, the Pact of Paris, and the United Nations Charter have restricted the right to make war to defense and sought to outlaw offensive warfare. (For discussion in the context of ideologically justified war see Johnson 1975, 259–74.) At the same time, much attention has been directed to achieving what Geoffrey Best (1980) has called "humanity in warfare," and Georg Schwarzenberger (1967, 197–99 and passim) describes as the requirements of "civilisation" in the practice of war through the development of moral doctrine, strategies and tactics of limited war, and especially, since the mid-nineteenth century, the creation of international treaties and conventions specifying the "laws of war" (cf. Roberts and Guelff 1989).[2]

This normative understanding of "civilized" war as it has taken shape in Western culture in the modern era explicitly seeks to rule out appeals to transcendent points of reference such as provided by religion for the justification and authority to fight; the rules for such warfare, moreover, define restraints that apply to all belligerents regardless of creed or any other dividing characteristic. The *jus in bello* restraints of international law apply even to belligerents fighting without proper *jus ad bellum*, as well as to their victims. Because this understanding of war is intentionally secular and universal, it leaves no room for arguments, claims, or behavior based in sectarian belief structures. Not only does this normative conception of war preclude war for religion, the fact that it is understood to express universal standards of "civilization" or "humanity" means that it has no place for different normative conceptions in which war for religion might be a possibility.[3]

The normative rejection of war for religion has been reinforced by the success of the secular state in modern Western society and the experience of the West in colonial rule of nonsecular societies. This colonial experience shaped a connection between the idea of the superiority of Western culture, the rejection of war for religion, and the concept of civilization itself. Any culture that practiced war for religion, on this view, was less civilized and hence inferior to the culture of the West. That religion was often the rallying-point for anticolonialist efforts simply underscored the Western scorn for religiously motivated warfare and for the religious leaders who often led the efforts in question. As a result of the fundamental cultural rejection of war for religion by the West early in the modern period, it has been especially difficult for Western culture to accept and make sense of the ongoing presence of the phenomenon of jihad as war for the faith in modern Muslim societies.

Approaching War for Religion in the Context of Islam

In distinct contrast with the West, and for deeply embedded reasons, war for religion has retained a meaningful place in Islamic religion and culture, where a different set of understandings about the justification for war, the proper authority for war, and the right conduct of war have developed. The cultural world of Islam experiences normative standards regarded in the West as objectively rational and universal but which contrast or conflict with those of Islam not as universal but as a hegemonic intrusion of Western culture. (For discussion in the context of international law see Mayer, in Kelsay and Johnson 1991, 195–226.) The deep difference between the two cultures in their normative conception of war for religion exemplifies the difficulty of finding common ground: while the West, rejecting holy war for theological, psychological, political, and later philosophical reasons, sees in jihad a threat to civilization itself, traditional Islamic culture finds in the Western concept of the secular state, the very political institution which makes holy war unthinkable, an offense to God's will for the right ordering of human community.

Various reasons exist for this cleavage, which is expressed through two competing sets of universal claims. Fundamental, and in sharp contrast with the relation between Western Christianity and the state, is the deep doctrinal and historical linkage between religion and politics found in Islam from the very first, that is, in the Qur'an and the practice of the Prophet Muhammad and the early Muslim community. Another reason is specifically historical: Islamic culture has not developed its own indigenous normative division between the secular and the sacred spheres and, indeed, has experienced such a division in practice mainly as a legacy of fragmentation and foreign domination. The result is that within normative Islamic tradition there is no theoretical place for the idea of a secular state, no place for a plurality of distinct states operating on a common functional level, and a tendency for individual empirical Muslim states to declare themselves the *true* Islamic state by contrast with all others. This tendency, well exemplified in the contemporary world by Iran, appeared very early in Islamic history and has been a recurrent theme in the self-definition of Muslim polities.

Tamara Sonn, linking the division of the religious and political spheres in Western culture to the historical experience of modernization, notes that for Islamic culture modernization has proceeded along a different course and according to a different schedule. "For Islam," she argues, "modernization began in the tenth and eleventh centuries C.E., when regional powers began to exercise virtually autonomous control over limited areas of the central caliphate's domain" (Sonn 1990, 131).[4] This was a process that might have produced a division between the religious and political spheres like that which developed in the West, with the religious unity of the world of Islam remaining centered in the caliph in Baghdad while political authority devolved to regional rulers. Yet within the self-understanding of Islamic culture the rise of regional powers did not produce that result. As Sonn observes, normative doctrine made no room for such a split between religious and political leadership; instead it continued to hold fast to the concept of a single Islamic religious and political community under a single ruler who had inherited the mantle of political and religious rule from the Prophet. The regional claims to independence were accordingly "tantamount to heresy" (131).

Decentralization and fragmentation of the 'Abbasid empire by indigenous forces nonetheless continued, Sonn observes (132), with the challenge to normative doctrine being further magnified and confused by the impact of a series of invasions of the core Islamic lands: that of the Seljuk Turks in the eleventh century, the Christian crusaders in the late eleventh and twelfth centuries, and the Mongols in the thirteenth. These were followed in turn by the creation of the Ottoman empire in the fifteenth and sixteenth centuries (leading to the assumption of the title of caliph by the sultan) and European conquest and colonial domination in the nineteenth and twentieth centuries. The result of this history is that the importance of the indigenous fragmentation of the unitary world of Islam has been overridden by the experience of invasion and domination, so that the problem such fragmentation poses for the doctrine of a single religio-political community of all Islam has come to be identified with the legacy of foreign domination. The reestablishment of a single Islamic community that is both religious and political in nature, thus making the world over in accord with normative Islamic doctrine, requires overcoming this legacy (132–33). On this view, the religion of Islam is not a threat to statecraft, as it tends to be seen from the perspective of the West; rather, it is the only way to an authentically Islamic statecraft free of foreign domination and able to reestablish the unity of the Muslim community.

Sonn's analysis and conclusion are aimed directly at providing a background from which to view the rise of contemporary Islamist movements—movements often as critical of the existing secular governments of traditionally Muslim states as of the West itself (see, for example, Jansen 1986). Her point is that while these movements make conscious use of historical normative tradition, they are nonetheless responses to modernity. A similar point is made by Sheila McDonough in commenting on the ethics of the Islamic fundamentalist theorist Abul Alla Mawdudi (McDonough 1984, 55–80).

Stressing the importance of the historical tradition, Emmanuel Sivan draws attention to the direct influence on contemporary Islamist movements of medieval Muslim theoreticians such as Ibn Tamiyya, who stressed the necessity of the connection between the religious and political within the normative Islamic community (Sivan 1985, ix–xi, 68–73, 90–107, and passim). The focus of Sivan's argument, like Sonn's, is on the rejection of secular societies and the embrace of a unified religious and political Islamic order as a central part of the contemporary quest for Islamic identity. Sonn calls this the "repoliticization" of the religion of Islam (Sonn 1990, 133); on the traditional normative view, though, Islam can never be truly *de*politicized; it is inherently political and religious at once, or it is not Islam.

Thus the actual relationship between religion and politics in the practice of statecraft within the historical experience of Islam is somewhat more diverse than what is allowed by the normative doctrine of the Sunni juristic schools. Adjustments *have* in fact historically been made, sometimes consciously and sometimes unconsciously, in understanding the force of this doctrine without the political communities in question considering themselves any the less Muslim or in any way distinct from the larger *dar al-islam*. But within the context of Sunni Islam no normative doctrine has emerged from this practical experience with enough force to replace that put together by the medieval jurists working in the context of the 'Abbasid caliphate at its height. And likewise within Shi'ism, which came into being as a rejection of the Sunni caliphate, the concept of the community of Islam as a single religio-political entity also remains robustly alive and well, though differently constituted from that defined by Sunni tradition.

Thus contemporary Muslims, whether Islamists or not, whether radicals or not, whether anti-Western or not, still must seek to come to terms with this conception of the ideal Muslim community as a single entity in which religious and political concerns are blended. In the context of Islamic culture this stands as the norm, just as in the context of Western culture during the modern era the norm has been independent states in which the religious and the political are distinguished and separated. Both are responses to the experience of modernity, but they are fundamentally different sorts of responses, with little appreciation of the other from either side. The attitude toward war in the name of religion concentrates and symbolizes this deep difference. Whereas Western culture's rejection of the idea of warfare for religion represents an effort to move beyond the destructive effects that may follow from religious difference when religion is mingled with statecraft, for Islamic culture the call to jihad represents a call to transcend differences and conflict in submission to the only true God. While for the West war for religion is divisive and terrible, for Islam jihad as war for religion is not divisive but unifying, and what is terrible is the world of strife jihad seeks to bring to an end.

Conflict or Dialogue Between Cultures?

As noted earlier, much debate has been occasioned by Samuel P. Huntington's vision of the future as likely to be characterized by a pattern of conflict fed by cultural or civilizational differences (Huntington et al. 1993). With particular reference to the relation between the cultures of the West and Islam, that a "clash of civilizations" is already under way is also the view of the respected scholar of Islam Bernard Lewis (cited in Huntington 1993, 32; cf. 30–33). Whatever the result of this particular debate, conflict over such differences is not new or simply a prospect for the future. In the relation between the cultures of the West and Islam their fundamental difference of perspective on the relation of religion, war, and statecraft has often come to a head within the framework of colonialism.

The colonial Western powers in the Muslim world in the nineteenth and early twentieth centuries experienced the call to jihad as the rallying cry of revolutionary movements against their rule—movements such as that of the self-proclaimed Mahdi, Muhammad Akhmad, against the British in Sudan in the mid-nineteenth century and that of the Moroccan tribal leaders against the French in the first two decades of the twentieth. In this context defeating the jihad was, from the Western perspective, not only part of maintaining colonial overlordship but an obligation of seeking to ensure the progress of civilization. In the contemporary period jihad has also been the war cry of revolutionary movements in the Arab world, movements whose methods have often been those of terrorism directed at the West. If the Western perception of jihad in the colonial period was of a struggle aimed at turning back the tide of civilization, the contemporary perception for practical purposes tends to reduce it to terrorism—uses of violence whose forms and targets make it deeply repugnant to Western sensibilities. As a result, between Western and Islamic culture there is possibly no other single issue at the same time as divisive or as poorly understood as that of jihad.

Yet an understanding of Islamic religion and culture reveals that this colonial and contemporary Western conception of jihad is not all there is to the idea of jihad in Islam, and the idea of jihad is not all Islamic tradition has to say about war. The concept of jihad, rooted in the very earliest stages of Islamic history, fundamentally denotes striving or effort expended by the individual Muslim to walk in the path of God. The jihad of the sword, the "lesser" form of striving according to one tradition associated with the Prophet Muhammad, is but one form alongside other, greater ones: the jihad of the heart (moral reformation), that of the tongue (proclaiming God's word abroad), and that of the hand (works in accord with the will of God). Where the idea of jihad centrally refers to war in classical Islamic tradition is in the statecraft of the Muslim community as it deals with the disorder and strife imposed by unbelief in the world. This jihad may be directed within the community at other Muslims (in special cases such as apostasy, heresy, or rebellion) or outside the community at non-Muslim political communities that pose a threat to Islam. Further, not all wars of the Muslim community are properly jihad, since they may lack religiously defined purpose or authorization.

Recent Western scholarship has probed the idea of jihad and its role in statecraft in the early stages of the Islamic community (e.g., Blankinship 1994; Ali 1977), in the critical period of the formation of normative juristic doctrine (e.g., Khadduri 1966; Sachedina 1988), from this foundational period through the Muslim response to the Crusades (e.g., Noth 1966), and (in the form of *ghaza*) in the rise of the Ottoman empire (e.g., Inalcik, in Holt, Lambton, and Lewis 1970, vol. 1). Other works have examined jihad in the context of nineteenth- and twentieth-century colonial wars (e.g., Peters 1979; Porch 1983) and contemporary Middle Eastern political and military conflicts (e.g., Sivan 1985; Wright 1985). Scholars of Islam have as yet provided no longitudinal study of the development of the idea of jihad and its role in statecraft in Islamic societies. Comparative study of possible thematic points of contact between the Islamic and Western cultural traditions on war have also been slow to develop. To establish a meaningful conversation between these traditions depends, however, on the continued pursuit of both kinds of inquiry.

At the same time, Western scholarship must examine anew its own historical experience and normative traditions on the relation of religion to statecraft and to warfare. The resolution reached in the modern period, that religion must be separated from politics and that it has no place in authorizing or justifying war, needs to be placed in its own historical and intellectual setting. Doing so is necessary to make possible a conversation with Islamic tradition on religion, statecraft, and war; it also is a fundamental contribution to such a conversation.

The idea of conversation, though, implies more than two separate inquiries; there must be interconnection and interaction between the inquiries. Comparison implies commonality; yet between Islamic and Western culture there are great asymmetries. What problems must be dealt with in carrying on this comparative conversation?

Problems of Comparison and Asymmetry

There is a fundamental difficulty in doing comparative study across major cultural lines. For the case of the two traditions examined in this book the first problem is to settle the matter of comparative sets. That is, just what are the two elements to be compared? In the previous section and throughout this book I distinguish "the West" and "Western culture" from "the world of Islam" and "Islamic culture." This is a terminology that is widely used and,

I think, the best general set of comparative terms when the aim is to think of the two cultures as a whole. Nonetheless, some Muslims and non-Muslim scholars of Islam would object that properly speaking Islam is part of the West. They are certainly right in many respects, but there are important differences between the two cultures, and other Muslims and non-Muslim scholars of Islam are satisfied with terminology that acknowledges these differences.

The available terms for comparison between these two cultures have somewhat variant meanings and valences in different contexts. For example, Islam is clearly a "Western" religion (or, as Muslims would put it, one of the "Abrahamic" religious traditions, alongside Judaism and Christianity) as compared with "Eastern" traditions such as Buddhism, Hinduism, Taoism, and Shinto. But making this kind of distinction is not the purpose of this book. Rather, this study focuses on the difference, not the similarity, between the cultural attitudes of the religion and culture of Islam and those of the West on the role of religion in relation to war.

Nor is this comparison limited only to the scope of the religions of Western Christianity (or Judaeo-Christianity) and Islam; rather, it examines religion and other elements of the two cultures as parts of a larger whole. The overall purpose, in this context, of examining religious ideas and issues is to place them in their relation to statecraft as conceived and practiced within the two cultures. So the set of terms "Christian-Islamic" or "Christian-Muslim" would be deeply inappropriate. While the comparative terminology I have chosen is not without its problems, it is the best available set of terms for the present project, and it is a comparative set that is widely in use and easily understood.[5]

A serious problem in comparative study of the relation of Western culture to Islam is posed by the legacy of Orientalism, which studied Islamic religion and culture comparatively with the result of representing it as inferior to the religion and culture of the West. Because of this legacy any comparative study at all is, for many Muslims and many contemporary non-Muslim students of Islam, inherently suspect. While sensitive to the problem this poses, I do not accept that this historical legacy voids all the possible benefits of comparative study. Indeed, comparative work is needed to overcome this inherited suspicion. If understanding and communication are to exist, then there must be elements of contact put into place through this sort of work. At the same time, the whole point of the effort would be lost unless both cultural traditions are taken equally seriously on their own terms and treated as equal subjects of critique and analysis. If the aim cannot be to degrade

Islamic culture and whitewash that of the West—criticisms often made of the Orientalists—neither can it be the opposite.

A further sort of difficulty is methodological. The whole purpose of a comparative dialogue requires identifying similar items and issues and bringing them into contact across cultural dividing lines. But how to do this evenhandedly and accurately? Unless one makes use of the categories familiar from one's own context, it is hard to comprehend what one is examining in the other culture. At the same time, use of one's own cultural categories may truncate, distort, or otherwise misrepresent the other culture. Nor is it possible to get around this problem by choosing the categories of that other culture, for this introduces the same questions in reverse. I have sought to minimize this difficulty, though I have not succeeded in erasing it fully, by organizing the comparison in terms of three focal concerns found in both traditions: warrant or justification, authority, and proper conduct of war in the name of religion. While these terms correspond to major just war categories, they also correspond to important themes in the treatment of war for the faith in Islamic tradition.

At the same time, it must be admitted that there are real theoretical advantages to beginning cross-cultural comparative study of traditions on war from the perspective of the just war categories, as was done in the collaborative studies mentioned earlier. This tradition is well understood in terms of its origins and development; it is widely spread through a range of subtraditions in Western culture; it is the focus of much recent and contemporary analysis of morality and war in the United States and Europe; and it incorporates values and attitudes derived from the core values and structures of Western culture as a whole. Scholarship on Islamic normative tradition on war is considerably less well developed. Thus while this present book is not an exercise in cross-cultural study through a just-war lens, there is value for the purposes of comparative study in making use of the full range of what is known about the nature and development of just war tradition in its relation to the practice of war and to statecraft.

A further methodological problem rises from the differences in the natures of the normative traditions of these two cultures. For the West, that tradition is quite eclectically based and conceived, with contributions from Christian canon law and theology but also from secular law, philosophy, the norms and customs of military culture, and the practical experience of statecraft and of war (see Johnson 1975, 25). For Islam what is understood to be normative is much narrower: in order of priority it is the Qur'an, the traditions associated with the Prophet Muhammad, and the interpretations of these sources laid down by the classical jurists who wrote on religion, statecraft, and war within the sphere of Islam. There has, of course, been a wealth of cultural experience that evinces transition and change in understanding and applying the meaning of this tradition. For a time in the Middle Ages, also, philosophical analysis and interpretation attempted to set out an understanding of war and Islamic statecraft at once more universal and more the product of rational reflection than the juristic model. Yet neither of these alternative cultural approaches to the problem of religion, war, and statecraft has shaken or changed the fundamental understanding of what is normative. For this reason the classical juristic texts and their use of the more primary texts, the *Hadith* of the Prophet and the Qur'an itself, remain at the center of the analysis. The comparison might be engaged more closely if it were framed as the normative tradition of the West versus what Muslims have done with the normative tradition of Islam, and accordingly in Chapter 6 I examine examples of the latter from the periods of the Crusades and the early Ottoman state. Yet a full account of this latter history remains to be written, and in any case it is truer to the core of the two cultures to admit the difference in the conception of normative tradition between them and to carry forward the comparison on this basis.

Besides the problems of comparative sets and of method, other sorts of difficulties are rooted in asymmetries between the traditions or in scholarship on them. Some of these kinds of difficulties have already been mentioned in other connections. Three deserve a closer look.

First, there is a considerable disproportion between what is known about the development of Islamic tradition on jihad as war for religion and as an element of statecraft and what is known about the relevant traditions in Western religion and culture, as well as in how these two cultural traditions are known. Unlike the case with the just war, pacifist, and international law traditions of the West, there exist no general histories treating the understanding of normative tradition on religion, statecraft, and war in Islamic societies or in Islamic religious thought. Many significant subjects remain unexplored for lack of researchers with the necessary training and language skills. Moreover, because of the high degree of specialization among scholars of Islamic religion or the history of Islamic societies, contemporary scholarly research (as noted in the previous section) tends to be highly targeted on particular periods, movements, or even individuals rather than being comprehensive and synthetic. Finally, there is in contemporary scholarship a dearth of efforts to explore the implications of historical antecedents in Muslim societies that might provide a deeper basis for normative reflection on the implications for statecraft of the classical doctrine on religion, the state, and war. By contrast, a substantial body of literature has been generated over the last thirty years analyzing the just war tradition in the West and variously applying it in debate over contemporary issues.

Second, the relation between the religious and the nonreligious is different in the two cultures, and their moral traditions relating to political life reflect this difference. In the West, secular political society ("civil society," in the classic term) began to develop autonomy relative to religion as early as the fourteenth century. That autonomy became a fact in the seventeenth century and has remained so ever since. Modern Western political theory presumes this autonomy. Scholars of Western traditions can speak easily about "religion versus culture" or about "the religious and the secular" and similar concepts. This does not mean, however, that these terms refer to separate realities with no interconnections. Rather, in the development of Western moral tradition relating to war, peace, and statecraft there are clearly definable elements that have come from religion and others that have come from nonreligious sources; each has influenced the other in various ways at various times, and the tradition as a whole has been carried and developed now by one, now by the other. Being able to distinguish the separate sorts of influence enriches analysis and understanding of the whole.

In Islamic societies, by contrast, there has been no comparable indigenous theoretical establishment of a separate space for the secular. Indeed, normative classical juristic doctrine moves in just the opposite direction, defining the Muslim community in terms of a unity between the religious and the temporal. In this definition the jurists made copious use of the religious centrality of the Qur'an, understood as direct and final divine revelation, and the traditions associated with the Prophet to establish the claim that the only proper state for Islam is a unified religio-temporal community, the *dar al-islam*. The autonomous, nontheocratic state, as it exists in the Islamic world today, is both in terms of its immediate history and in its perception by many contemporary Muslims a legacy of Western colonialism and the cold war. Critics assert that it lacks religious warrant, and, in some cases, this claim fuels fundamentalist or traditionalist efforts to overthrow the governments of such states. At the same time, though, other states founded on a secular basis are stable and successful. The claimed lack of religious warrant for autonomous, nontheocratic states also does not take into account the actual history of Muslim states in the past, which themselves would not have measured up to the standards of religious warrant imposed by contemporary fundamentalists and traditionalists.

A third asymmetry concerns the judgment on war in itself within the two traditions. In Western culture the concept of war for religion is but one theme in Christian judgment on war, and its role in Christian tradition overall has not been central but peripheral. A strong pacifist element in Christianity, reaching back to the very first, rejects war as such as contradictory to the message of Jesus. The idea of war for religion, in its development from the fourth century up to the beginning of the modern era, did not emerge historically as a distinct concept but rather formed one element in a broader tradition on just war. Within this broader tradition ideas of religious authority and justification developed in tension with definitions of authority and justification emphasizing the temporal, and the latter has played the dominant role. In the modern period, as noted above, war for religion has been rejected both by normative Christian doctrine and by Western culture as a whole.

In Islam, by contrast, there is no normative tradition of pacifism, and fighting has had a place in the defense and spread of Islam from the time of the Prophet himself. The concept of jihad, the striving in the path of God required of all Muslims, includes striving "by the sword." This concept was given formal definition in the normative juristic tradition in terms of war justified for simultaneously religious and political purposes and authorized by the power of supreme religious and political authority located in a single figure, the rightful head of the Muslim community. This concept, linking religious and political justifications and authority for war, continues to have normative force in contemporary Islam.

The Substantive Questions

The following chapters deal with five substantive questions. First, there is the problem of the exact nature of the subject of this inquiry: what is holy war, and how has it taken shape in the two traditions being examined here? The term "holy war" itself is problematical, since it is relatively late in Western usage and since it does not directly translate any of the regularly used Muslim terms, including the central term "jihad." These defects, however, in fact constitute an advantage: problematical from various specific angles, "holy war" turns out to be useful as a general, if not entirely neutral, term for the broad subject of this study. Other terms—war for the faith, religious war, war for God, war of God, war of religion, jihad of the sword, *qital* against unbelievers, crusade, *ghaza*, war of the church, war of Yahweh—all carry their own nuances, and some of them are limited to very particular applications. Sorting out some of the major differences and trying to identify elements in common in major conceptions of holy war is the task addressed in Chapter 2.

Second, there is the question of what constitutes a warrant or justification for holy war in the two traditions. This is the subject of Chapter 3. Once the possible meanings of holy war have been sorted out and the irrelevant ones put aside, it turns out that the two traditions examined here have well developed and quite specific conceptions of what justifies holy war or provides a warrant for waging such war. In both cases these warrants establish holy war as an activity of the community and by doing so reveal a great deal about the character of that community and the requirements of membership in it. Yet there is also some latitude in these conceptions of warrant, and this means that the judgment of a duly designated authority is necessary to identify when such a warrant exists and what the fact of its existence implies.

The third substantive question is that of the requisite authority for holy war. This is essentially, again, a question of the community—in this case, the nature of the leadership of the community that wages holy war. Either the leadership defines the community, or the community defines the nature of its leader, or some mixture of the two. Since both traditions define a role for the individual of faith to take up arms in defense of that faith, the question of authority for holy war includes that of the relation of individual members of the community to the governing authorities and thus gets to the central issue of how the community in question is defined within the two traditions. This question of authority for holy war also raises another central question about the community: what is the relation between temporal and spiritual authority there? The theoretical answer defines much of the difference between the two traditions in their conceptions of right politics; the empirical answer reveals that the two cultures are a good deal closer than the theoretical difference suggests. Chapter 4 focuses on the question of proper authority in the two traditions.

The fourth substantive question, the subject of Chapter 5, is what implication the idea of war for religion has for the conduct of war. Contrary to the contemporary association between holy war and terrorism, the fact that a given conflict falls into the category of holy war or war for religion bears implications both for the character of the combatants and for what they may do to those whom they are fighting. These constitute definite limits on what a holy warrior may do in the conduct of the war. While the Western and Islamic traditions differ on certain concepts of limitation, they converge on others. Discovering the points of convergence and divergence is substantively important for understanding the two traditions and the possibility for dialogue.

Finally, the fifth substantive question is how these issues have been played out over history through the actual practice of statecraft. This question is addressed in Chapter 6. Since I have already looked at this at considerable length for Western tradition (Johnson 1975), and since in any case the matter is of only historical interest there but still lives in the world of Islam, the last chapter of this study focuses on the question of the relation of holy war to the theory and practice of statecraft in the core Islamic lands and in the early Ottoman state. What is discovered is of interest for understanding the legitimacy and illegitimacy of jihad in the contemporary context, as well as for understanding some of the positive potential for secular Muslim states in the contemporary world.

2

THE IDEA
OF HOLY WAR

Passions and Misconceptions

Holy War. The term has the power to fire the blood, to cause passions to surge, to pump new life into otherwise dormant causes; conversely, the foreboding instilled by a threat of holy war can make the blood run cold and render the prudent timid. Almost forgotten for generations in Western countries by all but students of history, the concept of such warfare resurfaced as a reality of the contemporary world in the Hindu-Muslim conflicts that led to the birth of modern India and Pakistan and the war that attended the birth of the State of Israel soon after the end of World War II. In these two conflicts the term "holy war" translated into English the Arabic word *jihad*, and this latter term, now employed without translation in Western-language accounts of warfare and terrorism from Morocco through the Middle East to Afghanistan and on to the Punjab. To contemporary Western consciousness, "jihad" denotes a form of violence outside the ken of statecraft and even warfare as usual: terrorism, political polarization along confessional lines, clerical coups d'état, and *mujahidun*, warriors in the service of jihad.

Contemporary conflicts in which religion is important are not, however, limited to the Muslim world. The civil war in Northern Ireland is fueled by social, economic, political, and historical differences linked significantly to whether one is a Catholic or a Protestant. In Sri Lanka, in a conflict that has included terrorism, political and economic oppression, and open war, the protagonists are divided not only ethnically but also by the fact that one side is largely Hindu, the other largely Buddhist. Tensions among Catholics and two kinds of Orthodox Christians have troubled Ukraine. Three-way conflict among Catholics, Orthodox Christians, and Muslims helped to bring about the breakup of Yugoslavia and inflamed the conduct of the subsequent wars over the creation of Croatia and Bosnia. Religious ingredients in conflicts in the contemporary world are so numerous and so often important that the U.S. Institute of Peace has an ongoing study project aimed at identifying, understanding, and possibly ameliorating them.

The picture is complicated by the existence in the contemporary world of secular belief systems that have also served as sources for attitudes, passions, and practices now commonly associated with holy war. This has been true of Marxism in particular, as a secular ideology bent on fomenting revolution in the capitalist world, and links between Marxist groups and revolutionary movements also appealing to religious identity are widespread. More generally, the struggle of ideologies that marked the cold war has often been depicted in terms of its religious overtones.

In this book, however, I am concerned with the matter of holy war proper, that is, conflicts that have a strong ideological, motivational, social, or other connection with one major religious tradition or another. This means that secular quasi-religions and the struggles they have engendered are outside the focus of this book. To persons interested in the pattern of struggles generated by competing secular ideologies, this is no great loss; the cold war in particular has already been much studied from this perspective. But holy war itself has not, and that is the problem I hope to address. I am convinced that we in the West know less, in fact, than we think we do, as a group, about religiously motivated warfare, and that our ignorance about it often leads to unfortunate conclusions. In particular there is a problem in the common understanding of the Muslim jihad and in the lack of understanding of the roots of holy-war attitudes in Western culture itself. As journalist Robin Wright observed a decade ago,

> So far, attempts to understand the [Muslim] crusade have led to suggestions that a wrathful Muslim world is rising up in a holy war against Christianity or Judaism, capitalism or communism. An extension of this view warns of the "domino" or regional menace—that one state after another will "fall" if militant Islam makes further headway. Paradoxically, this way of thinking both exaggerates the phenomenon in some ways, and underrates it in others. (Wright 1985, 19)

Wright goes on with several caveats to counter this view but concludes nonetheless that "the Islamic crusade is the greatest single threat to the status quo" in the Middle East (20). Her book as a whole has more to do with supporting this latter judgment than with nuancing or rejecting the extreme position summarized in the quotation above. Indeed, recent books taking notice of the phenomenon of jihad in the contemporary Middle East have focused, not on this concept in itself, but on issues like the Iranian Revolution, the future of the supply of Persian Gulf oil, the Gulf War, the Israeli-Arab conflict, the war in Lebanon, and other matters of political or economic import. Jihad, where treated, is associated with "Islamic fundamentalism" (as in Wright's book), itself a shorthand phrase for a phenomenon not much explored or understood by the authors in question (or, I suspect, their readers).

There is, moreover, another question: what of the conceptions of holy war embedded in Western culture, drawn from the Bible and from Christian and Jewish history? How do these affect the understanding of the link between religion and war (or other forms of violence or conflict) in other cultures? The use of the term "crusade" by Wright in the passage above illustrates a dimension of the problem: technically, a crusade can only be fought by Christians, "cross-bearers." Applying the term to jihad assimilates two quite different religious concepts to each other, along with their respective social, political, and historical associations.

The use of the word "crusade," moreover, points to another factor: an association of warfare for religion with ages long past and presumptively more primitive than our own. The ongoing civil strife in Northern Ireland aside, the last time wars were fought for religion in the West was during the century after the Protestant Reformation, a period that included the religious wars in France, the Dutch Revolution, the Thirty Years War, and the Puritan Revolution in England. For Western scholars as well as in the common consciousness, holy war belongs to the past; today it is at best an anachronism, at worst an atavistic throwback to less enlightened times. Indeed, Western culture decisively rejected the concept of war for religion early in the modern period for reasons embedded in theology, revulsion at the horrors of religious war, and an inversion in the relation of the state to religion. This rejection is deeply embedded both in the institutions of the modern international order and in the modern theoretical conception of justified reasons for war and the limits to be set on warfare.

This is, however, misleading. While the cultural and political history of Western Europe and the Americas in the modern period has been dominated by the rise of the secular in law, philosophy, and politics, this pattern of development is neither inevitable nor universal. That is, cultures in which secularization has either not taken the same path or not as thoroughly penetrated the institutional structures of society as in the West are not thereby necessarily anachronisms, less modern, more primitive in a pejorative sense. Indeed, some of the most thoroughly secularized states in the contemporary world, including the old Soviet Union and the People's Republic of China, have promulgated conceptions and practices in international relations and warfare that closely compare to those characteristically advanced by contemporary proponents of holy war. In the case of the development of international law on war, for example, the focus on the state as actor is clearly a reflection of the emergence of the secular state in Europe in the early seventeenth century and its subsequent development to the present. But it is intelligible to argue that this focus has prevented positive international law on war from recognizing the need to address ideologically motivated warfare as a phenomenon somewhat different from that of the ideal secular state motivated by realpolitik, as well as the more recent phenomenon of resurgent claims of religious justification for violence and war so frequent over the last four decades (see further Johnson 1975, 259–74).

To be sure, it is impossible to comprehend the unknown except in terms of what is already known. This has led Western societies to misunderstand the contemporary phenomenon of holy war. We mistake it for an anachronism from the past, an expression of more primitive, less developed minds and societies. We consider it something that has no place in modern secular society, and so by definition alien and threatening. We confuse it with something we ourselves know very little about, the nature of holy war and its role in Western culture in history. And finally, we grasp it only dimly because it is rooted in a close connection between religion and politics, a connection we in the West either do not make or find uncomfortable.

In this book, then, I concentrate on the normative historical traditions in order to correct such misunderstandings. The exploration of those normative traditions as arising not only from the realm of theory but in the interaction of theory with practical statecraft points to the interdependence of the theoretical and the experiential in the shaping of cultural norms. For both the cultures being examined here, contemporary attitudes and judgments on the relation of religion, statecraft, and war are informed by their historical normative traditions. Bringing those traditions into dialogue, then, is a necessary step toward a contemporary dialogue on the relation of religion, statecraft, and war between these two cultures.

Yet before we turn to a focused analysis of these two normative traditions, we must come to terms with the variety of faces the idea of holy war has worn in the two cultures.

The Many Faces of Holy War

Holy war is not in fact a unitary concept but a complex of distinguishable but interrelated ideas. In any given historical phenomenon that may be described as holy war some mix of these ideas can be identified, but rarely if ever all of them, and the nature of the mix varies from historical case to case. The characteristic marks of holy war identified by previous scholarship vary according to the subject being examined. An effort to describe holy war as a general phenomenon, then, must take into account this variation from case to case and, in a comparative study such as this one, from culture to culture.

In Western culture the holy war idea appears in three major historical contexts: the Old Testament, the Crusades, and the religious wars of the post-Reformation era. The last of these was the historical context for the Western cultural rejection of the idea of war for religion, and it was during this era that the most widely recognized contemporary definition of holy war was composed. This definition, from church historian Roland Bainton in *Christian Attitudes toward War and Peace*, provides a convenient baseline from which to develop a fuller understanding of the phenomenon of holy war. On the basis of his study of the Puritan Revolution in England Bainton characterized "the crusading idea" as follows:

> The crusading idea requires that the cause shall be holy (and no cause is more holy than religion), that the war shall be fought under God and with his help, that the crusaders shall be godly and their enemies ungodly, that the war shall be prosecuted unsparingly. (Bainton 1960, 148)

While this statement is widely known and frequently cited, there are nonetheless problems with it as an attempt to characterize war as actually practiced by the Puritans (see further Johnson 1975, 134–46, and David Little in Kelsay and Johnson 1991, 121–40); it also is at some variance with definitions of holy war generated from other contexts.

A considerably different conception of holy war appears in Old Testament scholar Gerhard von Rad's classic *Holy War in Ancient Israel*. Here von Rad characterizes the original form of such war as a complex cultic phenomenon marked by nine distinguishable stages: the assembly of the host for war, in which participation was compulsory; consecration of the host, including sexual abstinence and other steps to ensure ritual purity among the warriors; sacrifice prior to taking the field; a divine oracle or sign; a resulting "unshakable certainty of victory, which was the characteristic defining all holy war"; the movement of Yahweh, God of Israel, in front of the host; "divine terror" seizing the enemy, so that his forces lose their courage and are thrown into confusion and rout; the *herem*, consecration of all booty to Yahweh; and ritual dismissal of the host (von Rad 1991, 41–50).

Later in the history of Israel, von Rad argues, a different concept of holy war appears: it loses its cultic character, becomes a "war of Yahweh" in which all that is required of the people is faith, and ultimately becomes a device of eschatological prophecy by which the last days of judgment on earth are rendered (von Rad 1991, 81, 89, 109, 114). He finds yet a third conception in Deuteronomy. Originally for the defense of the Israelite tribal confederacy, holy war becomes here an offensive "war of religion" aimed at conquering the holy land and setting Yahwism in place (118). All these conceptions of holy war are biblical, though characteristic of different stages and different social contexts in the history of Israel; all differ from the definition of holy war given by Bainton.

As for the third major historical context that has shaped Western thinking about holy war, the Crusades, it is useful to recall LeRoy B. Walters's argument that, in terms of the discourse employed to legitimate them, these wars are best understood as "analogies" rather than "antitheses" to just wars fought for secular purposes and with secular authority. He notes that the Crusades had specific characteristics of their own which distinguished them from purely temporal warfare: public authority for the Crusades came from the pope, while other forms of just war were authorized by a king or other duly situated secular official; the cause was religiously defined rather than being a way to settle quarrels between worldly rulers with no superior to adjudicate between them; the intentionality of the crusade was to be referred to God rather than merely to natural justice (Walters 1973, 586–90). He denies, with reference to Bainton's typology of holy war, that the Crusades involved a different "level of military violence" from wars for secular or political purposes (591–92). Yet the evidence here, as we have seen in the Introduction, is ambiguous. The limits on conduct in war that the church sought to impose were directed to conflicts among Christians, not warfare between Christians and Muslims. One result was, as Richard Barber has observed, that while the Truce of God (originally promulgated in 1054) made certain days and periods of the year illicit for battle among Christians, "in practice the First Crusade attacked Constantinople on Thursday of Holy Week." Yet Barber goes on to note that this churchly effort at restraint was mostly ignored in Europe as well: "It is hard to find a single instance where a battle was postponed because of the day" (Barber 1970, 213–14).

As these examples from the three major historical contexts show, recent interpretive scholarship has generated a richly diverse set of characteristic marks of holy war in Western culture. A considerable diversity is also found in recent work on the idea of holy war in Islam.

Robin Wright, as already noted, renders the concept of jihad as an "Islamic crusade." Her characterization of this Islamic form of holy war is useful not for providing an actual definition of jihad in Muslim thought and practice but for exemplifying a contemporary Western journalist's understanding of how this concept is currently employed by Muslims and a reflection of the understanding of the jihad idea in popular Western usage. Noting that the word originally meant "effort," Wright goes on, "It was a rallying cry for the masses to advance the world's newest monotheistic religion, under threat of the sword, against unbelievers." Over time the term came to mean, "more loosely, a 'righteous war.'" Strictly, she continues, because of the breakup of Islam into separate states, jihad "is no longer possible, except perhaps against Israel"; nonetheless, "many Shia have broadly interpreted jihad. . . . To Ayatollah Khomeini, the war with neighboring Iraq has been a jihad." So have other forms of violence, she continues, including hostage-taking and terrorism (Wright 1985, 55).

Scholarly characterizations of jihad provide a more detailed account of the traditional juristic meaning of this term. These characterizations have certain major features in common, some of which reinforce the popular contemporary conception of jihad as rendered by Wright. A familiar point is that in the Qur'an the fundamental meaning of jihad is not war at all but internal effort or striving "in the path of God" (e.g., Qur'an 22:78). In one tradition from the *hadith* the Prophet Mohammed tells his followers, on return from battle, that they have now returned from the "lesser jihad" (battle) and must turn to the "greater jihad" (the inner struggle for true submission to God). When the Qur'an provides a direct injunction to Muslims to fight, the word used is not jihad but *qital* ("fighting") or another word built from the same root (e.g., Qur'an 2:190: "Fight [*qatilu*] in the way

of God against those who fight you"; cf. Qur'an 9:13, 4:91–93). Moulavi
Cherágh Ali writes, "Jihad, as signifying the waging of war, is a post-Koranic
usage, and . . . in the Koran it is used classically and literally in its natural
sense" (Ali 1977, 165).

Abdulaziz A. Sachedina argues that the Qur'an provides a moral justification for defense and retaliation against attacks by others, but he notes that
the conception of jihad as "a war to increase the 'sphere of Islam'" originates
only later, with the classical jurists (Sachedina 1988, 106). Sachedina goes on
to distinguish between the orthodox Sunni and Shi'ite views; the former, in
theory, allows offensive jihad by a "just ruler," but in Shi'ite Islam there is no
such person until the hidden Imam reappears or appoints a deputy for the
purpose of waging war. Thus for the Shi'a offensive jihad—war to establish
an order in line with right religion—is not a possibility, though defensive
jihad, waged to defend Islamic persons or territory against attack, is "ur-
gently necessary" (110–11).

Rudolph Peters, developing a comprehensive synthetic description of
jihad out of diverse elements of classical Islamic law, highlights four characteristics: its definition in terms of a sense of perpetual enmity between the
sphere of Islam (*dar al-islam*) and the world outside, the "sphere of war"
(*dar al-harb*); the requirement that when formal war is waged in the sense of
jihad it is a collective duty of the community as a whole, with specific
categories of people required to fight and others exempted from this
obligation; that before battle the *da'wah* (summons to become Muslims) is
always to be issued to the enemy; and that once fighting actually begins, it
must be carried on according to certain rules and limits (Peters 1979,
11–24). Peters also notes that the contemporary Muslim literature widely
rejects the translation of "jihad" as "holy war" because of the broader
meaning of jihad as striving in the path of God by means other than war
(118). He further identifies a distinction between the "modernists" and the
"fundamentalists" on the question of offensive vs. defensive jihad: the
modernists emphasize the defensive aspect, whereas "the fundamentalists
are of the opinion that one cannot apply the categories 'offensive' or
'defensive' to jihad, because . . . jihad is universal revolutionary struggle"
(124, 132–33).

Finally, it is important to note that jihad against the outside world,
however defined, does not exhaust the possibility of religious cause for
taking up arms in Islamic tradition: there is also the matter of punishing and
correcting rebels and dissenters against the established authority, which in
classical Islam was religious and political at once. Specific conditions and

rules apply here which differ in important respects from those associated with jihad against the "sphere of war"; yet this too is a form of warfare for religion (cf. Kelsay 1990, 205–7, and Abou El Fadl 1990). This is not only an issue for Islam. In medieval Europe mobilization for the Crusades was often accompanied by violence directed against Jews and dissident Christian groups (cf. Previté-Orton 1952, 1:521); early in the thirteenth century Pope Innocent III declared the Albigensian Crusade, which was directed entirely at destroying the Cathar heresy in southern France (Walker 1959, 231). A related, but far from identical, point is made by von Rad about holy war in ancient Israel: according to the prophets of the eighth century B.C.E. God causes war to be waged against Israel for its unfaithfulness (von Rad 1991, 109–10).

Ten Meanings Associated with Holy War

As noted earlier, the sampling of scholarly characterizations of holy war in Hebraic-Christian tradition and in Islam I have given here is intended not to be systematic or comprehensive, but rather to render the diversity and commonality that exists both in holy war phenomena and in what scholars take to be definitive of holy war. From these samples, we can identify at least ten possible meanings associated with the concept of holy war in the Western and Islamic traditions:

1. *Holy war as war fought at God's command.* This is the sense of the original idea of holy war in ancient Israel, as depicted by von Rad. This meaning is also prominent in the holy war idea of the English Puritans. In the broad sense, it is the core also of the Islamic idea of jihad as the response to God's command to all humankind to submit to him; yet as already noted, this response does not entail a specific call to arms but implies in first place a command to strive for faithfulness.

2. *Holy war as war fought on God's behalf by his duly authorized representative.* This is the core meaning of papal authorization of the Crusades. It is also the core meaning of the authorization of jihad, in the specifically military sense, by the combined religio-political leaders of Islamic states according to Sunni tradition, and in the Shi'ite

tradition by the hidden Imam himself or by his specifically designated representative.

3. *Holy war as war fought by God himself.* This is the interpretation assigned to the idea of holy war by Old Testament writers such as Isaiah and, with an increasingly eschatological meaning, by the prophets of the eighth century B.C.E. The idea of God actively being present in battle, not as sole combatant but as one who is personally present and assists the forces of good, is found very widely in Hebraic and later Christian tradition. This idea is not a factor in Islamic understandings of holy war: the faithful, the Muslims, fight on behalf of God's dominion over the world, but God himself does not engage in the fighting.

4. *Holy war as war fought to defend religion against its enemies, without and within.* This defensive concept of holy war is quite pervasive in the ancient Hebraic, Christian, and Islamic traditions; in the last it is a major component of the contemporary concept of jihad across a broad spectrum of Muslim thought.

5. *Holy war as war fought to propagate right religion or establish a social order in line with divine authority.* This offensive understanding of holy war is the one that most quickly stirs contemporary concern, but it is in fact on balance less important than defense of religion in the Hebrew Bible, Christian tradition, and Islam. In the traditions and in contemporary thought, it is condemned as often and as fervently as it is praised. Yet in various forms it is nonetheless an element in the concept of holy war as historically defined in all these traditions, and it must be examined seriously for its place within the whole.

6. *Holy war as war fought to enforce religious conformity and/or to punish deviation.* This is the sense of holy war found in Ambrose's suggestion that war might be waged for the purpose of protecting Christian orthodoxy (Ambrose of Milan, *On the Christian Faith* 2.14.136–43, in Schaff et al. 1896; cf. Swift 1970, 534), in Augustine's urging of the use of Roman military power against the Donatists and other heretics (see Russell 1975, 23–25), in the crusades against the Albigensians/Cathari and broadly elsewhere in medieval Europe, and also broadly on both sides of the Protestant-Catholic warfare in the Reformation era (see further Johnson 1975, chap. 2). In Islamic tradition this is the kind of use of force widely treated by the jurists under the category of *ahkam al-bughat*. But warfare against apostates

can also be termed jihad (Abraham and Haddad 1989, 33–39). The point in all these cases is that whether external or domestic the use of military force for religious purposes is justified to ensure religious conformity and/or punish heresy.

7. *Holy war as warfare in which the participants are themselves ritually and/or morally "holy."* This is a complicated category. Three distinct meanings may be distinguished, though in practice they tend to be woven together or intermixed in diverse ways: cultic holiness, conferred by particular acts performed by the warriors individually or collectively and/or by specific acts of blessing by duly authorized religious leaders; moral uprightness, such as expressed in vows of renunciation of certain types of activity (e.g., sexual relations) for the duration of the conflict or, more generally, in strict observance of particular rules for fighting the enemy and/or disposing of booty seized in the fighting; and holiness or righteousness as conferred simply by being one of the designated people of God.

Understood in terms of all three of these meanings, holy war as the warfare of the holy is a quite widely distributed notion. Von Rad, as already noted, identifies all three types of holiness in holy war in ancient Israel. The medieval crusaders took religious vows before departing for the theater of war, and new religious orders of knights were specifically founded for the purpose of war against enemies of the Christian faith or to seek to protect the Holy Land (e.g., the Templars, the Knights of Malta, the Hospitallers). The influential English Puritan divine William Gouge distinguished between wars among the ungodly, in which the outcome is always uncertain, and wars in which the soldiers on one side are righteous and thus can be sure of God's blessing of victory. By definition, for Gouge, the Puritans were of the godly, but they had to prove it by their moral conduct and their manner of fighting as well (Gouge 1631, 290). Within Islam jihad in a fundamental sense is always understood as a war of the righteous, those who have submitted to God (Muslims of the *dar al-islam*), against the unrighteous (non-Muslims in the *dar al-harb*); in practice this meant for classical theorists that all adult males in good standing within the Islamic community were fit to fight in a jihad (al-Shaybani, secs. 21–25, in Khadduri 1966, 84–85; cf. Kelsay 1990, 200, and Peters 1979, 12). More comparable to the ancient Hebraic and Christian views is the position of Shi'ite Islam as described by Sachedina, that jihad has an essential moral base as a combat against dangerous and lawless persons by defenders of the moral order who are themselves moral (Sachedina 1988, 105–17). The specific training of the Iranian Revolutionary Guards during the war with Iraq stressed both rigorous commitment to religious duty and the particular blessing of the religious authorities.

8. *Holy war as the militant struggle of faith by means of arms alongside nonviolent means*. Adolf Harnack's classic study, *Militia Christi*, demonstrates the breadth and importance of military symbolism in the early Christian definition of true faithfulness. Widespread in the New Testament and throughout the early Christian movement, prior to the Constantinian era the military images were used to refer to the inner battles for faith within the individual soul; the *miles Christi*, the "soldier of Christ," was thus the individual warring against sin in his own beliefs and behavior. Beginning in the fourth century, though, the concept of soldiering for Christ was extended to actual military action against enemies of the church (27–66). The same tension remains in later Christianity up to the present. Similarly, the fundamental meaning of jihad as striving or effort "in the path of God" has been taken in Islamic tradition as embracing the personal struggle for faithfulness as well as military action against the unfaithful. In this the priority is clearly given to inner transformation. The later tradition expressed this priority by distinguishing not two but four different types of jihad: that of the heart (faith), that of the tongue (speech), that of the hand (good works), and that of the sword (holy war) (Peters 1979, 10; cf. Abraham and Haddad 1989, 26). The first three of these are all directed to self-discipline, internal striving in the path of God. But they are linked, as in Christian tradition, to the active taking up of arms against external unbelief, though the internal struggle can never be reduced to that form of militancy alone.

9. *Holy war as warfare under religiously inspired (charismatic) leadership*. In some respects this assimilates to the second possible meaning of holy war, war authorized by a duly appointed representative of God. But while that notion refers to the cultic status of the authorizing person or persons (e.g., the priests of the Israelite confederacy, the pope, the supreme imam of the *dar al-islam*), this present concept refers to something different: the *personal* rather than cultic character of the leader. He (or she) is able to lead on behalf of God because of a recognizably special presence of divine inspiration or personal

faithfulness. This notion includes the wars waged under the leadership of the judges of the Old Testament, the wars von Rad takes as the original form of holy war in the history of Israel (von Rad 1991, chap. 2); it includes a whole variety of phenomena from the medieval and early modern periods in Europe in which priests, monks, and self-described holy men took the lead in raising and leading bands of armed men for one cause or another. In Islam a characteristic expression is mahdism, the belief in a particular religious leader as the Mahdi, the "rightly guided one," who is expected to appear shortly before the End of Time, and who will act to end corruption and oppression and restore justice on earth. Peters notes that typically mahdism features in revolutionary movements; the examples he cites include those of 'Ubayd Allah (d. 934), founder of the Almohad dynasty, Ibn Tumart (1077–1130), founder of the Fatimid dynasty, "several *Mahdí* revolts" in Algeria in the latter half of the nineteenth century, a number of cases from India and upper Egypt also during the nineteenth century, the Mahdi Revolt in the Sudan (1881–85), and the struggle of Muhammad ibn 'Abd Allah against the British and the Italians in Somalia (1899–1920) (Peters 1979, 42–44). But the leader does not have to be perceived as the Mahdi to fit the category of charismatic leader; Douglas Porch cites a number of revolutionary leaders who fought against the French in Algeria and Morocco, whose leadership was founded in their followers' belief that they possessed *baraka*, a divine blessing, which gave them authenticity and would enable them to triumph over their foes (Porch 1983, chaps. 5, 7, 8, 19).

10. *Holy war as a phenomenon recognized during or after the fact as an "absolute miracle."* The phrase is von Rad's and, in context of his book, refers specifically to the account in 2 Chronicles 20 of the war of Jehoshaphat, king of Judah, against the peoples of the East (von Rad 1991, 129–31). The point of distinguishing this from the other meanings associated with the idea of holy war is to say that holy war may sometimes be recognized after the fact, by its results, not before or during the conflict of arms. For von Rad, describing the development of the idea of holy war in the Old Testament, the particular account cited in 2 Chronicles 20 exemplifies a theological interpretation given to holy war beginning at the time of Solomon and continuing into the postexilic period, by which human involvement in actual fighting is minimized and God's role is magnified to the point at which it becomes absolute. Under this interpretation the idea of holy

war as the war of Yahweh becomes a vehicle to encourage faith, not military action. But there is another line of meaning here that is more general: a particular war may be recognized as a holy war despite the lack of authorization by proper religious authority, a recognizable holy cause, uprightness on the part of the warriors, or other characteristics identified above. It is one thing, for example, to believe a war is holy because of the charisma or *baraka* of its leader; it is another thing entirely to be brought to believe that the leader does in fact possess a special blessing from God because the war turned out favorably despite great odds. Old Testament eschatological use of the concept of holy war mixes retrospection with foreknowledge of Yahweh's triumph over the nations and the forces of evil in the world: Israel knows of this triumph in advance through faith; the nations know it only after catastrophe comes upon them, and by then it is too late. Before the end of time, however, the result may be just the opposite: false faith can be proven wrong by the experience of defeat. The various mahdist revolts had this experience of *dénouement*. But when the results turn out unexpectedly positively, when, for some reason, the anticipated catastrophe does not occur, the result may be interpreted as miraculous, and the wartime leader given new prestige; a related contemporary example is Saddam Hussein's claim to glory in the aftermath of the defeat of the Iraqi army in the Gulf War.

Comparing Holy War to the Idea of Just War

What is one to make of these ten possible meanings to which the idea of holy war has been attached historically? The most general thing to say is that this listing reinforces an observation already made: that holy war is not a single phenomenon but a related group of phenomena. Nor can the Muslim theme of jihad be distinguished from the concepts of holy war found in Hebraic tradition and in the Christianized West; rather, this set of diverse meanings cuts across the religious and cultural boundaries, arguing implicitly that there is much in common between Islamic and Hebraic-Christian ideas of holy war.

It is also important to note what is absent or deemphasized in the various conceptions of holy war sketched by means of this listing. The just war tradition of the West distinguishes between two problems, that of justification in the resort to war and that of justified prosecution of war (denoted by the Latin terms *jus ad bellum* and *jus in bello*), with specific concerns or restraints defining the content of each. The *jus ad bellum*, as traditionally defined, requires a right authority to initiate force, a justifying cause, a right intention toward the enemy (hating the evil but not the enemy as persons), an overall calculation that the good brought about by this action will outweigh the evil that would result from failing to act, a situation of last resort, a calculation that there is reasonable hope of success in achieving the ends sought, and an overall purpose of restoring peace. To restrain the harm actually done in war, the *jus in bello* set limits on who might legitimately be attacked (the idea of noncombatant immunity, often expressed by moralists as the principle of discrimination) and the means that could legitimately be employed (including diverse efforts to limit various weapons, the days of fighting, certain strategies, and some tactics—often expressed by moralists as the principle of proportionality). A review of the above listing of meanings attaching to holy war shows that some, but hardly all, these concerns are also reflected there: on the question of whether to initiate war the requirements that there be right authority, a justifying cause, a purpose of restoring order by punishing and correcting evil, and a proper intentionality toward the enemy; on the question of how to fight such a war a concern for righteousness on the part of the warriors, a concern expressed diversely in cultic and/or moral restraints on the conduct of the soldiers during the conflict.

One should not make too much of this apparent discrepancy between the just war tradition and the historical understanding of holy war. The just war criteria are the product of several centuries of careful shaping through theological, moral, and legal debate, the developing customs of statecraft, and experience in soldiering and warfare. Holy war has been a sporadic theme in this debate and related historical experience; it simply has not received concerted attention as a separate and distinct phenomenon. Accordingly, where theoretical attention has been given to the idea of holy war in the West, it has been treated via the categories and purposes of the developing just war tradition. Effectively this means, as I have argued elsewhere, that within Western culture holy war has developed as a subcategory within just war tradition; they are, in Walters's (1973) words, "analogous" rather than antithetical. Specifically what this has meant is that warfare for religion can be described by substituting religious content for secular within the applicable categories: for example, right authority defined as that of pope rather than king or emperor; just cause as defense of religion, not defense of feudal rights or national borders. By the same method the categories of just war tradition can even be used to examine Islamic ideas of holy war (cf. Johnson and Kelsay 1990 and Kelsay and Johnson 1991).

Applying the just war categories in this way to holy war appears to assume that these categories are in fact able to be emptied of the specific content assigned to them by just war tradition and then refilled with content drawn from traditions expressing the idea of holy war. As an element in a comparative methodology this is a useful tool, but it tends to obscure the historical origins of the categories themselves and present them as empty frameworks rather than as what they are: ideas that have been historically defined by their concrete exemplifications. "Right authority," for example, is useful for understanding both warfare for religion and warfare for nonreligious purposes, not because it is an empty concept waiting to be filled with specific meaning, but because what is "right" authority to initiate war has been fought out intellectually and experientially through claims that have been made by both religious and secular authorities. Whether "just cause" should include the use of force to propagate religion or enforce religious claims or behavior has similarly been a subject of considerable and repeated focus in the development of this category within the just war tradition. When influential just war theorists at the beginning of the modern era rejected war for religion, they specifically had in mind the idea that propagation of religion or of religiously defined behavior should be recognized as a just cause for war; they did not reject war in defense of religion, because they understood self-defense to include protecting the right to be left in peace according to the laws and customs of one's own land, including its religion.

These considerations suggest that the reason at least some of the just war categories are useful for understanding holy war is that they have been shaped by historical experiences of holy war and debates over the proper role of religion in relation to statecraft and the practice of war. It also suggests that a more nuanced understanding of historical phenomena associated with holy war can be gained by attending to what the historical debates have been about. The discrediting of holy war in the developing just war tradition of the West, as well as the particular dimensions of this discrediting, are directly associated with the rise of the secular state at the beginning of the modern period. Secular states may have an interest in protecting the freedom of their citizens to practice one or another religion, but it is contrary to their interest to use their power to propagate religion or enforce religious truth claims, because doing so would implicitly give too prominent a role to religious institutions and authorities within their social and political structure. The discrediting of holy war in the West since the beginning of the modern period has, in practical terms, had a great deal more to do with the mutual decision of secular states that they have much more to lose than to gain by fighting wars for religion than with the proscribing of wars for religion by theorists such as Victoria and Grotius. Victoria, indeed, was somewhat ahead of his own time; Grotius more nearly reflected the growing consensus of his age. The fact that the relationship between religion and the state has taken its own course within Islamic societies alerts us to the possibility that holy war has a different role relative to the state in such societies, but this increases rather than decreases the importance of examining conceptions of holy war in the context of the political unit and its governance.

All of what has just been said reflects the experience of the West but also bears importantly on the study of holy war in Islamic culture. The key is the need to use the categories of analysis as windows through which to view the concerns represented by holy war in theory and practice, recognizing the differences from as well as the similarities with Western ideas and experiences in the process.

Apart from the question of categories is the question of emphasis: what concerns are of greatest collective importance in the various understandings attached to holy war, and how do these compare to those of just war tradition? In the foregoing characterizations of holy war three distinct concerns stand out: that the war have a transcendent authority, either given directly from God or mediated through the religious institutions in some way; that the war have a purpose directly associated with religion, either its defense or its propagation or the establishment of a social order in accord with religious requirements; and that the war be waged by people who are in some sense set apart, whether cultically or morally or simply by membership in the religious community, from those against whom the war is waged. The first two correspond to the just war requirements of right authority and just cause, but the third is uniquely associated with holy war. Exactly what it means, whether this meaning is universal, and how it relates to the other emphases will be examined more fully later in this book.

Not included in the list of meanings associated with holy war provided above is the matter of how the war should be waged; yet this too is an important emphasis in holy war thought in the traditions being examined here. Bainton, I think, is wrong in his characterization of "the crusading idea" to define holy war as a conflict which is "prosecuted unsparingly." This particular element in his characterization does not hold up, as I have argued elsewhere, even for the English Puritans whose practice of warfare he was directly describing (Johnson 1975, 134–46), and neither is it a useful concept for understanding holy war in a broader context as a phenomenon in itself. Rather, certain particular rules for fighting and for disposition of the spoils of war apply to holy war in specific cultural contexts, and these rules provide a useful perspective on the phenomenon of holy war itself in these contexts.

3

HOLY WAR AND THE
QUESTION OF JUSTIFICATION

Central in holy war debates, both historical and contemporary, is the question of the cause or purpose for which holy war can be waged. In both the Western and Islamic traditions these debates have had much to do with whether the religious community is coextensive with the political and undifferentiated from it or not, and if not, then with how to understand the proper extent and dynamics of the relation between the ruler and the religion or religions practiced within his or her domain. Broadly, where the two forms of community are entirely coextensive, no distinction is made between religious and nonreligious causes or purposes of war, and in practice any war engaged in by the community seems holy. When the political and the religious orders are distinguishable, whether entirely distinct or not, the justifications for war may be sought in either or both spheres. Finally, in cases where the political community is dominant over the religious, only secular causes for resort to war are acceptable. Appeals to religious reasons are, in such cases, transformed into justifying ideologies by the state.

The Two Worlds Concept
in Christian and Islamic Tradition

In both Christian and Islamic tradition the idea of holy war is closely linked to a religiously defined theoretical separation between two worlds, one ordered toward God and the other not. While Christian normative tradition on war was influenced heavily by other sources, in Islamic thought the two worlds distinction provides the basic context for developing the idea of jihad as the war of the faithful against the disorder, evil, and danger of the unbeliever. For Christian tradition the distinction between the two worlds is theological, whereas for Islam it is juridical; for both, however, it is moral, imposing a claim on how believers should act in the world, and political, bearing on how the political community should rightly be structured and governed. For both it is also a statement about how the past, present, and future are to be understood. The classic statement of this conception in Christian thought is that of Augustine in *The City of God* and the tradition of interpretation following from it; the classic statement in Islamic thought is that of the jurists of the early 'Abbasid dynasty, together with the tradition of interpretation built on it. These two traditions, and the two worlds distinction peculiar to each—the Christian built on Augustinian theology and the Islamic built on the work of the classic jurists—are important in many ways for understanding the idea of holy war in these two cultures.

Classical Islamic juristic thought, as noted in Chapter 1, makes a central distinction between two spheres or territories, the *dar al-islam* and the *dar al-harb*. The former is that region within which Islam holds sway, that is, where submission to God is observed; as a result, the *dar al-islam* is a territory of peace: Majid Khadduri calls it the realm of the *Pax Islamica* (Khadduri 1966, 13). By contrast, the world outside Islam is by definition one in which the divine will is not observed, and the result is continuing strife; *dar al-harb* is literally the "territory of war." It is continually at war within itself, and it is in a perpetual state of conflict with the *dar al-islam*. As part of their obedience to God Muslims are charged with extending that obedience over the entire earth, thus eliminating this perpetual state of war and instituting a universal reign of peace.

In Christian thought through the Middle Ages Augustine's distinction between two "cities," that ordered to the things of earth (the *civitas terrenae*) and that ordered to God (the *civitas dei*), provided a framework for understanding the progress of history and how to assist God's purpose through the ordering of the Christian state and the use of its power. By the *civitas terrenae* Augustine meant to specifically refer to the Roman state, which to him represented the apex of historical political communities in both its positive and its negative achievements. This "city" sought justice but erred fundamentally in one essential way: it did not give God his due. To remedy this God set salvation in motion, by means of grace gradually transforming human motivations toward being rightly ordered through love for God. The City of God will come into full being only at the end of time, when all things have been transformed and perfect justice is established. While throughout the remainder of history this gradual transformation will proceed invisibly, both in individual human hearts and in the communities they make up, the church stands as a visible presence of the promise of the City of God and as a particular community of those who believe they have begun to be transformed by grace.

In important respects this division of the world into two spheres is directly comparable to the Islamic distinction between the *dar al-harb* and the *dar al-islam*. Neither the *dar al-harb* nor the *civitas terrenae* is rightly ordered toward God: as a result even their best efforts are frustrated by human striving toward the wrong goals; their justice is always injustice; and their essential state is one of conflict, both internal and external. By contrast, the *dar al-islam* and the *civitas dei* are characterized by their right orientation: their *islam* or submission to God in the former case, demonstrated by behavior in accord with Islamic law; their *caritas* or rightly directed love of God over all else in the latter, an orientation which ultimately only God is able to judge. In both cases these are descriptions of the attitudes and behavior of individuals, the persons in whom the necessary change has taken place, but they are also descriptions of the society made up of these individuals: rightly directed individuals produce a rightly directed society. Further, both these concepts have a historical and an eschatological sense. The *dar al-islam* exists now in Muslim societies, with its ultimate destiny being to encompass the entire world, and the *civitas dei* exists now in the church, but its destiny is the heavenly community of the saints; in both cases this historical presence is imperfect, and the full realization of both awaits fulfillment at some future time now unknown.

Yet despite these major similarities, there are deep differences between the Muslim jurists' distinction between *dar al-harb* and *dar al-islam* and the Augustinian Christian distinction between *civitas terrenae* and *civitas dei*.

Augustine's idea of the two "cities" is fundamentally a theological attempt to render the history of humanity from the fall through the coming of Christ and a period of transformation by the grace of Christ until the fall is finally undone and salvation of the world is complete. From within this theological perspective the *civitas terrenae* no longer exists in itself because Christ has already ushered in the age of transformation by grace. But neither does the *civitas dei* yet fully exist, for even the church, the visible sign of its presence in the world, is not yet perfect as the community of those who love God. The present age, that of the ongoing transformation initiated by Christ, is characterized by a mixture of the two cities. Rome, for Augustine, was no longer simply an example of the *civitas terrenae*, because it had within it the presence of the *civitas dei* both at the level of the community (the church) and within individual citizens who were in the process of being transformed by grace. Similarly the church was not yet the full realization of the *civitas dei* both because its "city" was not yet universal in fact and because the individual Christians within it were themselves still in the process of being transformed.

This theological conception of the history of salvation provided the basis for the dominant political theory of the Middle Ages. Medieval authors seeking to enhance the power of the pope were more inclined than Augustine to characterize the church as both a visible presence of the *civitas dei* and the perfected form of human political community. Opponents of this view, who were seeking to justify the independence of secular authority, were more inclined than Augustine to stress the role of the state as a *civitas terrenae* already well on its way to perfection and the imperfection of the church's realization of the *civitas dei*. Both were able to find theological warrant for the defense of religion and for the punishment and correction of heterodoxy, though they differed in assigning authority for doing so. More important, though, in both cases this warrant was interpreted principally as applying domestically: for prince and pope alike, within the territories through which their authority extended. This meant that its major force was against rebellion and heresy or schism within a prince's domains or, for the pope, within Catholic Christendom.

The outstanding exception was the apologetic for the Crusades, which acknowledged the pope's claim to universal authority. Yet even the apologists knew this was far from true in actuality, and so the official rationale for the Crusades accordingly emphasized aid to allies in the Eastern church in defending against attacks on Christians. This rationale did not seek to justify the Crusades as for the purpose of spreading Christianity, but rather as for the purpose of repelling attacks on Christian territory, punishing the Muslim attackers, and retaking the lands, properties, and persons unjustly seized in these attacks. In other words, the crusaders invoked not the propagation of Christian religion but the three just causes for war known by the Romans: defense against attack, punishment of the attackers, and retaking things wrongly taken by the attackers.[1]

The Islamic distinction between the *dar al-harb* and the *dar al-islam* was fundamentally different in origin and conception; not only was it juristic rather than theological, aiming at insuring right behavior rather than right motivation, but it defined the world in terms of control of territory rather than the invisible progress of divine grace, and it defined membership in the two spheres by behavior (submission to God's will, *islam*, whether or not this was accompanied by faith, *iman*) and not the invisible presence of divine grace. Its political meaning was built into the concept of a distinction between the two spheres, not developed out of it as was the case with medieval political theory based on Augustine's thought, and the juristic concept of two worlds directly addressed the political character of the Muslim state. Ali (1977, 165) notes that the terms *dar al-islam* and *dar al-harb* are not found in the Qur'an but "only in the Mohammedan Common Law, and are only used in the question of jurisdiction." Khadduri likewise underscores the political character of the *dar al-islam*: "We should recall that Islam is not merely a set of religious ideas and practices but also a political community (the umma) endowed with a central authority" (Khadduri 1966, 10).

The term *dar al-islam* designated all territories in which Muslim authority was recognized; its inhabitants included the Muslims who made up the *umma* as well as members of the tolerated religious communities known collectively as "People of the Book" who lived under Muslim sovereignty. All other territories were designated collectively as *dar al-harb*, the "territory of war." This latter was a territory of war in two senses. First, since it lacked adherence to the divinely promulgated legal and ethical standards observed by Islam, it was prone to internal strife. A superficial manifestation of this internal conflict within the *dar al-harb* was its division into separate states; the Islamic world, by contrast, was by definition internally at peace and at least in theory a single political and religious community. Second, the *dar al-harb* was conceived as being in perpetual and inherent conflict with the Islamic state. This conflict would end only when the *dar al-harb* had been eradicated and the entire world has become *dar al-islam*. The source of all specific cases of warfare with the *dar al-islam* was thus the very nature of the *dar al-harb*, the fact that it was not in submission to the law of Islam. The hostility between the *dar al-harb* and the *dar al-islam* was thus not in the first place the result of actual acts of war by the former against the latter, though in practice such acts might take place; rather that hostility was thematic and systematic, rooted in the disorder of the *dar al-harb* and the universal mission of Islam to bring the entire world into the *dar al-islam*. (See further Khadduri 1966, 10–14; Shaybani, sec. 4, in Khadduri 1966, 130–41; and Peters 1979, 11–12.)

While the juristic distinction was conceived in terms of control over territory, it was no less a statement of an ideal than the distinction between the two "cities" in Augustine's original thought. As we shall see further in Chapter 5, the political reality has never, even in the time of the classical jurists themselves, matched their neat typological division of the earth into two "territories." Nonetheless, the ideal was powerful enough in both Christian and Muslim traditions that the practice of politics strove to match what was laid out in theory, with the result that holy war became integrated into statecraft.

Justification of War for Religion in Christian Thought: From the Middle Ages to the Reformation

The Medieval Debate over Just Cause for War

Classical just war theory recognized three causes for resort to arms: defense against wrongdoing in progress, punishment of wrongdoing already completed, and recovery of property lost as a result of wrongdoing already accomplished. All of these were causes of just war already recognized in Roman practice, incorporated into Christian thought on war by Augustine and thus bequeathed to the Middle Ages. They were taken for granted as core concepts by medieval thinkers like the theologian Thomas Aquinas and the canonist Gratian. In both their Roman and their medieval Christian forms these justifications for resort to force were understood as both grounded in the natural concept of justice and warranted by religion. Defense included defense of religion; punishment of wrongdoing included punishment of heresy and of sinful behavior; retaking things wrongly taken included not only recovery of church property but also reestablishment of right belief in areas that had fallen into religious deviation. (See further Johnson 1975, chap. 2, and 1981, chaps. 4 and 5.)

Defense here, and for the main line of the just war tradition down to the present day, included not only resort to force in response to evil acts already under way, but also preemptive use of force against acts of war clearly intended but still in preparation. A familiar image for the concept of defense was the upraised sword: for just defense it was not necessary to wait for the sword to fall.

What might justly be defended? A full list would include lives and property, of course, but also certain rights granted by the customs of statecraft (such as the right of free passage for peaceable people through foreign territory), as well as religious belief and rights given by religion. Walters, comparing medieval just war and crusade theory, distinguishes four "political" from four corresponding "religious" justifications for defensive use of force: "defense of the fatherland" versus "defense of the Holy Land"; "aid to allies" versus "aid to the Eastern church"; defense of "the right of innocent passage" versus defense of "the right of missionaries to preach freely"; "defense of the innocent" versus "defense of Christian converts" (Walters 1973, 590). His argument is that the two lines of reasoning were analogical, not antithetical. But in fact the sources show that these two lines of reasoning were often intermingled, and no consistent distinction was made between them in general practice (cf. Johnson 1975, 48–53). The distinction Walters notes applies only to the special case of the Crusades proper, not to wars inside the sphere of Western Christendom.

Defense of religion, moreover, could entail military action even when the other party was not itself attacking or threatening to attack: "The enemies of the Church are to be coerced even by war," wrote the canonist Gratian, quoting from Augustine, who had used this argument to urge the use of the Roman army against the Donatist schismatics (Gratian, *Decretum* 2.23.8.48). This line of reasoning blurred the distinction between offensive and defensive use of force more thoroughly than that between preemptive and reactive resort to force. Whereas in the latter case the burden of decision is on the prince, in the former it is on the religious authority, with the prince's role subordinated to the church's concerns. This distinction might or might not be made in particular cases, since the normative understanding of the role of the prince was as given in Romans 13:4: "He [the prince] is minister of God to execute his wrath on the evildoer" (cf. Thomas Aquinas, *Summa Theologica* 2/2.40.1).

The justification of the use of force to coerce "the enemies of the Church" also blurred the distinction between defense and punishment of wrongdoing. When what is being defended against is wrong beliefs held within a group that themselves pose no military threat, the coercion in question is not defense of the beliefs of the orthodox so much as punishment of the unorthodox. The cases of the Waldensians and the Cathari are prominent medieval examples; there are numerous others (Walker 1959, 227–32).

By the same logic retaking something wrongly taken was assimilated into defense of religion and punishment of wrong religious belief and/or practice. What has been "taken" is, for the case of religion, defined as the true faith; "retaking" it means enforcing the doctrines and practices of the established church. In this way the classic justifications for resort to war were understood to include war to uphold and propagate religion as defined by the church of Rome. In the broad sense of the use of force to coerce "the enemies of the Church," then, canonical and theological writers on the idea of just war defined holy war as one form of justified war.

All this came together in what Alfred Vanderpol has called the concept of "vindicative justice" (Vanderpol 1919, 250–75). Tracing this idea through Thomas Aquinas back to Augustine, Vanderpol argues that through it the role of the prince as secular ruler was theologically justified by being assimilated to rights and authorities understood as reserved to God. The ruler had no authority of his own, on this rendering, but only insofar as he acted, in Paul's words from Romans 13:4, as a "minister of God." This did not entail a conception by which the ruler was subordinated to ecclesiastical leadership in all things; rather, the prince was expected to know God's will as expressed in the natural order, to defend against violations of that order, and to punish such violations. The concept of "vindicative justice" refers to positive acts, whether involving the use of force or not, to set things right wherever they have been set wrong, thus "vindicating" the rule of God. (The term itself comes from the Vulgate Latin version of Romans 13:4: "Minister enim Dei est, vindex in iram ei qui malum agit.") Justified use of force, then, included in all cases: (1) an actual fault on one side, whether against the faith of the church or against the natural order of things, and (2) a pure act of vindicative justice in God's stead on the other.

Augustine's Two "Cities" and Religious Justification for War

Given the foregoing, within the context of medieval Europe warfare in defense of religion was an inclusive and pervasive concept, the result of an intermingling of the political and religious aspects of society (it is incorrect at this stage to think of them as distinct "spheres"); the Crusades were only particular instances of such warfare. When medieval writers thought about religion and politics, they did so by means of a political theory rooted in Augustine's *City of God*, according to which the political community was understood in terms ultimately religious in nature.

The City of God was for Augustine an attempt to understand the history of the work of divine grace, the invisible but inexorable transformation going on in history as God draws human communities and individuals toward their ultimate destiny at the end of time. In the authoritative medieval interpretation of Augustine this theory became a blueprint for the contemporary structuring of society and a justification of the ordering of society in terms of the ideals promulgated by the church. This conception could be read to give the church, and its head the pope, as the visible presence of the City of God, supreme authority even in temporal matters: hence the idea that the pope might authorize resort to arms in certain matters. But the Augustinian model could also be used to argue that the role of the prince, as the person charged with the right ordering of his political community, extended to authorizing the resort to arms for maintaining and promulgating right religion, the source of all good order.

Ultimately, in the fourteenth century, these alternative interpretations of Augustine hardened into competing political theories in authors such as Dante and Marsilius of Padua, on the side of the independence of the secular realm, and John of Legnano, on the side of papal supremacy. These competing theories complemented a struggle simultaneously being waged on the battlefield in the Guelph-Ghibelline wars between the pope and Holy Roman Emperor. The eventual defeat of papal claims to general temporal supremacy and the triumph of a secular sphere understood as standing in its own right was one important step toward the elimination of war for religion from the just war tradition. But at the time, and for the next three centuries—measuring from Dante's *De Monarchia* (composed between 1311 and 1318) and Marsilius's *Defensor Pacis* (1324) to Grotius's *De Jure Belli ac Pacis* (1625) and the conclusion of the Thirty Years War (1648)— the result was quite different: to transfer to secular princes the right to make war for religious reasons as well as secular ones.

Indeed, this fourteenth-century conflict had nothing to do with the validity of waging war for religion, only with identifying who might have the authority to do so. Both parties to the conflict between the pope and the emperor cited the holy wars of the Old Testament as proof that supporting true religion by the sword was God's own will. Medieval writers typically read this example through earlier writers, not from the Bible directly, and in the case of war as in that of politics generally they depended heavily on Augustine. While his conception of justifiable Christian resort to war referred to both the Old and New Testaments, Augustine made a great deal out of the Old Testament idea of war commanded by God as a continuing warrant to use military force to punish wickedness. Frederick Russell sums up Augustine's interpretation of this biblical precedent as follows: "Some men [in ancient Israel] waged war in obedience to a direct divine command while others acting in conformity with God's ordinance put wicked men to death. In either case their obedience rendered them innocent of transgressing the Sixth Commandment [Thou shalt not kill]" (Russell 1975, 22–23). Augustine, in turn, urged the Roman state to use its military power to suppress the Donatist schism, thus providing a direct link between war for religion in ancient Israel and war for religion in his own time. With this authoritative precedent, Augustine's medieval readers easily made the same connection.

In medieval theory the prince was conceived as having an obligation to act in defense of religion whenever his own judgment or that of church authorities told him that true religion was threatened, whether by ungodly behavior or by deviant doctrine. The justification for the suppression of heresies and schisms by force should be understood from this perspective. We shall see that much debate in fact surrounded the question of who could authorize resort to force for such purposes, with the result that the right of the church to authorize war even for religion was gradually undercut and taken away in canon law and theology. This did not, though, imply rejection of the concept of justified war for religious causes: rather, the purpose was to give the prince the right to authorize war for offenses against the religious order as well as for offenses against the political order of his realm. With this right established as a norm by the fourteenth century, the doctrine justifying war for religion lasted essentially unchanged right up into the wars of religion of the post-Reformation era. And to reject the justice of war for religion, it was necessary by that time only to deny the prince the right to refer to differences over religion as providing warrant for making offensive war against other princes. The right of the church to authorize such resort to arms had been lost centuries earlier. What still remained to the prince, however, was his right to use force to defend religion against force of arms, understood as part of his general right to defend his realm against armed attack.

War for Religion as the Most Just War: Holy War Advocacy in the Reformation Era

During the warfare of the post-Reformation era, then, the arguments over the justification of war took place in categories and with assumptions that had originated in the Middle Ages. This can be seen clearly through the prism of one sphere of religious conflict, that of England from the era of the brief reign of Edward VI through the Puritan Revolution (ca. 1550–1650).

As the Reformation—along with religiously based conflicts—moved westward, the arguments for war for religion multiplied and accumulated among both Protestants and Catholics. The English Reformation, coming after the struggles in Germany, France, and the Low Countries, drew on these arguments and gave them new focus.[2]

The influence of the Continent can be seen clearly through the work of Heinrich Bullinger (1504–75), a Swiss Reformed theologian. His *Decades*, a collection of sermons on various topics, was mandated reading by English clergy for a time in 1586 and was widely popular among members of the Puritan party otherwise. Among these sermons, "On War" (number 9 of the Second Decade) laid out clearly the mix of political and religious justifications for war then accepted as orthodox among Protestants and Catholics alike: defense against armed attack, punishment of "men who are incurable, whom the very judgment of the Lord condemneth and biddeth to kill without pity or mercy" (Bullinger's examples are Israel's wars with the Midianites and the Amalechites), and correction of error (Israel's collective punishment of the Benjaminites by war). Bullinger continues by making clear that religion offers, in his judgment, the highest cause for making war: "Hereunto appertain the wars that are taken in hand for the defence of true religion against idolaters and enemies of the true and catholic faith [which he, of course, read through Protestant lenses]. They err, that are of opinion that no wars may be made in defense of religion" (Bullinger 1849, 376–77). If worldly things may be defended, Bullinger continues, then so also "things of greater account," and nothing is of greater weight than "sincere and true religion."

A direct contemporary of Bullinger was the English Catholic prelate William Cardinal Allen. In *A True, Sincere, and Modest Defense of English Catholiques*, published in 1583, he justified war for religion in equally strident terms: "There is no warre in the world so just or honorable be it civil or forraine, as that which is waged for Religion, . . . for the true, ancient, Catholique, Romane religion . . . and not for wilde condemned heresies"

(Allen 1583, 103). Thus both Bullinger and Allen held that religion permits the righteous, those who profess "true religion," to go to war against adherents of different faith—"idolaters" (a common epithet of the Reformers against Catholics), says Bullinger; "wilde condemned heresies," says Allen. The language of both also reveals that what Bullinger termed "the defence of true religion" includes firing the first shot, not simply waiting to fire the second, against those who threaten true religion by idolatry and heresy. Clearly with these two apologists for holy war, and implicitly for many others whom they influenced, religious difference itself was a sufficient threat to "true religion," justifying the resort to war for the varied purposes of defense of this religion, punishment of the heterodox, and correction of the wrong beliefs and practices. This sets in context Victoria's contemporary argument to the contrary, "Difference of religion is not a cause of just war." For Bullinger and Allen the opposite is emphatically true: wars based in difference of religion are the most just of wars, far more just than those fought for nonreligious reasons.

Both Bullinger and Allen referred their judgments on the justice of holy war to examples drawn from the Old Testament. Bullinger cited Moses against the Midianites and Joshua against the Amalechites; Allen cited the prophet Azariah's words to King Asa: "Whosoever seeketh not after the Lord God of Israel, let him be slaine" (Allen 1583, 103). Bullinger and Allen took such biblical references not simply as historical examples but as indications of the very will of God. Following a standard mode of biblical interpretation of their day, these writers saw in Israel's religious wars a type that had continuing and universal validity. Since God willed that Israel make war for the true faith, he continues to will that Christians do the same.

Fifty years later such reasoning was still alive in the writings of Puritan apologists such as the influential cleric William Gouge. His argument fairly overflows with biblical references, mainly to various parts of the Old Testament. The wars of Israel "extraordinarily made by expresse charge from God" are those with the "best warrant that could be" (Gouge 1631, 214–15). "Maintenance of Truth, and purity of Religion" moved Israel to make war on "their brethren on the other side of Jordan." "Saints" such as Abraham and Joshua, some of the judges, and "the best of the Kings" are cited as having waged war with God's approval. Gouge notes that priests went to war among the Israelites, that "God is said to teach mens hands to warre, and fingers to fight." Moreover, God himself fights in such war: "Battels are stiled warres of God, and the Lords battels"; "God himselfe is stiled A man of warre, and the Lord of hosts" (209–10).

Visible in Gouge's thought is not only the interpretation of biblical examples as universally valid types, as in Bullinger and Allen, but also a more characteristically Puritan emphasis on holy war as war commanded by God. Whereas in the case of Israel that command sometimes came directly, it comes to the Puritan Christians through the Bible by faith. The command is, though, no less absolutely binding, and soldiers who have received it may "go in faith, with much confidence, cheerfully, and courageously," not fearing death, for their souls are in God's hands (217). The outcome of "the battels of the Lord" is, moreover, known in advance, because in them Christians are not fighting alone but alongside God himself and by his direction (290).

Such reasoning to justify war for religion was spread broadly over English society in this period. The Scottish Presbyterian author Alexander Leighton, writing with the aim of getting England to join in the conflict now known as the Thirty Years War, describes just cause as "the maintenance of religion, or civil right, either for our selves, or our Christian confederates" (Leighton 1624, 9–10). Unlike Gouge, however, for whom God's command makes a war just in itself, Leighton argues that the wars of Israel show that God himself recognizes such just causes as grounds for war (6). Leighton and Gouge's contemporary Thomas Barnes cites the Old Testament to argue that God commands war in cases of "monstrous pride," "insolence against God," "insulting over the Church," "tumultousnesse and rebellion," and "false-heartednesse" (Barnes 1626, 29–30). For him these justifying causes for war, being grounded in the Bible, are of far greater importance than defense, which he mentions only later and then only in passing.

Bullinger, Allen, Gouge, Leighton, and Barnes all continued and built upon traditional medieval Christian justifications of war for the cause of religion. Contemporaneously, other authors, among them Victoria and Grotius, were advancing a contrary argument, also based in reasoning inherited from the Middle Ages, that rejected religious reasons as justifying causes for offensive war. The latter position ultimately carried the day and became the basis for the Western moral tradition on war as it has developed in the modern period (see further Kelsay and Johnson 1991, 16–25). This elimination of religion as a justification for war is tied closely to the modern Western conception of the state as a secular political entity within which the interests and rights represented by religion exist only as one set among many, all of which the state should seek to protect as far as possible. Under this scheme religiously rooted rights and interests compete with those from other sectors, and the state has no obligation to favor them over those of other sectors. However, when the state itself develops a state ideology, something very much like holy war reasoning reasserts itself in secular guise. Examples include the ideologies of nationalism, nazism, communism, ethnicity, and even democracy. The West, then, has not completely rejected war for religion, for something very like it lives on in the form of wars for various justifying ideologies.

The Justification of War for Religion in Classical Islamic Thought

While the distinction between the *dar al-islam* and the *dar al-harb* provides an essential element for understanding the juristic concept of jihad, there is more to the jihad idea than this. A closer look at the concept of the justification for jihad in itself as it developed in classical Islamic thought will make this apparent. The classical Islamic jurists treated the justification of war for religious purpose in two different contexts, that of the Muslim community in its external relations with non-Muslim societies and that of the internal order of the Muslim community. In the former context the endemic threat of the *dar al-harb* justified defensive jihad and the role of the *dar al-islam* in history justified offensive jihad. In the latter context, the jurists focused on the need to maintain peace, order, and conformity within the *dar al-islam*. While in principle they defined the *dar al-islam* as the territory of peace, in practice they recognized various forms of disruption that could justify the use of force: apostasy, dissent, schism, rebellion, highway robbery, and other disturbances of the peace of Islam. The use of military force to suppress such violations of the peace of Islam could also be termed jihad, provided the intention was to ensure right religion and eradicate the forces of unbelief. Our concern here is principally with the justification of war for religion in the international context.

The Justification of Jihad in Classical Islamic Juristic Thought: An Overview

As noted earlier, the concept of jihad as it is found in the Qur'an and in the writings of the Sunni jurists is defined generally as effort or striving in the path of God. The word "jihad" and its derivations, with this meaning, appear thirty-six times in the Qur'an (see Ali 1977, 166–67, for the full listing), whereas the term *qital* and its derivations are employed for the practice of warfare. Outside the Qur'an itself, though, Islamic tradition very early associated the two concepts. This is one implication of the distinction ascribed to the Prophet between the "lesser jihad," warfare, and the "greater jihad," the struggle to purify oneself and submit fully to God. A place for jihad in the sense of warfare for the faith was also secured by the juristic classification of four types of jihad, that of the heart (faith), that of the tongue (right speech), that of the hand (good works), and finally that of the sword (holy war). Thus while it may be only in a derivative sense that jihad entails the use of force (*qital*), when the classical jurists employed the term in the context of relations with the *dar al-harb*, it is clear that they meant actual warfare and not simply missionary work or personal efforts at self-purification to resist the temptations offered by the territory of unbelief. Like Clausewitz's concept of war as politics carried on by other means, the classical idea of jihad as war was the struggle to establish and spread Islamic faith and law by means other than self-discipline, persuasion, and example.

The warrant for jihad in the sense of warfare can be traced to the permission given the first Muslims in Medina to fight back against the "folk who broke their solemn pledges": "Will ye not fight a folk who broke their solemn pledges, and proposed to drive out the Messenger and did attack you first?" (Qur'an 9:13). The message telling how to treat such unbelievers is unmistakable: "If they withdraw not from you, and offer you not peace, and refrain not their hand, take them, and slay them wherever you come to them; against them We have given you a clear authority" (Qur'an 4:91–93). This is a warrant both for defense and for punishment of wrongdoing. The extent of the defensive warrant is also explicit in the following often-cited passage:

> Fight for the sake of [or "in the way of"] God those that fight against you, but do not attack them first. God does not love the aggressors. Slay them wherever you find them. Drive them out of the places from which they drove you. Idolatry is worse than carnage. . . . Fight against them until idolatry is no more and God's religion reigns supreme. But if they desist, fight none except the evil-doers. (Qur'an 2:190–93)

Warrant for jihad in the sense of *offensive* military action against unbelievers can be traced to passages such as the following:

Make war on them until idolatry shall cease and God's religion shall reign supreme. If they desist, God is cognizant of all their actions; but if they give no heed, know then that God will protect you. (Qur'an 8:39–40)

Fight those who do not believe in God or the last day, and do not hold forbidden that which has been forbidden by God and His Apostle, or acknowledge the religion of truth (even if they are) of the people of the book, until they pay *jizya* with willing submission, and feel themselves subdued. (Qur'an 9:29)

The point here is reducing the unbelievers to submission to Islamic order—the conception which in Western thought is rendered as the right to correct wrongdoing. Here, though, the wrongdoing in question is defined in specifically religious terms, whereas in the West religious wrongdoing was seen as only one of various forms of wrongdoing that justified the prince's resort to force.

For the jurists, Ann K. S. Lambton notes (1981, 208–9), the duty to wage jihad in the sense of offensive warfare was a collective duty (*fard kifaya*) of the Muslim community, and all male, free, mature, able-bodied Muslims physically able to take part in such war and able to provide the necessary weapons were expected to take part. At the same time, as an action of the community as a whole, this warfare had to be undertaken at the command of the *imam*, the community's religious and political leader, who had the responsibility to lead the community in military jihad (either through his personal presence or by appointing a military commander) and to decide when to initiate such fighting, when to avoid it, and when to bring it to an end (cf. Khadduri 1966, 16, and Watt in Murphy 1976, 152–53). Because of the collective nature of the communal duty, all persons not able to take part in the war could discharge their own religious obligation in other ways, each carrying out his or her own personal striving (jihad) of the heart, tongue, and hands.

Rudolph Peters, drawing on various juristic sources, lists the following as exempt from the requirement to participate in jihad as the offensive warfare of the Muslim community against the *dar al-harb*: minors and the insane, because they are not legally capable; slaves, because their masters would otherwise risk losing their property; women, "since their constitution is not fit for warfare"; the ill and handicapped ("These must be disabled to such an extent that they cannot walk or ride a horse"); those who do not possess the necessary means for a military expedition; those who have not obtained permission from their parents to engage in jihad; debtors without their creditors' permission to engage in jihad; and for the Hanafi school only, the best lawyer (*faqih*) in a town (Peters 1979, 15–18).

If Muslim territory is attacked, however, matters are different; defensive jihad is a binding duty (*fard 'ayn*) on all Muslims as individuals (cf. Lambton 1981, 209; Sachedina 1988, 110–11). This conception corresponds functionally to the later Western idea of the *levée en masse*, a mass uprising by the populace of a nation in response to invasion (for examples, see Johnson 1981, 66, 237, 245, 252, 282, 308, 315). The justification for the *levée en masse*, however, derives from the right of self-defense each person is assumed to possess as a gift of nature (as in the discussion of "private war" in Grotius 1949, bk. 1, chap. 3, par. 1, and chap. 5, and bk. 2, chaps. 2 and 3), whereas the justification for defensive jihad comes directly from the divine command (as in Qur'an 2:190ff.).[3]

So the distinction between offensive and defensive jihad, as developed by the jurists, turns out to hinge on the nature of the religious obligation that justifies it: offensive jihad, when properly authorized and directed against the *dar al-harb*, is a duty of the Islamic community as a unit, whereas defensive jihad is a duty incumbent on Muslims as individuals. This is a quite significant difference with broad implications. In the first place, it shows that warrant alone is not sufficient for the waging of offensive jihad and shifts the focus to the nature of the Muslim community and its governing authority. Second, the obligation to wage offensive warfare to enlarge the territory of Islam turns out not to mean all that the assumption of perpetual strife between the *dar al-harb* and the *dar al-islam* seems to imply. As Khadduri comments, "The state of war existing between the dar al-Islam and the dar al-harb . . . does not mean that actual hostilities must occur" (Khadduri 1966, 14). Since the jurists allowed the *imam* of the community a certain latitude in choosing when, where, and against what enemy to wage jihad, in practice this led to formal armistices that could last for up to ten years; an informal peace in a given region could last much longer. Third, in the absence of the conditions assumed by the juristic tradition as necessary for offensive jihad, the concept of defensive jihad has tended to enlarge in various ways. We will examine all these issues further in later chapters.

Abdulaziz Sachedina argues from Shi'ite tradition for another dimension in the difference between offensive and defensive jihad. Expanding the latter to include retaliation by force, he finds a "strictly moral" basis for the justification of defensive or retaliatory jihad in the Qur'anic injunctions to eradicate "corruption on earth" and "commanding good and forbidding evil" (Sachedina 1988, 106). By contrast, the warrant for offensive jihad is not moral alone, even though it seeks the general aim of universally establishing a just public order. Sachedina's point, however, is not that this kind of jihad is exclusively religious rather than moral, but rather that as conceived by the classical Muslim jurists it was fundamentally political. This conception, he argues, is a quite different concept from that found in the Qur'an: "In the final analysis, the [classical] Sunni jurists identified jihad in the direction of establishing a universal social and political order under a Muslim ruler. But the Qur'an clearly points toward the establishment of a universal *creed*" (107, emphasis added).

The Sunni jurists were certainly interested in the political aspect of the Muslim community; in historical context, though, the Shi'ite juristic tradition did not challenge the concept of a unitary *dar al-islam*, only the authority of the caliphs to rule over it. In any case, as Lambton (1981, 209) emphasizes, the jurists' conception was only a theoretical construct, and one that was not reflected in the actual course of history. The Muslim expansion did not continue relative to the *dar al-harb*; non-Muslim states continued to exist and prosper, and from time to time Muslim territory was lost to them; and the ostensibly united *dar al-islam* was fragmented by the rise of rival caliphates and *de facto* independent political entities. Khadduri (1966, 20) defines seven stages in the evolution of the Islamic state: (1) the city-state (622–32), (2) the imperial state (632–750), (3) the "universal" state (750–ca. 900), (4) "decentralization" (ca. 900–ca. 1500), (5) "fragmentation" (ca. 1500–1918), and (7) the national state (1918–present). The development of classic Islamic jurisprudence spanned the second and third of these stages; the gradual historical breakdown of Islamic unity spans the last three. Even the religious unity of the Islamic world was shattered early by the doctrinal division between the Sunnis and Shi'ites, as well as less extensive but important disputes such as that with the Kharijis. A significant result was the extension of the idea of jihad in the sense of war for religion to warfare against internal disturbers of the Islamic order. Al-Mawardi defined two types of jihad, that against unbelievers and that against believers. Within the latter he distinguished three categories: that against apostates (*ahl al-ridda*), that against rebels (*ahl al-baghi*), and that against those who renounce the authority of the *imam* (*al-muharabin*) (Lambton 1981, 211). After the fall of the caliphate, and in the absence of centralized religious authority, temporal rulers declared themselves to be *mujahiddin*, leaders of the faithful in holy war. But the lack of any theoretical recognition of the possibility of a plurality of distinct states within the *dar al-islam* meant that Muslim rulers in the various states "referred to themselves as lords of Islam or of the Muslims and their territories as Islamic lands" (212).

The same tendencies continue in the present day. Contemporary Islamic fundamentalists rage against the "secular" governments of states like Egypt and Algeria and attempt to create theocratic rule in cases like Sudan. The terms *jihad* and *mujahid* are evoked for causes as diverse as the assassination of Anwar al-Sadat, the war against Israel, the Iran-Iraq war, and the war in Afghanistan. In the Gulf War Iraqi leader Saddam Hussein termed the struggle a jihad against the forces of the West, while the Saudi *ulama* (assembly of clergy) declared a jihad against Saddam. The ideas of the unity of Islam, its superiority and predestined triumph over the *dar al-harb*, and the duty of jihad to bring about this triumph continue to prove their ability to stir strong emotions but do not, as they did in their classical formulation, correspond to the historical reality witnessed by those who evoke these ideas. The effect is that the contemporary use of these ideas has changed from what it was in the age of the classical jurists. It is important, then, to look closely at the idea of jihad in the sense of war for religion in its classical stage to understand what this idea meant there.

The Two Worlds Distinction as the Context of the Idea of Jihad in Islam

The war of the *dar al-islam* against the *dar al-harb* is jihad in all its senses, including the military one. Lambton comments:

> The first duty of the Islamic world is to exalt the word of God until it is supreme. Hence the only proper relationship to the non-Islamic world is one of perpetual warfare. . . . The universality of Islam thus imposes upon the *imam* the duty of *jihad* until the whole world is converted or submits to Islam. (Lambton 1981, 201)

Sachedina observes similarly,

> There is no doubt that the Muslim jurists conceived *jihad* in the sense of engaging in a war to increase the "sphere of Islam" (*dar al-islam*) as an integral part of Islamic faith. . . . [T]he sphere in which this *jihad* was to be waged was designated the "sphere of war" (*dar*

al-harb), with the essential aim of uprooting unbelief and preparing the way for the creation of Islamic order on earth. (Sachedina 1988, 106–7)

Sachedina continues by noting that for the jurists this jihad is aimed not at converting individuals or groups to Islam ("people of the Book" could be tolerated and incorporated into the *dar al-islam*; "idolaters" could be killed), but at subduing the "forces of unbelief," that is, the political order of the unbelievers and its military arm. Not only did such forces stand in the way of the eventual spread of Islam throughout the earth, but as embodiments of immorality and unsettledness they threatened the moral order of the *dar al-islam*. So the justification of jihad against the *dar al-harb* also had a defensive aspect. The Sunni jurists "identified *jihad* in the direction of establishing a universal social and political order under a Muslim ruler" (107). But the Shi'ite branch of Islam, because of its belief that until the return of the hidden Imam there is no rightly guided ruler, has restricted jihad essentially to its defensive meaning (116–17).

It is clear from the early juristic distinction between *dar al-harb* and *dar al-islam* that the question of jihad by military means was not the major concern. Instead of looking outward, this dichotomy was in the first place focused inward, on explaining how the Muslim community was set in the world and how it should behave in itself and relative to the non-Muslim world. Rather than seeking to divide the world, it sought to describe a division that was already a fact and set up parameters for how Muslims should act to make the best of it. (Cf. the table of contents of al-Shaybani's *Siyar*, or law of nations, in Khadduri 1966, xvi–xviii.)

Within this context, the division of the world into the *dar al-islam* and the *dar al-harb* served two general purposes: to define the relationship between the Muslim religio-political order and non-Muslim political entities and to define the relationship between the Muslim religio-political order and non-Muslim religious groups within it. The overriding assumption visible in the division of the world into two spheres was the uniqueness of the territory of Islam relative to the rest of the world: the *dar al-islam* was the territory of peace, while the remainder of the world was continually torn by strife. Now, while this undoubtedly idealized the peacefulness of the Muslim community, it was a not unrealistic characterization of the relationships and behavior visible in the world beyond this community.

Centuries later, in a different part of the world and with a different cultural heritage, Thomas Hobbes would characterize the behavior of nations as that of the state of nature, a "war of every man against every man." Such is the *dar al-harb* of classical Islamic jurisprudence. It is a territory perpetually at war because of its nature, and while some mitigation of this nature is effected in the laws of lands under the rule of the "people of the Book," the only way to deal with it ultimately is to bring it under the law of Islam, which is the law of peace. (Cf. Khadduri 1966, 12–13.) Agreements for trade and other interaction, even peace treaties, may be entered into with the *dar al-harb*, but they are expected to be only temporary affairs, because of the very nature of the territory of war. Again, this represents a fundamental realism that is reflected in the actual conduct of nations. Peace treaties, trade agreements, and other forms of interaction among nations come and go. From this perspective what is unrealistic is less the characterization of the *dar al-harb* than that of the *dar al-islam*, which, it turns out, also has its problems of internal strife.

The internal problems the jurists sought to confront were of several sorts: how to deal with inhabitants of the *dar al-harb* who came into the *dar al-islam* for commerce and other such purposes, how to deal with non-Muslim slaves brought into the *dar al-islam* as a result of war, how to deal with the communities of non-Muslim "people of the Book" who lived within the *dar al-islam*, and how to cope with the actual reality that Muslims themselves were not always at peace with one another. This last included persons who followed their own interpretation of one or more doctrines (*muta'awwils*), apostates (*ridda*), dissenters (*kharijis*), rebels (*baghis*), and simple bandits, who, while perhaps not denying Islamic faith, had transgressed Islamic law and disturbed the *pax Islamica*. (Cf. al-Shaybani, bks. 3 and 6–11, and Khadduri 1988, 106–29, 158–292.) Each group posed its own problems and had to be addressed in its own way by the interpreters of the law.

Since the classical jurists understood the law that bound Islam to be by definition immutable, having been given directly by God through the Prophet, they did not conceive these problems as requiring new legislation, but rather as requiring new understanding of how to apply divinely given law to each particular case. Since the Muslim community was at one and the same time political and religious, and since its religiously defined law (which the jurists sought to interpret) was the law of the Islamic state, it followed that the use of force against those who transgressed the law had the character of religious war. Thus a full understanding of classical Islamic doctrine on war for religion must take into account the provisions for such uses of force as well as for use of force against the *dar al-harb*.

Thus the jurists used the distinction between *dar al-islam* and *dar al-harb* to organize their reflections on the meaning of Islamic law and its application. While Augustine's *civitas terrenae* and *civitas dei* were originally conceptual vehicles for explaining theologically the presence of sin and grace, or more precisely the sinful love *cupiditas* as opposed to the perfect love *caritas*, the Islamic jurists' distinction was focused on behavior and its regulation; it was not a theological concept at all, but a functional distinction aimed at clarifying the implications of Islamic law.

In their understanding of this distinction the classical jurists differ from contemporary Muslim fundamentalists, for whom this non-Qur'anic separation of the world into two spheres has taken on the character of a distinction between the satanic and the righteous. The jurists did not begin from the same perspective as present-day Islamic fundamentalists. They approached the distinction between *dar al-islam* and *dar al-harb* from within an Islamic empire that was the master of great portions of the known world, an empire that was powerful, prosperous, and intellectually more than equal to the world outside its boundaries. They could look with confidence on the ultimate triumph of Islam as a social and political system. Present-day Islamic fundamentalists, by contrast, look on the distinction between *dar al-islam* and *dar al-harb* from within a truncated and politically fragmented residuum of that empire. Rather than enjoying power relative to the non-Muslim world, they have experienced colonial and other forms of political domination. Rather than controlling their own destinies, they have seen their laws, political structures, and social customs eroded or supplanted by Western influences. The *dar al-islam* has experienced the taking away of power, culture, and even territory. So for contemporary fundamentalists the nature of the *dar al-harb* and the threat posed by it have taken on a theological rather than juristic character, and the opposition between the two "abodes" is perceived as a battle between the forces of good and the forces of evil. Jihad, as the form this warfare takes, is thus a greatly intensified duty for the faithful.

A Representative Classical Statement: The Idea of Jihad in Shaybani's *Siyar*

A representative and particularly accessible source is the *Siyar* (law of nations) of the eighth-century jurist al-Shaybani (born probably in 132 A.H./750 C.E.; see Khadduri 1966, 28 n. 74), a student and follower of Abu

Hanifa, founder of the Hanafi school of Islamic law, and his disciple Abu Yusuf. "No other jurist in the formative period," comments Khadduri, "seems to have contributed more to [the developing idea of *siyar*] than Shaybani" (Khadduri 1966, 41). Shaybani's career includes a period devoted to lecturing and writing on jurisprudence and a period of service in the role of judge (*qadi*), a position in which he was expected to advise the ruling authorities on matters related to Islamic law. His life coincided with the period of the spread of influence of the teachings of the Hanafi school (29–35). In the last stage of his life Shaybani was summoned to live in Baghdad, then the center of government of the growing Islamic empire, and became a legal adviser to the caliph.

Shaybani's thought thus provides a window into one of the major streams of Islamic jurisprudence during the period of its formation and spread, an example reflecting practical experience of government as well as a keen intellectual ability to understand the tradition and draw new implications from it to apply to the reality at hand. Khadduri (1966, 57) notes that Shaybani has been called "the Hugo Grotius of Islam" for his formative influence on the developing Muslim juristic concept of the law of nations; in terms of his life, however, a better comparison is with another major figure in Western moral tradition on war, the Spanish Dominican schoolman Victoria, who after spending the majority of his career as a teacher, lecturer, and writer, concluded it as a consultant to his monarch, the emperor Charles V, on matters pertaining to the just use of force by the Spanish against the Indians in the New World (see Victoria 1917; cf. Johnson 1975, chap. 3).

The term *siyar*, as used by jurists, referred to the conduct of the state in its relationships with other communities (Khadduri 1966, 39). The full title of Shaybani's major work, *Kitab al-Siyar al-Kabir*, means the "law" of such relationships: hence the description of Shaybani's work by the Western term "law of nations."

Shaybani makes certain assumptions in his *Siyar*, among them the already established juristic division of the world into *dar al-islam* and *dar al-harb* and the conception that a perpetual state of war exists between the two. Unbelievers who live in the *dar al-harb* are *harbis*, belligerents. This state of belligerency means that any *harbi* who enters the *dar al-islam* may be killed, just as any belligerent would be in war. Nonetheless, in practice peaceful forms of interaction between the two territories are possible. While the political entities of the *dar al-harb* are not recognized as legitimate, tempo-rary peace treaties—perhaps more properly termed armistices, since the assumed state of war continues—may be concluded with them to facilitate

necessary interchanges (such as commerce) between the two territories or to
protect the Islamic lands from invasion if the power of the unbelievers in the
dar al-harb is (temporarily, it is assumed) greater. Likewise, *harbis* may be
admitted into the *dar al-islam* under a safe-conduct (*aman*) for particular
reasons advantageous to the *dar al-islam*. Shaybani in addition accepted the
position of Abu Hanifa that even in the absence of such formal arrange-
ments, Muslims should treat *harbis* according to the principle of reciprocity,
with specific examples including commerce, diplomatic immunity, and matters
associated with the exchange of prisoners (Shaybani, pars. 732–33, 774–
81, in Khadduri 1966, 170, 174–75; cf. Khadduri 1966, 52–53). Shaybani's
emphasis is on detailing the rules by which such peaceful interaction should
be ordered (Shaybani, chaps. 4–6, in Khadduri 1966, 130–94).

Like his teacher Abu Hanifa, Shaybani never says that the unbelievers are
to be attacked by the Muslims solely on account of their unbelief; they must
show themselves a hostile threat. Shaybani's conception of actual military
action against the *harbis* is that of defensive holy war, following the
injunction of the passage cited earlier, Qur'an 2:190: "Fight for the sake of
God those that fight against you, but do not attack them first. God does not
love the aggressors" (Shaybani, par. 1, in Khadduri 1966, 76).

Specifically on the waging of jihad, Shaybani opens the *Siyar* by citing the
Prophet's charge to his troops (Shaybani, par. 1, in Khadduri 1966, 75–77):
The Muslim *mujahiddin* are to fight "in the name of God and in the path of
God." They are to fight only unbelievers. They are neither to cheat, nor to
commit treachery, nor to mutilate, nor to kill children. Whenever they meet
their "polytheist enemies," they are first to invite them to accept Islam. If
they do, then they are no longer enemies, and specific directions are given for
dealing with them; if they do not, then they are to be fought against and
killed or subdued.

This charge establishes the proper order of the mission of the Islamic
community. It is most desirable that people accept Islam. While this acceptance must be "without compulsion" (Qur'an 2: 256), where "polytheists"
are concerned, they must in fact accept the religion of Islam or be killed. The
invitation to Islam is to be issued before fighting begins to allow them to
exercise this choice. The jihad of the sword, then, takes second place to that
of the tongue, the call to Islam. It is clear from this charge that in such
contexts the purpose of jihad, in the core sense of striving in the path of
Islam, is the conquest of unbelief through bringing unbelievers to accept
Islam. The increase of territory under Muslim rule is a function of this. If the
call to Islam is heeded by those to whom it is addressed, then their territory

falls under the rule of Islamic law and becomes part of the territory of the Muslim community—the *dar al-islam*, in the jurists' terminology. If the call to Islam is not heeded, then the next priority for the Muslim community is to extend the rule of Islamic law by force if necessary.

The priority of the call leads Shaybani to term it "commendable" for a Muslim army to renew the invitation to Islam after fighting has begun, though "if it fails to do so it is not wrong" (par. 55, in Khadduri 1966, 95). Beyond this, though, so long as the fighting continues, the war may be prosecuted as harshly as necessary as long as the Muslims do not resort to treachery. The Muslims may launch their attack "by night or by day" and may use fire or flooding against enemy fortifications. Because the *harbis* are unbelievers, they have no inherent rights relative to the Muslims once the war has begun; the only limits mentioned by Shaybani on the conduct of the Muslim force in fighting are those required by Islam or advantageous to the Muslims.

The religious purpose of such war is further indicated by Shaybani's references to "the Imam" as the one who authorizes the fighting, exercises overall leadership of the army (though does not necessarily command it in battle), and has the power of decision over such matters as the disposition of spoils of war (cf. chap. 2, passim, in Khadduri 1966, 55–105). The enemies, unbelievers belonging to the *dar al-harb*, have no rights at all in their persons; the only limits on what may be done to them, whatever their status, are derived from the words of the Prophet (such as the forbidding of treachery, intentional mutilation, and the killing of children) or the decision of the Imam on whatever else is "advantageous to the Muslims" (par. 97, in Khadduri 1966, 100). The members of the Muslim army are individually and collectively bound by religious rules of conduct specified in the Qur'an, though in the absence of the Imam or other high authority, such as the governor of a city or province, a specifically military commander does not have the authority to exact penalties under these rules (pars. 124–33, in Khadduri 1966, 103). Upon the return of the army to the *dar al-islam* it is the decision of the Imam, as religious leader and thus the highest authority in the *umma*, as to how to divide the spoil (chap. 3, in Khadduri 1966, 106–29).

We thus find in Shaybani's discussion of jihad against the *dar al-harb* several key elements of the idea of holy war already identified in other contexts: religious justification, religious authority, religious rules for conduct of the participants, and a definition of the enemy in terms of difference of religious belief, a definition that makes all the enemy, regardless of personal status, susceptible to being killed by the army in the course of the war. Nonetheless, this difference of belief alone is not itself warrant for war; that requires an active showing of hostility by the *harbis*. Shaybani's conception of jihad is thus fundamentally one of defensive war for the faith, though his concept of defense is a broad one due to the conception of the *dar al-harb* as a source of perennial enmity and danger. The idea that jihad is to be waged against unbelievers simply for their unbelief is not found in Shaybani; Khadduri notes that it can be traced to the later jurist Shafi'i (d. 204 A.H./820 C.E.). This latter interpretation, though not part of the early juristic understanding of jihad against the *dar al-harb*, became normative within the later Sunni tradition (Khadduri 1966, 57–58).

An Alternative to the Juristic Theory: The Concept of Jihad in Farabi's *Aphorisms*

As noted earlier, in Western Europe from the medieval through the early modern periods thinking about holy war developed as part of a broader tradition on the justification and limitation of war, one shaped by nonreligious as well as religious sources. In Islamic culture too there were efforts to define a conception of war for reasons apart from jihad, a conception generated not by religion but by the needs of good government as such. This reasoning was a contribution from the sphere of philosophy, not jurisprudence. The most prominent exponent of this way of thinking about war is the philosopher Abu Nasr al-Farabi (257 A.H./870 C.E.–339 A.H./950 C.E.) in his *Aphorisms of the Statesman*.

Farabi's thought, coming just as the Islamic state was decentralizing into increasingly autonomous regional powers, provided an alternative way to think about statecraft in those regional centers of power. While religious orthodoxy continued to hold to the concept of a single, religiously and politically coextensive Islamic community, Farabi focused on what was needed to be a good ruler of a single city-state, the emergent practical reality. Born over a century after Shaybani and fifty years after Shafi'i, Farabi lived in a time when the juristic tradition on jihad was well established; he also lived in a period in which the spread of Islam had made the borders between the *dar al-islam* and the *dar al-harb* relatively distant from the seat of the caliphate in Baghdad. His concern, then, was not with the warfare that might take place on those frontiers but with the uses of force that might be necessary for virtuous rulers of cities within the Islamic world. These differences produced a concept of warfare different in important respects from that of jihad as defined by the jurists. In the following brief summary of Farabi's thought on war and government I draw extensively on the discussion of Charles Butterworth in "Al-Farabi's Statecraft: War and the Well-Ordered Regime" (Butterworth 1990).

In the *Aphorisms* Farabi lists eleven kinds of war (*harb*) that may occur and the ends for which they are waged, distinguishing the unjust forms of war from the rest. His list begins with five kinds of warfare: that for defense, acquiring a good the city deserves, reforming others, subjecting those suited for it, and retaking what is rightfully the city's but has been taken from it, declaring that all these types of war serve two purposes: acquiring some good for the city and establishing justice. To this initial list he then adds two other types of war, arguing that they serve these same two ends: warfare to punish those who have committed some crime and warfare against implacable enemies of the city "to destroy them in their entirety and to extirpate them thoroughly because their survival is a harm for the people of the city" (54). While Farabi does not explicitly say that these seven types of war, all of which serve the same two good ends, are just, this is clearly his implication, since he explicitly labels the four remaining types of war unjust: that "for the sake of the ruler's increased honor or self-aggrandizement, pure conquest, venting of rage or achieving some other pleasure through victory, and overreaction to an injustice committed by others" (85).

Farabi's listing of (implicitly) just kinds of war is more extensive than the three justifying causes for war identified by the Christian theorist Augustine, which became normative in Western tradition: repelling an injury, retaking something wrongly taken, and punishment of evil (Augustine, *Quaestiones in Heptateuchum* 6.10; see further Johnson 1987, 60). The forms of unjust war identified by Farabi are closer to Augustine's list of "what is evil in war": "the love of violence, revengeful cruelty, fierce and implacable enmity, wild resistance and the lust of power, and such like" (Augustine, *Contra Faustum* 22.74; see further Johnson 1987, 61).

More to the present point of Islamic tradition on war, Farabi in this context makes no explicit mention of the concept of jihad and no attempt to relate it to his list of just and unjust forms of war. Butterworth (1990, 84) argues that Farabi's third type of war, that to subject "a certain people to what is best and most fortunate for them . . . when they have not known it on their own and have not submitted to someone who does know it and calls them to it by speech," is a possible reference to the juristic tradition and point of contact with the jihad idea. Certainly Farabi's language, though rather abstract, could be taken as a description of the *harbi*, the traditional object of jihad. If this was intentional on Farabi's part, then the effect is to redefine jihad as one form of just warfare among others which may be engaged in by the virtuous statesman. But Butterworth notes that neither the word "jihad" nor any of its derivatives appear in Farabi's discussion. Given Farabi's purpose, to define good statecraft for the rule of city-states within the world of Islam, it might be more appropriate to link this category of just war to the suppression of apostasy, heresy, or dissidence; yet the phrasing, to subject the people in question to "what is best and most fortunate for them," is quite generic and makes no explicit reference to religious heterodoxy or unbelief.

In any case, it is abundantly clear that Farabi's conception of types of warfare justified for the statesman to prosecute is much broader than that of jihad as defined by the juristic tradition. It is also more secular. The aims Farabi attaches to these just kinds of war, securing some good for the city and establishing justice, are aims of statecraft, not of religion. The virtuous ruler will presumably be a good Muslim, but he is to be guided in his practice of governing by philosophy, not the limits of Islamic juristic tradition.

At the same time, the tradition of jihad lives on in Farabi's concept of the virtuous man as, among other qualities, one who does not fear death in the service of the city; the virtuous warrior is *al mujahid al-fadil* (Butterworth 1990, 86). Further, within the plenitude of positive characteristics possessed by a virtuous ruler, one of them is "bodily capacity for *jihad*, and having nothing in his body that prevents him from carrying out things pertaining to jihad" (88). The use of the term "jihad" and its derivative *mujahid* in these contexts makes its absence in the discussion of just and unjust war the more noticeable. It is clear that Farabi knows the tradition of jihad and its implications, but that the kind of war he is discussing has a different focus.

Over the succeeding centuries the practice of statecraft within the *dar al-islam* became increasingly characterized by an acceptance of territorial pluralism and of conflicts among segments of what was in religious theory a single Islamic community. Farabi's work reflects the context of this development and reveals a form of self-understanding more closely attuned to the problems of ensuring the good of specific, and plural, Muslim political communities. In his conception jihad, war for religion, is more of an echo than a major concern. Yet in the religious tradition, represented forcefully by the jurists but also present in popular religion, jihad remained and could be invoked even for internal warfare of Muslims against Muslims. Farabi's work provides a point of contact between Islamic culture and those forces which in the West would eventually lead to a secularized conception of the justification and limitation of war, with war for religiously defined causes explicitly rejected. It might still be possible to construct an indigenously Muslim, though philosophical rather than juristic, understanding of state-craft on the base of such a conception as Farabi's. Within historical Islamic culture, however, despite the practical acceptance of territorial pluralism and uses of force justified by the concerns of politics rather than of religion, the theoretical innovations implicit in Farabi's work did not triumph. The official tradition remained that defined by the jurists, with jihad in the sense of holy war against the forces of unbelief a central element in the under-standing of the Islamic state and its relation to other states.

4

AUTHORITY TO
MAKE HOLY WAR

In both the Western Christian and Islamic traditions holy war requires religious justification as determined by religious authority. Such authority ensures that the warrants for war are sufficient and have been properly interpreted; it establishes a substantive link between the war and the power, blessings, and/or moral obligations associated with religion; and it makes clear whose decisions are to be regarded as final in waging the war. Failure to examine the justification for war opens the gates to wars or threats of war or calls to holy war in the service of nonreligious causes, but under the cover of spurious religious warrant. Failure to establish a link between war and religion deprives the participants and the community that supports them of much-needed psychological support. Without a sense of transcendent purpose, those waging the war and their supporters will question the cost and doubt the success of the undertaking. Failure to establish final decision-making authority begs the fundamental question of ultimate responsibility, both for initiating the resort to arms and the manner of prosecution of the war, as well as for the destruction that results and the benefits, if any, that accrue from the fighting.

How these problems are addressed reveals a good deal about the nature of the religion in question and the place of religion in the political community whose forces undertake the holy war. Accordingly, the Western Christian and the Islamic traditions differ significantly in how they speak to these issues. Thus it follows that holy war has a different status in the statecraft of the two traditions as well.

Authority to Wage War
for Religion in Western Christian Tradition

From Rejecting War to Authorizing War

What, exactly, does religious authority for holy war mean for Christian tradition? The answer is not simple. The earliest Christian communities, gathered in eschatological hope for the second coming of Christ, rejected participation in war as they rejected all participation in the politics of the age. For its part, the Roman state often persecuted Christians and sought to eradicate their communities. Gradually this attitude of separateness changed as the character of the church became less eschatological and as state treatment of Christians came to include periods of toleration and even encouragement. By the second century Christians were serving in government, and by the third quarter of that century there is evidence of a Christian legion in the Roman army, the so-called *Legio Fulminata* (Cadoux 1982, 229–31). Still, participation in the order of this world continued to be opposed in some circles. For the Latin-speaking North African theologian Tertullian, writing at the end of the second century, involvement in this world was, plainly and simply, "idolatry" (Tertullian, *On Idolatry*, in Roberts and Donaldson 1885, 2:61–78). For his Greek-speaking Alexandrian contemporary Origen, writing early in the third century, Christians ought to avoid participation in the political order and might not under any circumstances serve as soldiers; yet Christians too support the empire, argued Origen, because they pray for the emperor and for his forces in battle (Origen, *Contra Celsus*, 8.73; Roberts and Donaldson 1885, 4:395–669). Other theologians argued similarly (see Cadoux 1982, 209–11). This was a remarkable development, for while it was meant as a rationale for a continuation of separatism (Christians might not serve as soldiers), it accepted the idea of Christian intercession on behalf of the Roman state in war.

While actual relations between the church and the Roman state continued for some time to include a mixture of acceptance and rejection, toleration and persecution, the dominant pattern was that of a growing involvement by Christians in the life of the empire and an increasing acceptance of the church by the Roman state. Theologically, the rationale for this was an understanding of the state as "a useful and necessary institution, ordained by God for the security of life and property, the preservation of peace, and the prevention and punishment of the grosser forms of human sin" (Cadoux 1982, 195), a conception derived from Paul in Romans 13 and from other New Testament sources.

A decisive step in the bonding of religious to secular authority was taken in the battle of the Milvian Bridge in 312, when the Emperor Constantine (who was not himself a Christian at that time) adopted the device of the cross as a battle standard for his forces, which included a considerable number of Christian soldiers. Legend has it that a sign appeared in the sky: *In hoc signo vinces* ("By this sign conquer"). Constantine's forces went on to defeat those of his rival Maxentius, who was killed in the battle. Though fought, according to tradition, with divine approval and support and with the participation of Christians, this battle was formally waged on the authority of the secular ruler, Constantine. It was not a case of war formally authorized by the Christian leadership in the name of Christianity.

The development of a tradition of specific religious authority for the use of military force began later, at the end of the fourth and early fifth centuries, when Ambrose and Augustine called for the use of the Roman military against Christian heretics and schismatics. Later tradition took this as a case of their invoking their authority as bishops (of Milan and of Hippo Regius) to give formal sanction to such resort to force and all it might entail. In each of these cases a religious cause was clearly held up as warrant. Yet in both cases the forces in question were those of the Roman state, and neither Ambrose nor Augustine had any formal authority over those forces nor, indeed, any formal standing within the state. In this context, their calls for resort to force had the character of apologetic moral urging that the state authorities do what is right—right for the good of public order as well as for the church. Yet for the faithful the fact that Ambrose and Augustine were bishops could not be missed; their calls to arms amounted to episcopal authorization for war against enemies of the faith (Ambrose, *On the Christian Faith* 2.14.136–43; Augustine, *Contra Faustum* 22.74–75; Russell 1975, 22–26; Swift 1970).

A sharper focusing of the idea of religious authorization for war appears with the case of the First Crusade late in the eleventh century (Walker 1959, 219–22). Here papal authorization was present in such forms as explicit exhortation to Christian knights to join the crusade and indulgences (forgiveness of temporal punishment for sins) given to the crusaders. While some soldiers ultimately under papal command fought in this and later Crusades (including, for the latter, members of military religious orders whose leadership was directly responsible to the pope), they were not a central issue, and most of the soldiers were from the temporal sphere: feudal lords and their vassals and retainers, other persons who had received permission from their feudal superiors to participate in the crusade, and groups of peasants.

Finally, consider the fourteenth-century wars between papal and imperial forces in Italy. These were conflicts in which the pope himself had forces under his ultimate command and authorized their use against the armies of the emperor. The issue in question was ecclesiastical rather than doctrinal; that is, no fundamental Christian doctrines were in dispute, but instead whether the pope had a right as head of the church to exercise temporal lordship over territory as well as spiritual lordship over souls. In these wars papal authority essentially occupied the same place as that of the Emperor Constantine, the secular authority, at the battle of the Milvian Bridge. The cause, in both cases, was clearly secular. These are quite different sorts of cases, and others that might be cited relating to authority for holy war can be closely joined to one or another of them. The judgment of history varies considerably with respect to them: the case of the First Crusade provides the archetypal conception of holy war in Western culture; the late medieval struggle between the pope and the emperor exemplifies the illegitimate overreaching of religious authority into the temporal sphere; the case of Constantine exemplifies the use of religious symbols and warrant by a temporal ruler for an essentially temporal cause; and the type of case illustrated by Ambrose and Augustine illustrates the provision of moral and theological authority but not command authority for the waging of war for religious purpose.

The example of Ambrose and Augustine in fact set up the terms for theological and canonical debate and church practice regarding religious authority for war within Western culture right down to the rejection of war for religion in the seventeenth century. The key fact was their role as bishops. For Western culture in the Middle Ages the issue was posed this way: granted that bishops have spiritual authority and that the spiritual realm is higher than the temporal, does this mean that bishops can also exercise temporal authority? If so, does this right extend to all bishops, or is it limited only to the pope as the bishop of all bishops and head of the church? Does it reach downward to include lesser clergy or members of religious orders as representatives of the spiritual realm as well? The argument was complicated by two factors: the tradition, inherited from early Christian separationist pacifism, that monks and clergy (including bishops at all levels) could not personally bear arms even in a religious cause and the development of offices that joined temporal and spiritual authority in a single person, whereby the bishop of a city was also its feudal lord and the pope came to possess large portions of Italy as temporal suzerain.

Rival Claims to Authority

The medieval and early modern justification of holy war was carried out against this somewhat confused backdrop and was not always consistent in its appeals to authority. A full treatment of this subject would be the subject of a book on church and state during this period (but cf. Johnson 1975). In the present context the best that can be done is to identify the major issues and claims in contest, the principal lines of the argument over them, and the shape of the final resolution of the issues in question.

In most respects the easiest matter to resolve was that of monks and clergy below the rank of bishop. Theological and canonical positions were united and consistent on this. Monks, as a consequence of their calling, had renounced the temporal world and bound themselves by their vows to a life of nonviolence. Even in the world of the monastery (which was conceived as an enclave of the spiritual world, the *civitas dei*, inside yet apart from the temporal sphere), monks had no authority that was not given them by their religious superiors. Thus they could not bear arms or authorize others to do so, even in the best of causes, in support for the church or the Christian religion. Secular clergy, who had not received the same calling as the monks or taken monastic vows and served in the temporal world rather than within an enclave of the heavenly realm, were nonetheless bound by obedience to their superiors and a tradition, eventually formalized into canon law, that allowed them to accompany armies to minister to the soldiers' spiritual needs but forbade them to bear arms or participate in fighting. (See further Johnson 1975, 43–46, and Russell 1975, 105–12.)

These limitations did not prevent monks or priests from writing, preaching, and moral exhortation in support of the idea of war for religion or for actual warfare waged on behalf of the church or for religious reasons. (On the canonical limits placed on clergy and members of religious orders see Russell 1975, 105–12.) Indeed, after the proclamation of the First Crusade by Pope Urban II in 1095, religious and clergy of all levels, including the popular preacher Peter the Hermit, a monk, spread the word throughout Christendom and enlisted volunteers (cf. Walker 1959, 220). St. Bernard of Clairvaux, a monk who went on to found one of the strictest religious orders of the Western church, strongly supported the founding of the military order of the Templars and was a vigorous public advocate of the Second Crusade through public sermons and personal suasion (cf. Russell 1975, 36, and Walker 1959, 221–22). Many clergy and monks accompanied the armies of the Crusades (cf. Morris 1983, 79–87, and Walker 1959, 220–21), and clergy commonly accompanied medieval armies on campaign within Europe under temporal leadership and for entirely temporal reasons. While the primary purpose of the presence of clergy was to say mass, hear confessions, and perform last rites on the dying or dead, they also commonly led prayers for victory and blessed the soldiers and their arms prior to battle. Such activities were accepted by the church and society generally as right and proper manifestations of the priestly function, without contravening canon law or tradition and without in themselves representing the church's commitment to one belligerent's cause or another or implying the presence of religious cause in the conflict.

What overstepped the canonical boundaries were rather different activities, in which individual monks or priests, sometimes personally bearing arms and sometimes not, took the lead at the head of armed forces and personally authorized them. These were invariably affairs involving peasants or townsmen and typically were of one of three kinds: some form of revolt against the established authorities, organized persecution of Jews or heterodox Christians, or resistance against armed bands of robbers. Only in the second type of case was any specifically religious cause claimed, but a more general divine blessing was typically claimed for the other kinds of such warfare, comparable to the blessing claimed for members of armies led by feudal authorities.

Local uprisings led by individual priests or monks against Jews, heterodox Christians, and other such religiously defined "enemies" or "dangers" illustrate the danger of conceiving holy war only in terms of war justified by appeal to religious warrant or cause. Local monks and priests simply did not have the authority, in religious terms, to make such claims; the church claimed that authority but did not give it out at this level. For established Christian doctrine, then, individual priests and monks failed the test of right authority for holy war in all three of the respects identified earlier: they did not have the capacity to judge the presence of legitimate religious warrant, whatever they might have claimed; they did not, in orthodox doctrinal terms, have the right to guarantee divine support or a successful outcome, or assert that participation in the war was a religious obligation; and despite whatever charisma they might display in persuading followers to take up arms for a cause, they were illegitimate leaders who could not finally bear responsibility for their followers' actions.

The other forms of peasant uprisings led by priests or monks illustrate the same shortcomings and also pose other problems. The first sort of case mentioned above, rebellion against the established authorities under the claim of religious warrant, was simply treated as rebellion by the secular rulers and the religious warrant was denied. The reason the rulers could act in this way was that, in the absence of accepted religious authority, the warrant claimed was null and void. Uprisings against bands of marauders brought a mix of benefits and problems. Disposing of such marauders and ending their depredations was obviously advantageous to society generally, including the temporal authorities. But such manifestations of local initiative and autonomy also indirectly challenged the established pattern of rule as not being able to offer the protection and order that good rulers are supposed to provide. Again the issue boiled down to the authority of the individual priest or monk to lead such military action. Since such persons had the necessary authority neither from the church nor from the temporal rulers, their cause was by definition improper.

The case of bishops introduces a quite different set of issues. The term "bishop" (Greek *episcopos*) in the early Christian church referred to the spiritual and liturgical leader of the Christian congregation in a particular city or town. While the first bishops traced their authority to various of Jesus's disciples or to the Apostle Paul, over time bishops were ordained by other bishops. They were assisted by deacons and deaconesses, whose responsibilities included such duties as visiting the sick but not the liturgical functions or authority of the bishop. As the congregations grew and additional congregations were formed in neighboring areas, the local bishop (with the assistance of other bishops) ordained as helpers priests (presbyters), who could carry out most of the ritual responsibilities of the bishop and often were placed in charge of branch congregations. Thus the pattern grew of a metropolitan bishop (the term "metropolitan" is still used to designate this office in both the Orthodox and Catholic churches) in the principal church of a given area, reported to by priests who were in charge of lesser congregations in the surrounding area. Deacons and deaconesses might serve in any or all of the congregations, assisting the priest in charge. As Christianity spread into new regions, new bishops were created who had the same liturgical responsibilities and powers as the earliest bishops, but a higher level of authority continued to be associated with those earliest episcopal positions. Thus the metropolitan bishop (or archbishop) of a particular city might have oversight of a number of other bishops as well as priests and deacons/deaconesses directly reporting to him, as well as indirect authority over those reporting to bishops in his charge.

This increasingly complicated pattern metamorphosed into the ecclesiastical structure of both the Eastern and the Western churches. In the East a number of primal congregations existed in various regions divided by culture, language, and sometimes politics; as a result the Eastern system developed around a plurality of such bishops, who were technically equals. In the West, however, only a single primal episcopal see existed, that of Rome, and the bishop of Rome, who claimed direct descent through ordination from the disciple Peter and the apostle Paul and came to be known as pope (*papa*, "father"), developed as the primary figure with responsibility over all other bishops and other clergy in the Latin-speaking churches of the West.

The position of bishop is thus central to the development of Christianity in both its Catholic (Western) and Orthodox (Eastern) forms. While priests differ in having only a derivative position and a lesser liturgical role, all bishops are liturgically equal and differ only in functional respects.

Because of the centrality of their position bishops alone were conceived as able to propagate the church over time through the confirmation of new members and the ordination of clergy. Theirs was also the responsibility to maintain purity of doctrine and practice and to teach Christian belief and behavior to those in their charge. Bishops had the power of excommunication in their dioceses as well.

Thus by contrast with priests, whose authority was limited and derivative, the office of bishop carried with it an authority drawn ultimately from the disciples of Jesus or the Apostle Paul and through them from Jesus himself. This authority within the church did not, however, directly translate to authority over the sword, since bishops were subject to the same tradition as priests regarding the bearing or use of arms. Nonetheless, bishops could offer spiritual support to warriors and accompany armies in the field. While they could not personally bear arms or participate directly in the fighting, no prohibition prevented bishops from using their spiritual authority to urge the use of force for a particular cause. Thus the question whether they could formally authorize resort to war did not have a clear answer through much of the Middle Ages, being blurred by the activities of bishops in support of warriors and of particular uses of military force.

The matter was further confused by another medieval practice, that of regalian episcopacy, by which the same individual served simultaneously as bishop and as feudal lord of territories included in his see. Thus spiritual and temporal authority were brought together in the same individual for the territory in question. His role as feudal lord inevitably involved a regalian bishop in military activities, and bishops in such roles claimed and exercised to the right to authorize wars and to lead their armies on campaigns. In such circumstances it was difficult in practice to discern where the spiritual office left off and the temporal office began.

The case of the pope, the highest bishop in the Western church, raised special issues. All the authority claimed for bishops was of course maintained for the pope as well. In addition, the pope professed additional authority as the Vicar of Christ on Earth by virtue of his succession from Saints Peter and Paul. Papal supremacists argued that this office included temporal as well as spiritual overlordship, since it would be absurd to argue that the Divine Christ had authority only over the spirit and not over the body. In practice the exercise of temporal authority by the pope included quite real lordship over the papal lands and their military forces. More broadly, though, the pope claimed authority over all souls in Christendom, including those of soldiers and those in positions of responsibility over them. Whether this extended only to spiritual authority, or whether it also included temporal authority, required centuries to resolve.

The question of authority to bear and employ arms was further muddled by practice in the temporal sphere. Through the early Middle Ages individual knights claimed the right to bear arms and use them at their own discretion, subject only to the discipline of their feudal superiors. Bullying and lawlessness were inevitable results. (See further Johnson 1987, 75–79.) Feudal lords had a better claim to authority over force than individual knights, and it was generally in their interests to keep their knights and men-at-arms in good discipline within their own domains. At the same time, their authority was limited by the obligation owed to their own overlord, and his to his suzerain, on up to the level of king or emperor, who in theory had no feudal superior.[1]

In medieval Europe, then, temporal and spiritual authority was organized in two parallel hierarchies: one whose head was the pope, with cardinals, archbishops, bishops, and priests beneath; the other whose head bore the title king or emperor (or in special cases lesser feudal titles, if by tradition the office in question had no feudal superior), with the various ranks of the feudal nobility beneath him, on down to the rank of knight. Actual authority was muddled by a host of factors, including conflicting lines of responsibility and claims to authority at all levels of the two hierarchies.

Over a period of roughly three centuries, from the latter part of the tenth through the thirteenth, this muddle of conflicting claims of authority to use force was gradually brought into a scheme of order. Over this period, by an accumulation of efforts in both the churchly and the temporal spheres, right authority to use force was pushed higher and higher up the levels of the two parallel hierarchies, until finally such authority was defined to exist only in those persons with no earthly superiors: within the temporal order, kings and the emperor, as well as the special cases of lesser princes referred to above; and in the churchly realm, the pope. (See further Johnson 1981, 150–75, and Russell 1975, 138–55.) Within the church the debate was focused most sharply in the twelfth and thirteenth centuries by two generations of canonists working from a basis in Gratian's *Decretum*, the Decretists and the Decretalists.

For the Decretists warfare for the faith was, as Frederick Russell has characterized it, "the just war of the church" (Russell 1975, 112). Eager to support the Crusades, the Decretists qualified the general prohibition of clerical participation in warfare to allow such participation in battles waged on superior authority against enemies of the church. Focusing on the idea of punishment of evil as the most just cause they drew warrant from Christian tradition for use of force against heretics and infidels, differing among themselves only over whether a prior act of violence was necessary or whether mere "divergence from orthodox Christianity coupled with *de facto* possession of property and dominion was sufficient to justify war" (Russell 1975, 112). The precedents to which they appealed included Ambrose and Augustine but most of all the Old Testament wars of the people of Israel against their enemies. Russell summarizes their consensus: "In the minds of the canonists all pagans, infidels, heretics, schismatics and excommunicates posed an almost collective threat to Christianity from within and without. Defense of the church was not always consciously distinguished from defense of the Holy Land, defense of hierarchy and clerics, and defense of the faith and faithful" (112–13). He concludes, "The Decretists developed in effect a religiously motivated just cause for war out of the Old Testament, Roman legal principles, and patristic writings" (113–14).

Authority for such warfare, for the Decretists, lay ultimately with the church itself. Despite limits on clerical participation in war, they acknowledged "the right of the church on its own authority to initiate wars both within and without Christendom" (Russell 1975, 116). For the Decretists this right was shared with the pope by other bishops. Non-regalian bishops might exhort the temporal authorities to make war, while regalian bishops might themselves make war on enemies of the church (117). But their authority was limited by the extent of their see or their temporal territories. The supreme position of the pope at the pinnacle of the churchly hierarchy meant that he possessed authority to call all of Christendom to holy war, though the actual waging of such war would still be under the command of temporal leaders.

Partly because the Decretists had resolved certain questions and partly because the historical context had changed, the Decretalists' emphasis shifted more centrally to the problem of limiting resort to violence. Accepting the Decretists' basic position that, under the right circumstances, both churchly and temporal officials could authorize use of force, the Decretalists effectively restricted the initiation of such use to those persons with no superiors—the highest temporal princes and the pope. Persons of lower ranks might respond with force defensively against attack, but this was not formally war, and these persons had no authority to initiate resort to force or to attack outside their own territories. This position established by the Decretalists was one aspect of a generalized movement within both the state and the church to deny independent authority and power to the lower ranks while centralizing it at the top. (See further Russell 1975, 147–55.)

The Decretalists' limitation on authority for war affected church and state alike, undercutting the claims of the bishops as well as those of the barons: neither had legitimate authority to initiate a just war. But in another respect their arguments affected church and state differently, redefining what authority over the use of force meant at the top of each of these two orders. Regarding the secular sphere, the Decretalists had a great deal to say justifying the authority of the prince to initiate just war; their purpose was not merely to shore up the prince's position but to deny such authority to lesser persons. With regard to the church, though, while the Decretalists accepted the Decretists' position that the pope could authorize resort to war, they did not emphasize this. Rather, they shifted the meaning of this authority, with influential Decretalists arguing for the pope's right, as head of the church, to pronounce judgment on the justice of particular wars (Russell 1975, 180–81). This effectively divided authority for war into two aspects, the executive, possessed by the secular prince with no superior, and the judicial, possessed by the pope. But the division did not affect the two sides equally: the pope lost executive authority, but secular princes retained the authority to judge for themselves in matters affecting the temporal security and well-being of their realms.

The practice of subsequent centuries ratified this division of powers. While wars continued to be waged between Christians and Muslims on the seas and in the border territories, and while some of them were denominated crusades by the church, these wars were in practice the wars of secular princes who happened to be Christian against a foe who increasingly could be described in similar terms, secular princes who happened to be Muslim. Within Europe the church continued to claim the right to authorize violence against heretics, schismatics, Jews, and others identified as enemies of the faith, but it was in fact secular officials who were in charge of the violent measures taken, and secular reasons for these measures were laid alongside the religious ones.

Thus during the last great upsurge of holy war fervor in Western Europe, the century of internecine warfare between Protestants and Catholics that was launched by the Reformation, the focus in religious quarters, Protestant and Catholic alike, was to support the role of the secular authorities in using force to protect the true faith, punish dissenters, and establish right religion (however these were defined). The religious apologists on both sides did not claim for themselves or for the church the authority to wage war but rather the authority to justify waging war—an important difference underscoring the increasing separation of the religious and secular spheres and the growing autonomy of the secular in statecraft.

In Chapter 3, I argued that the demise of holy war in the West after the Thirty Years War follows from a new understanding of the state, revulsion at the destruction experienced in the post-Reformation religious wars, and the denial that difference of religion constitutes a just cause for war on the part of the state. Now something further needs to be added: this demise of holy war can also be traced to the medieval redefinition of the church's authority over war to that of a judge, not an executive. By contrast, the secular ruler could be his own judge in matters affecting his state as well as executive over his own armed forces. The judgments of religious authorities might have moral force, or they might not, depending on circumstances. In practice, even the role of judge, conceived as impartial arbiter, has eroded as the secular nature of Western society has increased, and positions taken by spokespersons for institutional Christianity have become elements in partisan support or criticism directed at particular conflicts.

In the contemporary period the role of religious authority to pronounce on the justice of war has been revived within the mainstream churches, but the emphasis has been on limitation of war, not justification, and arguments for religious authorization of war have not figured or have been explicitly rejected. Only within apocalyptic sects does the ideal of religious war remain part of accepted doctrine, and it is associated explicitly with the conflicts of the end of the world. Except for this extremely narrow portion of the whole, contemporary christianity no longer maintains the doctrine of holy war, war authorized by religious figures for religious cause.

Authority to Wage War for Religion in Islamic Tradition: The Classical Juristic Concept

In contrast to Christianity, Islam was from the very first a political as well as a religious community, and the Prophet Muhammad was at once a religious and a political leader. Fazlur Rahman observes that Muhammad's earliest efforts reveal an "active strategy" that took account of the political reality in North Arabia and attempted to use it to the advantage of the faith he preached. This strategy aimed at control of Mecca, the religious center of the Arabs, and conversion of his own tribe, the Quraysh, which exercised "great power and influence" in the region (Rahman 1966, 20). The Prophet's emigration to Medina with his followers in 622 (the *hijra*) was undertaken after failure to overcome political opposition in Mecca and after the people of Medina had asked him to become their political and religious head. The subsequent spread of Islam was at the same time a political and a religious triumph: the two were not separated but linked inseparably together.

All this followed from a conception of obedience to God as implying the spreading of submission to the divine will throughout the world, thereby eradicating "corruption on earth" and fulfilling the directive of "enjoining the good and forbidding the evil" (Qur'an 3:104, 110; 9:33–34, 71). This was not to be done by divine intervention, according to the Qur'an, but by the work of the Prophet and his followers. While early Christians rejected the orders of the existing world as sinful and looked forward to their being wiped away and replaced by Christ when he came again, Muslim religion developed around a hatred for unbelief as the source of evil in the world and looked forward to the spread of the Qur'anic faith as the vehicle for eradication of this evil and transformation of the world. In short, for Muslim tradition from the very first, it is not the world that is to be hated but unbelievers. Proper submission to God does not entail withdrawal from the world to wait for God's action but taking power in the world to foster good and prevent evil.

From the beginning the Muslim community was engaged in warfare against hostile forces, and it responded in a military manner. The Prophet himself sent his forces into battle and fought with them. After the *hijra* or emigration from Mecca to Medina the Prophet Muhammad and his followers for several years were the objects of attacks from various quarters, with the Meccans' continuing acts of hostility the most serious (Rahman 1966, 21–23; Holt, Lambton, and Lewis 1970, vol. 1, part 1, chap. 2). The Qur'anic injunction, "Fight for the sake of God those that fight against you, but do not attack them first. God does not love the aggressors" (2:190), reflects this experience. The Qur'an depicts the enemies in religious terms: they are unbelievers, enemies of God, idolaters, and "idolatry is worse than carnage" (2:191). The nature of the enemy and of the fighting are clearly depicted: if the unbelievers attack, they are to be put to the sword. "Fight against them," the Qur'an commands, "until idolatry is no more and God's religion reigns supreme. But if they desist, fight none except the evil-doers. . . . Have fear of God, and know that God is with the righteous" (2:193–94).

It should be noted that the cultural context in which Islam came into being was one that accepted intergroup hostilities as a reality of life (Holt, Lambton, and Lewis 1970, vol. 1, part 1, chap. 1). Fred Donner observes that among the North Arabian tribes at the time of the rise of Islam a " 'state of war' was assumed to exist between one's own tribe and all others" in the absence of a peace treaty, and intertribal raiding (*ghazw*) seems to have been "a frequent, almost routine part of life" (Donner 1991, 34). The spread of Islam took advantage of this warlike context and transformed it so that the enemies were no longer defined by tribal membership but by acceptance or rejection of Islam. The later juristic distinction between the *dar al-islam* and the *dar al-harb* reflects the sense of Donner's description of intertribal hostility and projects it upon the world as a whole. The triumph of good will come with the conquest of the evil part of the world, which is defined by its unbelief and is the ultimate origin of all conflict. Whereas Christian theology put the war of the forces of good against the forces of evil into apocalyptic context, for the faithful of Islam in its early development this warfare was actually going on in the world they knew, involved real people, the Muslims and the unbelievers, and would go on through history until the world is brought under the rule of Islam.

War against the hostile military forces of non-Muslims, then, was from the very beginning of Islam political and religious at once. Jihad in its military sense developed around two possibilities: that the hostile forces of the unbelievers might attack, in which defensive "striving in the path of God" would be necessary to repel the attack and protect Muslim lives and territory; and that the military forces of the Muslim community, knowing of the perpetual hostility of the unbelievers and the conflictual nature of their world, might preemptively take up arms against them in an effort to spread the dominion of Islam. By the example of the Prophet himself, the authorization and leadership of the Muslim forces in either case belonged with the head of the Muslim community, who was at once a religious and political figure: the *imam*. Thus as the classical jurists developed the theory of jihad in its military sense, the authority for waging such war was that of the *imam*, though he might delegate the actual command of the Muslim forces to others. The tradition made clear, moreover, that the *imam* was to engage in offensive jihad once a year, unless unfavorable circumstances prevented doing so (Lambton 1981, 208–9).

Can the religious and the temporal or political be separated here in the concept of authority for war? Another way of asking the same question is whether a temporal state can be separated conceptually from the Muslim community (*umma*). For classical Islam the formal answer is no: there is one Muslim community, and it has both a political and a religious character. Rudolph Peters comments of Islamic society, "In a society where politics are entirely dominated by religion, there is no articulate distinction between politics and religion, and political aims will always be represented as religious aims" (Peters 1979, 4). Such a conceptual distinction depends on a Westernized differentiation between the spheres of politics and religion; only when understood as separate can religion dominate politics or vice versa. Such a distinction, though, simply would not have occurred to Muhammad or his followers in the formative period, or to the classical jurists a century and more later, or to anyone in between. For them religion and politics belonged to a single sphere, the ongoing life of the community of Islam. This community's wars were conceived as at one and the same time justified and authorized according to the religion of Islam and justified and authorized according to the political interests of the Muslim state. The authority for them was the highest authority of the *umma*, an authority simultaneously religious and political. To seek to understand jihad in only a religious framework is thus wrongly to force it into a differentiated category that is foreign to Islamic tradition as it took shape in the formative period.

This helps to explain why jihad in its military sense quickly became extended beyond war with outsiders to conflicts within the Islamic community involving apostasy, heresy, and rebellion. These all threatened the unity of the *umma* by challenging either the religious or the political authority, for a challenge to one was understood as a challenge to both. The later jurists accordingly extended the category of jihad to cover these conflicts, creating three new subcategories of defensive jihad. But this response covered over the more substantial problem that the *dar al-islam* was not the single community of all Muslims that was assumed in the juristic definition; rather, Muslims were divided into various communities, some defined by religious differences, some by separate political entities, others by both. So underneath the conceptual linkage between the political and the religious in classical Islamic thought there were in fact fissures within the ostensibly unitary Muslim community that in some cases took the form of a *de facto* separation between the two. What the jurists were describing was an ideal, not the reality.

In normative Islamic tradition the distinction between offensive and defensive jihad is fundamental to both the nature of the obligation and the nature of the authority required. As for the matter of authority to undertake such war, offensive military jihad was defined as a community obligation, only to be undertaken by the authority of the head of the community, the *imam*. As we have seen, not all members of the community were required to fight, but those who did not do so retained the obligation to wage the jihad of heart, tongue, and hand. Defensive jihad, on the other hand, was an individual obligation. Such war might be waged by the community and on community authority, but the duty to defend Islam was an obligation of each individual Muslim, not just of the community as a whole, and when fighting defensive jihad each Muslim accordingly was conceived to possess his own authority to do so.

Even in the case of defensive jihad the logic of the tradition pointed toward community action under the authority of the *imam*, because of his responsibility for promoting good and forbidding evil within the community. The possibility of setting himself at the head of a defensive jihad actually gave the *imam* a great deal more power to draw on the entire resources of the community because of the difference of obligation imposed and felt by the members of the *umma* in offensive and defensive jihad. If the *imam* issued a call to offensive jihad against a neighbor in the *dar al-harb*, many in the community, as we have seen, had no personal obligation to take up arms. Yet if the *imam* declared a need to wage jihad to defend the *dar al-islam* against attack, every Muslim had a personal obligation to join in.

The idea of jihad for the purpose of defending Islam thus incorporated a powerful motivational tool for mobilizing the populace as a whole to make whatever sacrifices might be necessary for a successful struggle.

During the period of Islam's expansion, however, the implications of the tradition's distinction between offensive and defensive jihad had little opportunity for play. The Muslim state had the military advantage over its actual and potential enemies, and these adversaries were not strong enough to make any serious and long-term inroads on the *dar al-islam*. During this period of growth a more significant issue within the concept of jihad was the nature of the authority at the head of the Muslim community, the authority by which the community could wage jihad, and thus the nature of the wars that were waged under the banner of jihad.

According to the tradition, only the *imam*, the heir of the Prophet, as simultaneously religious and political leader, could authorize the waging of jihad by the community. So long as Muhammad was alive, he fulfilled this dual role. On his death in 632, leadership of the community was taken up by others in turn, who were known by the title *khalifa*, caliph (literally "deputy" or "successor"). Each caliph was also *imam* for the community as a whole, though the caliphs were admitted to lack the special divine guidance received by Muhammad. They did, however, have the Qur'an as the record of that guidance, and they and their supporters employed it to justify the military and political actions they took to consolidate their central authority over the extended Muslim community. Such actions were necessary immediately, because upon Muhammad's death the religio-political community he had formed quickly began to fragment: sometimes for political reasons, sometimes for religious reasons, sometimes for both. The consolidation of caliphal authority was, in its structure, both religious and political. It was political in that it established that there would be a single Muslim political community with the caliph at its head, not a regression to the pattern of independent tribes and cities that had been normative in Arabia before Muhammad. It was religious in that it established the Qur'an as the ongoing presence of revelatory guidance for that political community. This appeal to the Qur'an gave the caliphs a legitimacy as successors to Muhammad that they would not otherwise have had, since it compensated for the fact that, unlike the Prophet, they lacked direct divine guidance.

Among the minorities within the Muslim community who, for various reasons, disputed the caliphal succession and the nature of caliphal rule, historically the most significant was the group who later came to be known as Shi'ites. This party's objection attacked caliphal rule from two directions at once: by claiming that the Prophet had in fact designated his successor, and that succession should follow in the direct line of blood descent from Muhammad; and by insisting that only persons who themselves received direct divine guidance could legitimately exercise leadership of the Muslim community.

The opposition of this group came to a head during a struggle for power between the third caliph, 'Ali, whom they supported as the Prophet's designate, and Mu'awiyya, governor of Syria (cf. Holt, Lambton, and Lewis 1970, 68–72). In 661, five years after 'Ali's succession to the caliphate, supporters of Mu'awiyya murdered 'Ali, and Mu'awiyya seized power as caliph. 'Ali's supporters rejected him as a usurper and continued to fight, led by the Prophet's grandson, Husayn, whom they regarded as the true *imam*, bearing the prophetic mantle of divine inspiration. In 680, at the battle of Karbala, the Party of 'Ali (*shi'at 'ali*, hence Shi'a) were defeated and Husayn killed. This effectively ended the military phase of the conflict and caused the Shi'a to concentrate on their religious differences with the caliph and the dominant party. Until 1501, when Shi'ism was declared the official religion of Persia by the new Safavid shah, Isma'il, partisans of this understanding of Islam lived by *taqiyya*, or "precautionary dissimulation," under caliphal rule (Sachedina 1988, 114–15). Though they rose in rebellion from time to time, the Shi'ites lacked power to overthrow the caliphate. At the same time they regarded this rule as unjust and illegitimate, holding that the only true authority, given by God, lay in their religious leader, to whom they gave the title *imam*. Each imam passed this authority directly to his successor. Without such designation, legitimate authority did not exist. Sachedina writes, "The cornerstone of the Imamite theory of political authority is the existence of an Imam from among the progeny of Muhammad, clearly designated by the latter to assume the leadership of the Muslim community. . . . [G]overnment belonged to the Imam alone, for he was equally entitled to political leadership *and* religious authority" (89). While the Imamate lasted, the Shi'ite sect in effect knew two distinct ruling authorities. The caliphs were *khulafa' al-jawr* or *al-zalama*, "tyrannical or unjust" caliphs, distinguished from the leadership of the imams, who alone were *'adil*, "just" (89, 94). This led to the development of a distinctively Shi'ite conception of political authority distinguishing between the just ruler, the *sultan al-'adil*, who was the divinely guided imam, and the *sultan ja'ir*, the unjust or tyrannical ruler, identified with the caliphs and the caliphal system (94). After the disappearance or "occultation" of the Twelfth Imam in 874 the concept of the Imam as *sultan al-'adil* became eschatological: there would be no just ruler in the world until the Twelfth Imam returned as Mahdi, the rightly guided one sent by God to rule the world in the end of time. But only God knows when that will be. In the face of this need to live in the world for an indeterminate period, Shi'ite theorists acknowledged that the rule of the *sultan ja'ir* might be accepted for the temporal sphere, but only in matters of the law and only so far as he did not break that law. Religiously, however, Shi'ites were to hold to "sound belief," defined as upholding the rightness of the twelve imams in succession from the Prophet, and "sound knowledge," defined as the tradition of knowledge originating in the teaching of the imams (58).

The majority of Muslims, however, continued to accept the legitimacy of caliphal rule. The line of religious belief that developed in this context came to be known as Sunni from its dependence on the *sunna*, "custom," referring specifically to traditions associated with the Prophet's words and acts. A number of distinctive elements in later Sunni Islam follow directly from the system set up by the early caliphs. The concept of the *dar al-islam* as a religious and political entity with a single head idealizes the caliphal system more than it reflects the nature of the Muslim community under Muhammad (or, indeed, the historical reality of that community even in the time of the classical jurists). The emphasis on the Qur'an as the completed record of God's revelatory guidance was not possible so long as the Prophet was alive and continued to receive revelations. The role given the Qur'an as infallible revelatory guidance for the community (and ultimately for the world) led to its being understood legalistically and to the rise of jurisprudence as the definitive means of interpreting its meaning for both religious and political purposes. While the caliphs continued to claim the role of *imam* for the entire community, in practice their actual behavior was more clearly political, and the term *imam* gradually took on the more specialized religious meaning it has today for Sunni Muslims, the title of the prayer leader of a local mosque.

Two distinct traditions of ruling authority have thus developed in the two major divisions of Islam, the Sunni and the Shi'i. For Sunni tradition the caliphate and its successors represented the union of political and religious rule initiated by Muhammad. In practice, however, the caliphs functioned as temporal rulers, having recourse to their religious authority as required for state purposes. For the Shi'ites the same was true of the imamate, though in reverse: the imam was held to be the only legitimate heir to both religious and political power, but in practice the imams were restricted to religious leadership of the Shi'ite community while the caliphs and not the imams held actual power in the Islamic community as a whole. (This pattern held under the Safavid shahs, despite their adoption of Shi'ism as the state religion; see Holt, Lambton, and Lewis 1970, vol. 1, part 3, chap. 5.) And further for the Shi'ites, the occultation of the Twelfth Imam drove a wedge between religious and political authority. Religious authority, in Shi'ite theory, is held by interpreters in the tradition of "sound knowledge," but these do not hold political authority; that authority is wielded by temporal rulers whose leadership can never be truly just, only at best a tolerably unjust rule. These latter hold no authority in religious matters.

These divergent conceptions of legitimate authority bear significantly on the conception of authority for jihad. For Sunni tradition the caliph, in his dual religious-political role, can authorize offensive jihad; indeed, by the tradition that requires an annual offensive jihad by the *imam*, he has an obligation to wage such war against the enemies of Islam. Throughout the caliphate and even late in the Ottoman empire, the rulers employed the call to jihad to mobilize and motivate their armies and to secure the support of the populace. Jihad thus provided a rationale for offensive war as well as defense. Despite this invoking of religious authority for war, the causes of the wars in question were essentially temporal; despite being termed jihad, they were wars of the state, not wars of religion. So in Sunni tradition the theoretical union of religious and political authority in the person of the caliph devolved into a rationale for the caliph's temporal rule. Within a theoretical framework that denied the possibility of a Muslim state founded on a temporal basis alone, the conception of the caliph as highest religious authority in the community he governed gave legitimacy to his rule as highest authority in the state.

For Shi'ite tradition the divide between temporal and spiritual leadership means that there is no longer any temporal ruler authorized to initiate offensive jihad, and there will not be until the return of the Twelfth Imam at the end of time. While some Shi'ite jurists argued that the Hidden Imam might, in specific circumstances of need, appoint a "deputy" (*khalifa*) who, like the Imam himself, would be a "just ruler" (by contrast to the "unjust" and "tyrannical" rule of the caliphs) and could thus authorize offensive jihad, this concept was shrouded by ambiguity. Admitting this as a theoretical possibility, Abdulaziz A. Sachedina, writing on the concept of the "just ruler" in Shi'ite Islam, argues that in practice defensive jihad is the only option open to Shi'ites; there is no legitimate leader able to authorize offensive jihad (Sachedina 1988, 105–17).

The Shi'ite conception of authority to wage jihad was more than an implication of the Qur'an as the Shi'ite jurists read it; it was a reflection of the position of the Shi'ite community as threatened by Sunni-dominated political rulers, who did not hesitate to invoke jihad in order to punish religious dissidence. Thus it was clearly in the interest of the Shi'ites to deny the right to wage offensive jihad in the sense of war to compel religious conformity. Citing the Qur'anic passage, "There is no compulsion in religion" (2:256), Sachedina argues that the Qur'an sanctions jihad, whether against external or internal enemies, only against aggressors (9:33) and persons who reveal their unbelief by breaking oaths (9:12) and not forbidding "what God and His messenger have forbidden" (9:29), thereby obstructing the success of God's cause. He summarizes:

> So construed, to advocate the use of force by an Islamic authority in the name of *jihad* would require rigorous demonstration that the purpose of *jihad* is nothing but "enjoining the good and forbidding the evil." . . . Muslim authority . . . , like *al-sultan al-'adil*, must shoulder the burden of proof and establish that the *jihad* was not undertaken primarily for territorial expansion, but in order to usher in the ethico-social world order that the Qur'an requires. (Sachedina 1988, 109)

Or again, citing the Shi'ite jurist Tusi, "It is a pernicious error to engage in jihad under the leadership of unjust rulers for the purpose of conversion" (Sachedina 1988, 111). In the context of Shi'ite juristic writings, this reasoning directly targeted the caliphal leadership.

The right to wage jihad in defense, however, the Shi'ites protected as absolute. "The second purpose of jihad—protection of the basic welfare of the community against those who have threatened it—makes jihad a defensive measure, and the Imamite jurists have ruled its needfulness unrestrictedly" (Sachedina 1988, 111). This form of jihad does not require the authority of the absent Imam but is authorized by the Qur'an itself. "When the community is in danger, it has the responsibility to defend Muslim families, children, and property" (112).

The Sunni jurists lived in a quite different relationship to the state, and their conception of authority in the state extended that authority to include precisely that rationale for jihad which the Shi'ites rejected: offensive war against entities in the *dar al-harb* defined as enemies precisely because of their unbelief. Territorial expansion of the sphere of Islam was justified because it brought unbelievers under the order of Islam. So if the caliph declared war on a neighboring territory in the *dar al-harb* it was legitimate for him to do this as jihad both because the warrant was already there (the need to overcome the rule of unbelief and replace it with the rule of Islam) and because he possessed the necessary religious authority to do so in the name of Islam. To say this is to admit the possibility of using jihad as a pretense for nonreligious designs. This was in fact the Shi'ite judgment on the behavior of the Sunni rulers, and it is also apparently what Rudolph Peters has in mind when he writes, "Historical research . . . has proved that the wars of the Islamic states were fought for perfectly secular reasons" (Peters 1979, 4). But while some Muslim rulers over history have undoubtedly invoked jihad for its propaganda value, and while the jihad idea has clearly developed as a tool of statecraft for Muslim rulers, the record is not so one-sided as Peters's statement or the Shi'ite witness suggests. The Shi'ites, as noted already, had their own reasons apart from religious doctrine for opposing the caliphal rulers: as Sunnis, these rulers represented a threat to the Shi'ite community and its beliefs. But in the case of the 'Abbasid caliphs who ruled during the development of classical Islamic juristic thought and who were in fact the immediate source of the threat to the Shi'ites during this period, one must turn the matter around: to an important degree their statecraft was motivated by their religious piety (cf. Holt, Lambton, and Lewis 1970, vol. 1, part 1, chap. 4). Similarly the early Ottomans understood the proper expression of their faith to be the undertaking of holy war to increase the sphere of Islam (Holt, Lambton, and Lewis 1970, vol. 1, part 2, chaps. 3, 4; cf. Chapter 5 herein).

Both the Sunni and the Shi'ite traditions agree on the fundamental conception of right authority in the Islamic community: it is unified even as the community of Muslims is itself one, and it is simultaneously political and religious. Both positions are theories establishing the ideal of just authority, and neither is refuted as an ideal by pointing to historical actualities such as the fact that the Muslim community has been divided into numerous independent states and Muslim rulers have often served their own private ends or the ends of those states as secular political units. The idealism of the Shi'ite theory is internally clear in its projection of just rule onto the person of the Imam-Mahdi of the end of history: until then unjust rule is the norm, not the exception. The idealism of the Sunni theory is revealed in comparison with the actual course of Islamic history and in the divergence between the juristic account and the actual nature of the Islamic world at the same time the jurists were writing. Yet both conceptions of the ideal serve historical purposes, though those purposes are diametrically opposite: providing a "prophetic" critical perspective on political rule for the Shi'ites, providing a higher yet realizable standard for such rule on the part of the Sunnis. Both theoretical conceptions of authority are thus tied to history, and both have their uses there as well as their embarrassments.

5

THE CONDUCT OF
HOLY WAR

We in the modern West tend to think that holy war is waged without limit or restraint. In his influential typology of the Western crusade theme, Roland Bainton says as much: the cause of such war shall be holy, that is, above any earthly reasons for fighting; the participants "shall be godly and their enemies ungodly," and "the war shall be prosecuted unsparingly" (Bainton 1960, 148). The example he provides, that of the Puritan sack of the Irish city of Drogheda, involved killing Bainton clearly regards as a massacre. Richard Barber, commenting on medieval efforts to limit warfare, such as the Truce of God, which forbade fighting on certain holy days, and ecclesiastical bans on the use of certain weapons, highlights the fact that these were directed to conflicts among Christian adversaries only and were not regarded as applying in the Crusades (see Barber 1970, 213). The religious wars of the century following the onset of the Protestant Reformation offer many examples of the disregard of limits by that time long established in just war tradition, culminating in the devastation of much of northern Europe during the Thirty Years War.

Looking to the case of Islam, past instances of extremism such as occurred during the Mahdist rebellion in Sudan in the 1880s and present-day acts of terrorism by groups who style themselves by such names as "Islamic Jihad" reinforce the conception that in a holy war the enemies are all those of different faith and no limits restrain the harm that may be done them.

This is not the case. Both the Christian and Islamic normative traditions on war, taken as a whole, put limits on the conduct of war. Classical Islamic

juristic tradition applied these to jihad from the beginning; for the case of
Christianity, consensus on the limits to war was not reached until after the
era of the Crusades, but judging the post-Reformation wars of religion by
the *jus in bello* concepts in place by that time was commonplace. Thus the
proper normative comparison is between the standards set by the classical
jurists of Islam and the just war consensus established in Western culture by
the end of the medieval period. Neither tradition countenances wanton
slaughter. Both limit the means that may be used in warfare and the persons
against whom even the allowed means may be directed. Both insist that a
war for religion be undertaken only under a firmly established legitimate
authority, and that this authority bear responsibility for the actions of the
troops under its leadership.

At the same time, however, the restraints set in place within the two
traditions differ in important respects. Though each tradition has a conception of the difference between combatants and noncombatants and the
treatment appropriate for each, these conceptions are not the same. Calcu-
lations of proportionality applied to the inflicting of harm are affected by
dissimilar prior assumptions. Each of the two religious traditions shows,
moreover, the lingering influence of two divergent cultural traditions on
warfare, the Germanic for the Christian and the Arabian for the Islamic.
Indeed, the differences between the two cultures figure strongly in each
tradition's conception of the enemy in holy war as one who is beyond the
pale of the right order of things: the unbeliever, the infidel, the inhabitant of
the "territory of war."

Such differences are typical in wars across major cultural boundaries.
These wars are especially prone to disregard limits set within the distinct
cultural frameworks of the warring adversaries, because the accepted limits
do not always mesh and a new regime of reciprocity has to be worked out
(cf. Johnson 1981, chap. 3). But all this is still far from saying that holy war
by its nature is total and unrestrained.

Restraints on Holy War in Western Tradition

In the West holy war doctrine has developed as an element of the just war
tradition, and while the justifying causes and the requisite authorities for
holy war and just war differ, there is no difference between holy war and the
larger tradition in the matter of the restraints on war adopted as normative
in Western culture. As a matter of history those restraints have come into

being in considerable part as a result of nonreligious influences, notably the effect of knightly conceptions of warriorhood and combat, the influence of classical traditions on war carried and mediated by the public law, and the actual experience of warfare and statecraft. The church contributed to the development of the *jus in bello*, the law of war, but its influence was but one element in a larger whole as Western culture moved toward a normative consensus on warfare. (See further Johnson 1985, chap. 1, and 1981, chap. 5.)

Medieval Efforts at Restraint

The critical historical period for the coalescence of Western normative tradition on war was the Middle Ages, more specifically the period from the late tenth century through the fourteenth. During this period the church's contribution to normative restraints on resort to armed force paralleled those of Western society at large, restricting the legitimizing causes for use of force and insisting that only the highest authorities, those with no superior, could authorize war. The aim of these restraints, which formed the core of the developing *jus ad bellum*, the law on the right to go to war, was to dampen the violence endemic to medieval society by restricting the right of the sword to relatively few persons, and then for only a limited number of reasons. The two approaches to limiting resort to violence coalesced in the characteristic emphasis on the New Testament passage Romans 13:4, read as establishing the right of the prince to use arms to punish evil, thereby creating and maintaining a peaceful order.[1]

The Crusades, occasioned by Islamic gains in the Holy Land and against the Byzantine empire, provided a focus for turning violent tendencies in society outward (thus anticipating Machiavelli's advice to his Prince by several centuries) and also for beginning the process of consolidating authority and cause for war into a single consensual doctrine applicable and accepted in both the religious and the secular spheres.[2] (For discussion in the broader context of the medieval and early modern development of just war tradition as a whole, see Johnson 1975 and 1981, chaps. 5 and 6.) Within the medieval European church these matters were treated at the highest levels, by the most respected canonists and theologians and by the highest authorities, including the pope himself.

By contrast, the church's effort to restrain the conduct of war took shape mainly at lower levels in the ecclesiastical hierarchy. This effort took three major forms: the Peace of God, first declared at the Council of Le Puy in 975; the Truce of God, first promulgated by the Council of Toulouges in 1027;

and a ban on certain weapons first adopted at the Second Lateran Council in 1139. Each of these initiatives was periodically renewed by subsequent church councils. All were canonical; that is, they set up penalties in church law for those who transgressed the limits. All focused on restraining the effects of widespread use of arms within Christendom, that is, the area where the Church's authority to enforce these rulings extended. In fact the enforcement was even less widespread, being dependent on the support of local bishops and regional councils of bishops. In any case, they were not aimed at limiting warfare with non-Christian belligerents, who were not participants in the violence found in the areas covered by these efforts and over whose conduct the church authorities had no direct influence. All three approaches were motivated to a considerable extent by self-interest on the part of the church, since a principal effect was to protect ecclesiastical persons, property, and concerns. And while these *jus in bello* efforts endured for some time, church intellectuals gave more concerted attention to the problem of just resort to war, the *jus ad bellum*.

The Peace of God originated in the French regions of Anjou and Aquitaine (Contamine 1984, 271ff.; Bull 1993, 23–39) as a response of local and regional church authorities, in close cooperation with senior nobles and representatives of the king, to a rise in lawlessness and the overall level of violence associated with a breakdown in governing authority. Two particular forms of lawlessness were typically targeted: the bullying behavior of mercenary knights and other soldiers (*milites* and *adjutores*) in the service of local barons during times when they were not employed in war and the depredations of armed bands who lived on the fringes of settled areas and periodically raided those areas for food and goods. The churches were the victims both directly and indirectly: directly, in that as unprotected repositories of wealth they were tempting targets for raiders; and indirectly, in that theft from the supporting population limited their ability to give to the church.

The original Peace of God was an initiative of the French bishop Guy of Anjou, who at the Council of Le Puy in 975 assembled the peasants and *milites* of his diocese "to hear from them what their advice was for the maintenance of peace." After hearing them, and before the *milites* dispersed, he required them to take an oath "to respect the Church's possessions and those of the peasants" (Contamine 1984, 271). Though they had taken this oath, some of the *milites* subsequently resisted, and they were brought in order by the force of arms of two local counts, both relatives of the bishop. Subsequently other regional bishops and church councils (cf. Bull 1993,

34–35, 43–46) adopted similar measures, in some cases also targeting higher levels of society. The bishops at the Council of Limoges in 1031 excommunicated "those *milites* from this diocese of Limoges who refuse, or have refused, to swear peace and justice to their bishop," but also singled out for complaint the *seculares potestates* (the secular powers; that is, the nobility of the region) "who do not allow God's church to be at rest, who interfere with the property of the sanctuary, who afflict the poor . . . and the servants of the church" (Bull 1993, 45).

The most important contribution of the Peace of God movement to restraining the conduct of war was to establish the immunity in war of ecclesiastical persons and property. Typically other classes of persons and their property were protected only insofar as they were the responsibility of the church. The culmination of this trend was reached in the statement on noncombatant immunity in Gratian's *Decretum* (ca. 1148), which lists as protected classes of people only those related directly to the church: clergy (including bishops), monks, and pilgrims. A century later, however, another landmark in the development of the canon law, *De Treuga et Pace* (Of Truces and Peace), went beyond this to include peasants, together with their goods and their lands, in the list of those who do not make war and thus should not have war made against them. (See further Johnson 1975, 42–45.)

Taken as a whole, the Peace of God effort made an important contribution to the development of the ideas of noncombatancy and noncombatant immunity in Western moral tradition on war. Influences from other sectors of medieval culture, some more powerful and more far-reaching in their effect, contributed to this development as well. In particular, chivalric ideals and practices extended noncombatant status and noncombatant immunity to those without the ability to bear arms (women, children, the aged, and the infirm) and to those who by virtue of social status normally did not bear arms or participate in war (that is, persons who were not of the knightly class) (see further Johnson 1981, 131–50). But the Peace of God, as a specifically religious effort to declare certain classes of persons and associated property off-limits to attack by force of arms, is especially interesting from the perspective of holy war thought. In this connection four points in particular deserve to be noticed (see further Johnson 1987, 83–86).

First, the restraints of the Peace of God were directed at persons who engaged in violence without public authority. By contrast, the church depended on violent force in the hands of public authority to enforce the terms of the Peace. While one of the long-term important positive effects of the Peace of God movement was to establish the *jus ad bellum* idea that only force in the hands of a "right authority" was justified, the short-term effect was to establish the idea that the temporal authorities might serve as enforcers of the rights of the church when these were transgressed against. In southern France where the Peace was promulgated in the twelfth and thirteenth centuries, but also in the apologetic for the Crusades, this translated into the use of violence by temporal authority to punish enemies of the church.

Second, the geographical scope of the Peace of God was, as noted above, limited by the range of authority within which it was promulgated: if by a single bishop, then for his diocese only; if by a council of bishops, only for their dioceses; if by a council of bishops of the church at large or on papal authority, then only within the bounds of Christendom. The conception of noncombatancy and noncombatant immunity the Peace put in place was thus not a general one for all wars everywhere, but only for troubled regions of Christendom. Thus in the form that the Peace of God existed at the time of the first three Crusades, it did not extend, by its very nature, to such wars outside the bounds of Christendom.

Third, the development of the Peace of God idea in the specific direction of protecting the church's own interests—the lives of priests, bishops, monks, and pilgrims and property owned by the church or dedicated to it—was not extended to protection of religion in general. It did not, for example, include protection of Jews, heretics, or dissenters within Christendom or their personal or communal property. There is no record of the Peace of God being invoked to restrain harm to churchmen and others who were part of religiously dissident groups inside Christendom, such as the Waldensians and the Cathari, and certainly not harm to infidels (the favorite medieval term for Muslims) outside Christendom.

Fourth, the Peace of God movement, despite being aimed at reducing violence within Christendom, contributed to the shaping of the historical context in which the Crusades became possible. By making temporal peace a religious cause the church made fighting to protect such peace a religious duty, and church authorities were not slow to identify enemies of the peace for the pious to make war against. This originally unintended consequence of the Peace of God movement thus was to legitimize unrestrained war against enemies of the faith.

Thus the Peace of God movement tended to encourage holy war, not restrain it. While it set limits on warfare between Christians within Christendom, it placed no restraints on war for religion against unbelievers, wherever they might be found. In its medieval context a more important element of restraint on war generally, reinforcing that side of the Peace of God which bore on creating a concept of noncombatant immunity, was the influence of the chivalric code and the chivalric practice of warfare (Johnson 1981, 131–50). The coalescence of these two approaches, that of the Peace of God and that of chivalric ideals and practice, can already be glimpsed in *De Treuga et Pace* and had become quite clear by the time of the Hundred Years War (mid-fourteenth century) (Johnson 1975, 66–74). Yet even chivalric ideals and practice pertained only to warfare within Christendom.

The second effort to restrain war that originated within the medieval church was the Truce of God, a declaration that forbade fighting on certain days and during certain periods of the year. Like the Peace of God this originated at the local level and only gradually spread to other regions. Unlike the Peace, which sought to limit use of armed force not under proper authority and to protect certain classes of people and their property from attack, the Truce sought to rule out all uses of force, whatever the authority, purpose, and targets, during times the church regarded as holy: every week between Saturday at the ninth hour and prime on Monday, according to the Council of Toulouges in 1027; from vespers on Wednesday until sunrise on Monday, according to a council of the bishops of Provence in 1041. From this beginning whole seasons of the Christian year were added to the times in which war was proscribed: Christmas, Lent, the period from Rogations to Pentecost, the feasts and vigils of the Virgin, some saints' festivals (Contamine 1984, 271, 436; cf. Russell 1975, 183). Similarly the geographical scope of the Truce was enlarged, but it applied only "amongst all Christians, friend or foe" (Contamine 1984, 271, citing a letter from the bishops of Provence to bishops in Italy asking them to "maintain" this truce), even after a papal Truce of God was promulgated by Urban II at the Council of Troia in 1093 (Russell 1975, 35). As noted earlier, Richard Barber has pointed out that the Truce of God did not restrain the Crusaders (Barber 1970, 213), but the full story is that the Truce did not work particularly well at restraining warfare between Christian belligerents either. It aimed mostly at preventing battles, and medieval European warfare produced comparatively few pitched battles. Wars were carried on chiefly by sieges, and the Truce of God allowed sieges to continue even during the days proscribed for fighting.

But the particular structure of the Truce of God shows that it had other purposes than placing limits on warfare. The Truce belongs together with other efforts by the medieval church to control sin by ruling out specific behavior on certain days: for a period before and after mass on Sundays not only was fighting prohibited, but also sexual intercourse with one's spouse, for example; during Lent not only was fighting proscribed, but also certain foods. Viewed in context with such other canonical rules imposed on the Christian life, the prohibition of fighting on certain days looks rather different. From this perspective it was an internal restraint directed at the individual soul, and it might have effect wherever that soul might be, within Christendom or without, in conflicts with other Christians or with non-Christian enemies. The historical evidence, however, does not allow any judgment on this internal moral effect on individual Christian soldiers.

In fact the effort to rule out specific periods for fighting by canonical decree turned out to be a dead end. The idea of such a truce itself was in direct conflict with a canon included in Gratian's *Decretum* (C. 23, q. 8, c. 15), which was understood as allowing a just war to be waged at any time (Russell 1975, 183). This meant that the only wars the Truce might interrupt were those that were unjust for one reason or another; yet Christians were not supposed to wage unjust wars at *any* time. Working from the *Decretum*, succeeding generations of canonists interpreted the various statements of the Truce so narrowly that it was effectively nullified. Accordingly, the Truce waned and effectively disappeared in the period after the *Decretum*.[3] That the Truce was hedged about in various ways even before Gratian implies that we should not read too much into the Crusaders' attack on Constantinople during Holy Week, cited by Barber as evidence that the Crusaders did not observe the same limits on the conduct of war when they were fighting infidels as Western Christians did when fighting each other. According to the canon cited by Gratian (which antedates the *Decretum*, since Gratian was only a compiler), there was no general limit on just wars within Europe among Christians that would have prohibited such an attack.

The third canonical effort to restrain the practice of war in the medieval period took the form of a ban on certain weapons: crossbows, bows and arrows, and siege weapons. First promulgated at the Second Lateran Council in 1139, this ban, like the Peace and Truce of God, applied only to warfare among Christians. Like the other two canonical efforts already treated, this one had as its target the armed violence endemic to Christendom in this period. Like the Peace of God it was supported by the temporal authorities; indeed, the ban strongly benefited these authorities, as well as landed nobles and knights generally. The weapons singled out by the ban were not the classical arms of the knight: the sword, lance, and mace or battle-ax. Rather, they were weapons typically used by soldiers not of the knightly class and, at the time of the ban, often employed as the weapons of choice by bands of mercenaries, who hired themselves out as specialists in their use. With the bolt from a crossbow or an arrow from a bow, a commoner could wound or kill a knight; by means of a siege machine a band of mercenary "mechanics" could batter down the walls of a fortress and cause much loss of valuable property, perhaps even deposing the ruling lord. So this weapons ban was, like the Peace of God, aimed not at the feudal authorities and the landed knights and nobility, who were generally perceived as a source of order with whom the church could cooperate, but rather at the rise of specialized mercenary armies that threatened that order. (See further Johnson 1981, 128–30, and Russell 1975, 241–43, 246, 277.)

This ban was undercut, however, by the fact that these very mercenaries and their specialized weapons were of great use to the legitimate authorities in their wars. Thus, as in the case of the Peace of God, the effect was to strengthen the authorities' hand in the use of force at the expense of groups that might pose a threat to that authority. The simple fact is that the ban did not work. The use of bows, crossbows, and siege weapons continued, though the former were often the target of chivalric grumbling (as at the Battle of Agincourt, for example, when English bowmen cut down the flower of the French nobility, who, apart from a small body of crossbowmen, had no corresponding force of archers on their side).

In warfare with the Muslims additional factors undermined the weapons ban. Bows and arrows and siege weapons were among the arms of choice for the Muslim armies, and the principle of reciprocity meant that they were immediately in use on the Christian side as well. Further, in the Crusades the specialized mercenaries were present in the army under command authority, not operating on their own without such authority. And third, none of the Christian authorities, ecclesiastical or secular, cared much if such mercenaries preyed on the local population in this theater of war; these people were not the peasants whose labor supported them back in Europe.

All this argues that the medieval ecclesiastical restraints on war had little if any effect in the religiously motivated and authorized Crusades. But the full story of these efforts at imposing restraints is that they did not work very well in limiting the conduct of war within medieval Europe either. While the Peace of God, the Truce of God, and the weapons ban were efforts toward defining a *jus in bello*, a major part of their collective effect was on the developing *jus ad bellum*: to strengthen the hand of the authorities (temporal and ecclesiastical) at the expense of armed persons and groups that posed a threat to their authority and power. So, not without some irony, the medieval church's three major efforts to restrain war in Europe were not understood to apply to the church's own just wars, the Crusades.

Were there any restraints abroad in the culture of medieval Christendom that did extend to the holy wars against Muslim forces? The answer is yes, but it is difficult to judge how much effect they had. The first has been alluded to already: the quest for avoidance of sin on the part of the pious individual. The second, which we now will examine, was the concept of knighthood and its implications for conduct in combat.

The Christian acceptance of warfare was always somewhat conditional. The use of force was justified only if it was undertaken against evil, and the soldier was enjoined to hate the sin against which he was fighting, not the sinner. Through much of the medieval period canon law required that soldiers do penance after battle as a precaution against having sinned by allowing themselves to be overcome by such wrong intentions as listed by Augustine as "what is to be blamed in war"—"the desire for harming, the cruelty of avenging, an unruly and implacable animosity, the rage of rebellion, the lust of domination and the like" (*Contra Faustum* 22.74; also see Verkamp 1988, 224–25). Right or wrong intention was understood as independent of the enemy or the cause; it had to do rather with the moral character of the soldier as an individual. After a battle in which wrong intentions surfaced, a soldier was to refrain from the sacrament of the eucharist, for he was unworthy, and to partake of the body and blood of Christ in such a condition would dishonor Christ himself.

Alongside this conception of the moral soldier as one who fights without base passion developed other ideals rooted in the customs and attitudes of chivalry, notably prowess, courtesy, and the desire for glory or prestige (cf. Painter 1940, 33). The first of these referred to the goal of the knight to develop skill in the use of arms; the second and third referred to his relation to others and his perception by others. Briefly stated, the knight gained glory by demonstrating his prowess in arms courteously, that is, against worthy opponents and for the protection of the weak and innocent. This is the cultural root of the protection given to women, children, the aged, and the infirm in the fully developed conception of noncombatant immunity achieved in Western tradition by the fourteenth century. It was this conception—built on the canonical list of noncombatants provided in *De Treuga et Pace* on the one hand and on the additions to this list developed in the context of chivalry—that was passed on to the early modern period as a main element in the *jus in bello* of the cultural consensus on just war.

These two themes—the concept of good moral character in combat as measured by right intention and the chivalric ideals for knightly conduct—tended to reinforce each other and to inculcate a carefulness in the use of armed force. Within the just war tradition this link between the concept of right intention and the development of a concept of noncombatant immunity determined by weakness and inability to protect oneself is clear, and we know this conception was in place by the fourteenth century (cf. Johnson 1981, 131–50). What is less certain is how much of it was in place at the time of the Crusades, or how far these restraints were taken as applying in wars with non-Christians.

The general conclusion from examination of efforts to restrain war in the Middle Ages must be that the various positive cultural efforts to legislate limits on the conduct of warfare—its means, its targets, and the times in which it could be waged—were defined as applying only within Christendom and were not understood as extending to the Crusades against the Muslims. To set this lack of explicit canonical restraints on the conduct of holy war in perspective, however, the canonical restraints set in place for warfare inside Christendom had only very mixed results there too. By contrast with the ecclesiastical limits, the themes of restraint derived from focus on the character of the warrior were not limited by geography, since wherever the warrior fought, there he was required to embody these ideals. Thus these in principle applied to warfare outside as well as inside Christendom: the good knight protected the weak and innocent and avoided dehumanizing hatred of the enemy everywhere. Yet it is not clear from the historical evidence how much influence these ideals may in fact have had during the Crusades. We are left with a somewhat indistinct picture of norms bearing on conduct of holy war in the Middle Ages. In sum, there are three elements to this picture. First, at the time of the Crusades there was no consensual set of normative restraints on war (that is, no *jus in bello*) yet in place within Europe to limit the conduct of war among Christians within Christendom. Second, the formal canonical efforts at restraining warfare within Christendom had only limited territorial validity, and they did not in any case because of their structure extend to warfare outside Christendom and with non-Christians. The issue was not whether the war was for religion or not but whether it was outside or inside the territory where the canonical restraints applied. Third, there were certain moral restraints on the conduct of Christian soldiers that in principle had force everywhere, but since these were often disregarded in intra-Christian warfare, nothing conclusive can be derived from evidence of disregard of these restraints in the wars with the Muslims.

While there was no *jus in bello* consensus in Christendom at the time of the Crusades, by the end of the Middle Ages such a consensus had formed and was generally accepted in European warfare. Based mainly in canon law and chivalric practice, it included a broad conception of noncombatant immunity and an extension of the requirement that the good achieved by the war exceed the harm done during the waging of it.

At the same time, after the initial crusading fervor wore off, the wars on the borders between Christendom and the *dar al-islam* gradually came less to exemplify holy warfare (though they were often still called such) and more to resemble the struggle of competing temporal empires in which religion was but one of the issues at stake. The issue of holy warfare would not arise again in Europe until the wars for religion that followed the Reformation, wars fought well after the just war *jus in bello* consensus had been established.

The Question of Restraint in the Post-Reformation Wars of Religion

In the religious warfare of the post-Reformation period defining major new restraints on war was not an issue; such restraints were already in existence in the form of the just war tradition that both Protestants and Catholics inherited. The question was whether these restraints applied to this kind of war (cf. Bainton 1960, 148, and Johnson 1975, 134–46). These conflicts were fought out with varying degrees of ferocity in various theaters of conflict—the German states of the Holy Roman Empire, the Low Countries, France, England, Ireland, Central Europe. In each case religion was an added element to partisan conflict over other issues—in Germany, a running dispute over the rights of local princes versus those of the emperor; in the Low Countries, local autonomy versus Spanish hegemony; in France, a dispute over succession to the throne; in England, the rights of Parliament versus those of the king; in Ireland, resistance by the Irish to English domination; in Central Europe, the rights of the lower nobility and their followers against the higher nobles and their foreign supporters. The common theme in all these cases was a link between the religious reformers and forces seeking more local autonomy. The result was what we would today recognize as an ideological use of religion to bolster claims essentially political and economic in nature. (On these issues see Clark 1958; Johnson 1975, 81–133; Mosse 1957; Salmon 1959; and Walzer 1965.)

It is ultimately impossible to separate the religious elements in these wars from the other causative forces, and it is misleading to try. What stands out most obviously is something else: the revolutionary aspect of these struggles. This bears directly on the nature of their conduct. Apologists for the forces in authority excoriated their opponents as rebels, declared that they had forfeited all rights by their rebellion, and urged the authorities to use the harshest possible measures against them—measures extreme by the standards of the received cultural consensus on war, but normal by the standards of police actions against criminals. Since the authority in power was, by the standards of the time, assumed also to have the right to set standards for religious practice, to profess the contrary religion was taken in itself by the apologists as evidence of criminal rebellion worthy of harsh punishment. On the other side of the conflicts, the forces of reform cited the autonomy of local princes (Germany), "ancient rights and privileges" (the Low Countries), the "rights of Parliament" (England), and other such rights as inalienable and termed the higher authority an unjust usurper not worthy to rule. It did not matter whether the authority in power was Catholic or Protestant, or whether the rebels were Protestant or Catholic: when the sides changed, the same arguments were used, but with their valences reversed. Thus in England Catholic apologists accused Elizabeth I of being a "usurper," and her Protestant partisans depicted English Catholics as disloyal and rebellious toward the throne. Later, Protestants denounced the pro-Catholic Charles I as unworthy to rule, and his Catholic supporters accused the Protestants of being disloyal rebels.

The least restrained warfare during the post-Reformation period was that which most closely resembled civil war of the forces of order against rebellion; by contrast, warfare in which the belligerents were formally equal and both possessed *compétence de guerre* tended to observe the received tradition on restraint in combat. The wars in Germany early in the period of Lutheran reform exemplify the latter case, since the belligerents were formally independent princes and their states. The religious issue was settled in a way that preserved this independence, according to the principle "Cuius regio, eius religio" whereby each prince determined the religion of his state, while the emperor's civil authority over the whole empire was reaffirmed. Similarly, the English Civil War was one in which each side in practice generally treated the other according to the established *jus in bello*, despite inflamed rhetoric on both sides that depicted the war as one of rebellion or just resistance against an unjust ruler. By contrast the French Wars of Religion, the warfare in the Low Countries, and the conflicts that escalated into the Thirty Years War all exhibited the character of disputes over authority to impose order. In these conflicts the standards of order themselves were in dispute, and this was manifested in a frequent and often general lack of restraint in conduct on the battlefield, disregard of noncombatant immunity, and disproportionate destruction.

The warfare of this period did not produce new restraints, but it did not do away with the existing ones either. Rather, the ferocity of religiously tinged warfare led to a general rejection of the legitimacy of such warfare. A major factor in this rejection was criticism, on the basis of the just war *jus in bello*, of indiscriminate and disproportionate violence in the name of religion. The reaction to violations of the inherited tradition of restraint might have been to lay the tradition aside as irrelevant; instead, as exemplified by Grotius's *De Jure Belli ac Pacis* and subsequent developments, the *jus in bello* was reaffirmed and given new emphasis. What was rejected was rather war for religion, identified as war without *in bello* restraints. Legitimate warfare was redefined to include only wars of sovereign princes and states for reasons of state—territorial disputes, economics, claims of authority, and the like—warfare limited in principle by the terms of the consensual *jus in bello*.

Not a new feature, but a prominent one in the arguments of some apologists in the context of the post-Reformation religious wars, was the insistence on a more scrupulous kind of behavior in warfare on the part of the righteous than that defined in the received just war tradition, a more scrupulous standard than could be expected of the unrighteous enemies. By this reasoning, the soldiers of God were held to higher standards than in wars for merely temporal reasons—standards of personal purity that maintained their ritual worthiness to serve alongside God in combat. "Oh then that wee would make a holy Warre indeed, that is, to be holy in our selves," prayed one Protestant holy war advocate from the era of the Puritan Revolution and the Thirty Years War (Leighton 1624, 9).

Thus in the wars of the post-Reformation era, the last period before the main line of Western moral tradition rejected warfare for religion, the standards for conduct in religious war derived mainly not from the religious factor itself but from the type of temporal conflict to which this warfare was assimilated: war of rebellion or war between sovereign equals. The only specific holy war influence on conduct in these wars which cuts across these two types is the notion that the soldier of righteousness is himself to be a righteous soldier—even though the enemy cannot be expected to behave the same way, because he is fighting in the cause of evil. This concept echoes the medieval moral restraints on knightly conduct and makes them more explicit.

It is important to note finally that even when the apologists for these early modern wars were speaking and writing in language evoking holy war tradition, they were on a more fundamental level already thinking about these wars in temporal terms as wars for a just public order, and they were employing religion as an ideological tool to argue for a conception of that order as rooted in an established authority or as dependent on reform that would change the nature or person of that authority.

The Conduct of War
for Religion in Normative Islamic Tradition

On the conduct of war for religion in Islamic tradition Majid Khadduri observes that since the fundamental objective of jihad is to universalize the Islamic faith, the faithful participating in the military form of jihad "were advised to refrain from the shedding of blood or the destruction of property unnecessary for the achievement of their objective. This general rule is based on Abu Bakr's address to the first expedition sent to the Syrian borders as well as . . . other similar utterances by succeeding caliphs" (Khadduri 1955, 102).

Khadduri goes on to identify three general areas regarding conduct of war on which the later juristic tradition commented: destruction of property, including animals; treatment of enemy persons; and times when fighting is not allowed. These three areas correspond directly to concerns that developed in Western moral tradition on war, though the content differs. Indeed, as Khadduri notes, the various jurists, while agreeing on the fundamentals, differed among themselves on the particulars.

Exemplifying such differences, Khadduri cites three jurists on limits to the destruction of property. Malik, he observes, prohibited only "the slaying of the flock and the destruction of beehives," whereas Abu Hanifa allowed destruction of everything the Muslim army could not bring under its control, including "houses, churches, trees, flocks, and herds," and Shafiʿi allowed animals to be slain only if not doing so would strengthen the enemy (Khadduri 1955, 103). The underlying idea in all three cases is that these are goods from which the Muslims might be able to benefit. Only Abu Hanifa's approach, though, makes this plain.

On the treatment of enemy persons, the fundamental principle was that after unbelievers in the *dar al-harb* had been issued the call to Islam (the *da'wa*) and refused it, they might be killed, combatants and noncombatants alike. Within the scope of this general principle, though, the jurists defined a place for different treatment of noncombatants: those "who did not take part in the fighting, such as women, children, monks and hermits, the aged, blind, and insane, were excluded from molestation" unless they actively aided the enemy, in which case they forfeited their noncombatant status (Khadduri 1955, 103–4). Also, killing by treachery and mutilation were forbidden. The general principle that all enemies might nonetheless be killed provided the rationale that permitted besieging of enemy cities, along with the use of inherently indiscriminate weapons like catapults and bows and arrows, even though this led to the harming of noncombatants. If Muslims were mixed with *harbis*, Khadduri finds a version of argument from the rule of double effect in Sufyan al-Thawri and Abu Hanifa: killing Muslims in such cases "would be regarded as killing by mistake" (Khadduri 1955, 106–7).

As noted in the previous section, the Truce of God in medieval Europe sought to prohibit fighting during particular periods defined as sacrosanct. Similarly, Islamic juristic tradition, building on the Qur'an, held that fighting should be *avoided* during the sacred months. The tradition did not, though, actually prohibit fighting during this period. The obligation to spread Islam took precedence, and this might entail war during the sacred season; similarly, if Muslims are attacked during this period, they may fight to defend themselves. Khadduri sums up the jurists' position: "abstention [during the sacred time of year] is recommended [but not required]" (Khadduri 1955, 105).

John Kelsay, who has examined in some detail the subject of restraint in classical Islamic juristic doctrine (Kelsay 1990, and 1993, chap. 4), argues forcefully that the juristic concept of jihad as war includes definite rules for its conduct, rules that distinguish classes of noncombatants from legitimate combatants and define what measures of harm are permitted against the enemy. These rules, Kelsay argues, can be recognized as analogous to those of the *jus in bello* of Western just war tradition and similar though not identical in content. Kelsay's discussion, which takes Shaybani's teaching in the *Siyar* as its starting-point, focuses and extends the basic understanding of proper conduct in war summarized by Khadduri.

As noted earlier, Shaybani's treatment of jihad as war begins by recalling the Prophet Muhammad's charge to his warriors whenever he sent them out:

Combat only those who disbelieve in God. Do not cheat or commit treachery, nor should you mutilate anyone or kill children. Whenever you meet your polytheist enemies, invite them [first] to accept Islam. If they do so, accept it and let them alone. . . . If they refuse [to accept Islam], then call upon them to pay the *jizya* [poll tax]; if they do, accept it and leave them alone. (Shaybani, par. 1, cited by Kelsay 1990, 198–99)

This passage compares directly with those Qur'anic passages examined in Chapter 3 in connection with the question of justification or warrant: 2:190–93, 4:91–93, 8:39–40, and 9:29. Elements in these passages seem to indicate that the Muslims are to make unrestrained war against such enemies so long as their unbelief lasts: "Idolatry is worse than carnage. . . . Fight against them until idolatry is no more and God's religion reigns supreme" (Qur'an 2:192); "Make war on them until idolatry shall cease and God's religion reign supreme" (Qur'an 8:39). Yet in fact the Qur'an itself and traditions associated with the Prophet limit what may be done in fighting with unbelievers, even idolaters. Thus Kelsay notes that elsewhere in the *Siyar* Shaybani cites further teachings ascribed to the Prophet:

He [of the enemy] who has reached puberty should be killed, but he who has not should be spared.
The Apostle of God prohibited the killing of women.
The Apostle of God said, "You may kill the adults of the unbelievers, but spare their minors—their youth."
Whenever the Apostle of God sent forth a detachment he said to it, "Do not cheat or commit treachery, nor should you mutilate or kill children, women, or old men." (Shaybani, pars. 28, 29, 30, and 47, cited by Kelsay 1990, 199)

Kelsay comments in summary: "This is consonant with the general approach of classical Sunni jurisprudence, which was still in a developmental stage when al-Shaybani wrote" (199).

These passages limit the conduct of war by specifying the enemy, by distinguishing combatants from noncombatants, and by prescribing limits to what harm may be done to combatants and noncombatants among the enemies.

1. The enemies, those against whom war may be waged, are the unbelievers, "those who disbelieve in God." If an unbeliever accepts the call to Islam

or submits to the order of Islam by paying the poll tax, he is no longer an enemy and war may not be made against him. Elsewhere the latter is qualified: only "people of the Book" and not "polytheists" may live in peace with Islam by paying the poll tax; "polytheists" must convert on pain of death.

2. Among the enemies, only the men of fighting age—those past puberty and not yet too old to bear arms—may be killed. Women, children (including male children who have not reached puberty), and old men are specifically excluded, though they may be taken captive and enslaved. This constitutes a limited doctrine of noncombatant immunity.

3. The means of injuring the enemy are limited in two ways: by a general prohibition against cheating and treachery and by a prohibition not only of killing noncombatants but also of mutilating them. This last is necessary because, in general, the permission to kill may be argued to include permission to do harm up to and including killing. The prohibition of mutilation thus lowers the threshold of harm that can be done to noncombatants. Fundamentally, since the arms in ordinary use in warfare of the period mutilated by their very nature, this restriction inhibits the direct, intentional use of such arms against noncombatants.

Several other observations may be made, beginning with the passages cited.

First, the texts Shaybani cites simply state the restrictions, giving no rationale for them. These restrictions, because of their source, have an immediate and inherent authority: the command, "Do not cheat or commit treachery, nor should you mutilate or kill children, women, or old men" is the rule for Muslims, not because it can be derived in some way from reason or nature or the customs of honorable war but because this is what the Prophet said "whenever [he] sent forth a detachment" (Shaybani, par. 47, in Khadduri 1966, 91–92), and it is therefore binding on all Muslims.

At the same time, attempting to move beyond these spare texts to their meaning for a more general conception of how properly to wage war requires some effort at explaining the nature of these restraints and what they imply.

One issue is whether the distinction between adult males of fighting age and women, children, and old men should be understood as implying a difference in degree of culpability between them. This is a problem closely bound up with the reason for fighting in the first place, which is defined by the unbelief of the enemy. The general conception of the enemy, those against whom war may be waged, is defined in *religious* terms within these traditions associated with the Prophet: "Combat only those who disbelieve in God." Do the restrictions on harm to women, children, and old men imply that they bear a lesser degree of religious guilt than males of fighting age?

One possible line of reasoning, applicable however only to very young children, follows from the Qur'anic doctrine that all children are born Muslim, and that unbelief comes later as a matter of free, if wrong, choice. On this reasoning very young children are to be spared in war because they are not yet properly among the unbelievers against whom the war is fought. Yet the traditional restriction includes older children up to the age of puberty, by which time they too have fallen into unbelief. There is a distinction between the very young and older children up to the age of puberty in terms of unbelief, but it is a distinction that turns out to make no difference in the restriction on harming children in war.

Exploring another possible line of reasoning, Kelsay suggests, following the twelfth-century philosopher Ibn Rushd (Averroes), that the traditional provisions for restraint in the treatment of women and children correlate with their status as the property of the adult men. This socially defined subordination of women and children establishes a presumption of lesser responsibility, and for this reason they are subject to lesser forms of harm by the Muslims (Kelsay 1993, 62–63).

This argument of Ibn Rushd, while suggestive for an effort to develop a more general theory on the conduct of war than is provided in the early traditions, comes from four centuries after Shaybani and is set in a philosophical, not juristic, context. It is useful more as an example of how the meaning of the tradition might be drawn out rather than as a vehicle for understanding the classical juristic position itself. Another problem with employing it to examine the reasoning implicit in the texts on which Shaybani based his teaching is that, in terms of its substance, this argument does not address why old men among the enemies, and not only women and children, are to be spared killing and mutilation. Indeed, if anything it works against including old men in the category of those to be spared such harm. If as Ibn Rushd argues women and children have lesser responsibility and thus bear lesser guilt as a result of their subordinate social status relative to men, then old men, who have a superior social status due to their age and who have lived a lifetime of full social responsibility as males, would seem all the more deserving of death in case of war. Yet they are in fact grouped with the women and children as to be treated more leniently than men of fighting age.

The most general concept of noncombatant immunity visible in the texts in question, the only one that accounts for all the classes of people named, is a *functional* one: those sorts of persons named—women, children, old men—are the members of the enemy's society who are generally unable to bear arms and do not do so.

This functional distinction does not assume any difference in level of unbelief or the guilt associated with it, though it does assume differing levels of war guilt. Islamic tradition in fact (like that of the West) accepted the presence of women in war with functions other than bearing arms, and this presence did not affect their noncombatant status. Like women of the *harbi* societies against which they made war, Muslim women all through the classical period accompanied the Islamic armies on jihad, not to bear arms but to keep the army fed and clothed and to care for the wounded. The same phenomenon may be observed as late as the Moroccan *harka* of the early twentieth century (Porch 1982, 68 and passim). So the prohibition of mutilation or killing of enemy women, and by the same reasoning also children and old men, correlates with their not bearing arms and could be revoked in cases in which they did so.

Such a functional definition of noncombatancy is also found in Western tradition on war (Johnson 1981, 132–33). In either culture it leads to a conception of noncombatant protection that is less than absolute, since it depends on contingent factors. Thus a functional approach to noncombatancy differs importantly from another rationale prominently in use within the Western tradition: that of noncombatant status as a right by possession. On this conception, as illustrated by John Locke's description of the state of nature, the rights to life and to freedom from harm are vested in each individual by nature, and only when the individual gives up these rights, notably by wrongly harming or threatening to harm another, may harm be directed to him or her. Here noncombatant status is the fundamental state of all persons, and the status of combatant is an exceptional state achieved by individuals on the basis of their behavior (Locke 1924, bk. 2, secs. 179–83). The rights of noncombatancy are absolute, the rights over combatants conditional. Another form of argument for an absolute conception of noncombatant immunity, a specifically religious one made on the basis of Christian charity rather than natural rights, is found in the contemporary just war theorist Paul Ramsey (Ramsey 1961, chap. 3). Normative Islamic tradition on war against unbelievers does not appear to include such a concept of noncombatancy as an absolute.

A functional approach to the definition of noncombatancy, whether that of Western or of Islamic tradition, begins with an opposite assumption from that of noncombatancy as an absolute and moves away from it. From the functional perspective, the state of war establishes a fundamental status of enmity between the belligerents, which extends to all the populace on both sides and gives each belligerent the right to harm or kill the enemy. That right is mitigated, but not entirely taken away, by the behavior of individual members of the enemy populace. Such is the argument identified above in Islamic tradition. For Western tradition it is illustrated by the following passage from the Western theorist Emmerich de Vattel:

> Women, children, the sick and aged, are in the number of enemies. And there are rights with regard to them, as belonging to the nation with which another is at war, and the rights and pretensions between nation and nation affect the body of the society, together with all its members. But these are members who make no resistance, and consequently give us no right to treat their persons ill, or use any violence against them, much less to take away their lives. . . . However, if women are desirous of being spared, they are to employ themselves in the occupation of their sex, and not play the men in taking arms. (Vattel 1916, sec. 145)

For Islamic tradition the closest social analogy to Locke's state of nature—or better, to the societies created by social contract which protect rights rooted in the state of nature—is the status of life inside the *dar al-islam*, where God's will for human behavior is the norm and the practice to which believers aspire, and within which believers and others who subject themselves to God's law live, in principle, at peace with one another. In this peace no one has any right to harm another. But specific behavior against God's law, up to and including apostasy, changes this, giving those who would uphold that law the right to use force to punish, correct, and in the extreme case, kill those persons who manifest such behavior.

The concept of the *dar al-harb* is a reflection of this link between right behavior and belief: the *dar al-harb* is the territory of unbelief and thereby the territory in which conflict and enmity are the norm. The rights of Muslims over unbelievers in the *dar al-harb* follow from this: these rights are essentially the same whether given in the language of Shaybani or that of Vattel commenting on the meaning of the state of enmity in the context of Western tradition. It is the assumption of enmity and the derivative, functional definition of noncombatancy that are the important factors here, and they are the same in both traditions.

In Western tradition a functional definition of noncombatancy is often joined to a rationale based on an invocation of justice or fairness: the classes named as noncombatants do not normally participate in war and so do not deserve to have war made against them (see further Johnson 1975, 42–44). This again assumes that noncombatants have certain rights that enemy soldiers are obliged to respect.

The reasoning in Islamic tradition, as well exemplified by Shaybani's discussion in the *Siyar*, is different. All enemies, by their refusal of the invitation to accept Islam and by their resistance to the Islamic mission, are by definition in a state of rebellion against God and God's Prophet, and hence may be killed; yet some among them, namely the classes of people mentioned, are normally to be spared killing and the lesser damage of mutilation. The reason given in the text is not that these have rights of their own to be spared harm, rights derived either from nature or from considerations of fairness or justice, but rather that they are potentially of value to the Muslims. Such persons are subject to being taken captive and returned as slaves to the *dar al-islam*. Killing them would make them valueless for this purpose, and mutilation would reduce their value. Their being spared the sword is thus not a matter of some obligation of the Muslim soldiers toward them but a matter of the soldiers' obligation to bring the greatest benefit to the Muslim community (cf. Shaybani, chaps. 2 and 3, in Khadduri 1966, 95–129).

Because benefit to the Muslim community is the overriding criterion for what measures may be taken against the enemy, even men of fighting age do not *have* to be killed; they too may be taken captive and returned to the *dar al-islam* as slaves. Shaybani writes, recalling the teaching of Abu Hanifa:

> I asked: If male captives of war were taken from the territory of war, do you think that the Imam should kill them all or divide them as slaves among the Muslims?
>
> He replied: The Imam is entitled to a choice between taking them to the territory of Islam to be divided [among the warriors] and killing them [while in the territory of war].
>
> I asked: Which is preferable?
>
> He replied: [The Imam] should examine the situation *and decide whatever he deems to be advantageous to the Muslims.* (Shaybani, pars. 94–97, in Khadduri 1966, 100; emphasis added)

The passage continues with further qualifications of the general right to kill males of fighting age. If captives taken in jihad within the *dar al-harb* become Muslims, they may not be killed, but they remain slaves and should be returned to the *dar al-islam* "as booty to be divided among the Muslims" (Shaybani, pars. 100–101, in Khadduri 1966, 101). Elsewhere Shaybani notes an exception to this, determined by the criterion of benefit as well as by the general power of life or death over men of fighting age: if the captives include such men and women, and if no transportation is available, the captives should all be made to walk back to the *dar al-islam*; if they are unable to walk, the Imam "should kill the men and spare the women and children, for whom he should hire means for carrying them" (Shaybani, pars. 80–81, in Khadduri 1966, 98). Men from the *dar al-harb* who have been given a safe-conduct prior to battle are not to be taken back as slaves but set free (Shaybani, pars. 106–9 in Khadduri 1966, 101). If "the blind, the crippled, the helpless insane" are taken as prisoners of war, they should not be killed, even though they have little or no value as slaves (Shaybani, pars. 110–11, in Khadduri 1966, 101).

The result of these qualifications is to temper the general right of life or death possessed by the Muslim force over men of age to bear arms during jihad in the *dar al-harb*. The criterion of benefit—an example of functional reasoning—implies mitigation of the general right to kill the men in the case that they will be useful as slaves and can be returned to the *dar al-islam* either by walking or by transportation that is in hand. The mitigation of this right in the case of prisoners who have a safe-conduct follows from another principle, that of *pacta sunt servanda*: agreements are to be honored. This principle holds even in relations with the *dar al-harb*. Finally, not killing blind, crippled, and insane captives, though they are of little or no value as slaves, seems a pure act of moderation outside considerations of benefit.

Mitigation of harm to males of fighting age once they have been taken captive follows from the fact that prisoners are no longer capable of engaging in combat and are thus functionally noncombatants. Thus the criterion of functionality by which women, children, and the aged are defined as noncombatants extends also to men captured in war. At the point at which noncombatancy is defined, then, the next concern is how noncombatants are to be treated, and the answer is given by another functional criterion: whether they can benefit the Muslim community as slaves. The decision on this is the *imam*'s, and no further criterion is mentioned by which he might decide the fate of the captives.

It is especially interesting, given the general definition of the enemy by the criterion of unbelief, that Shaybani offers the above judgments for enemy prisoners of war *despite* the fact that they remain unbelievers. Their captive status has removed the threat they pose to the mission of Islam even though their unbelief remains. Conversion only eliminates the option of putting them to death: male captives of war who become Muslims may not be killed but "should be regarded as booty to be divided among the Muslims" (Shaybani, pars. 100–101, in Khadduri 1966, 101).

In general, for Shaybani the treatment of human captives from the *dar al-harb* is directly parallel with that of animals and property taken by the Muslim army on jihad. These are to be taken back to the *dar al-islam* if that is possible, but otherwise destroyed. Mutilation of animals (such as hamstringing) and leaving them behind is expressly forbidden; if they cannot be returned to the *dar al-islam* they are to be slaughtered (Shaybani, pars. 82–87, in Khadduri 1966, 98–99).

All the above concerns the direct, intentional treatment of enemy persons and property. Within the general framework of the conduct of war as *jihad* against and within the *dar al-harb* the limits discussed above are not taken to imply restrictions on combat that is otherwise of an acceptable sort. In a siege or in the storming of an enemy city whatever measures are necessary to subdue the city may be taken: it would be "permissible to inundate a city in the territory of war with water, to burn it with fire, or to attack [its people] with mangonels, even though there may be slaves, women, old men, and children," or even Muslim merchants or, at the extreme, Muslim children in the city (Shaybani, pars. 112–23, in Khadduri 1966, 101–2). Shaybani, referring to Abu Hanifa's teaching, gives the reason: if the presence of such persons meant that the Muslims could not besiege the city or attack it, then they could not make war at all, for "there is no city in the territory of war in which there is not one at all of these you have mentioned" (Shaybani, par. 117, in Khadduri 1966, 102). But while Muslims may carry on their warfare against the city, they should not intend to harm those who should not be harmed. If such harm occurs, that is the result of war, and the Muslim soldiers do not incur guilt from it.

Exactly the same reasoning is found in Western tradition on war: the concept of mitigation of harm to noncombatants refers only to direct, intentional harm done them. If noncombatants are caught in a context within which they may be harmed, such as the siege of a city in a just war, then the siege may continue despite the presence of the noncombatants, because damage to them is not the aim of the military action under way. So long as the city is defended the attack may continue, even by such indiscriminate means as those named by Shaybani, fire, bombardment by mangonels, or flooding, because the aim is to capture the city, not to harm the noncombatants in it.

Taken all together, there are significant points of connection in the overall understanding of what is allowable in war within the classical Western and Islamic traditions. The conception of noncombatancy and the treatment allowed noncombatants, however, take somewhat different form in these two traditions. While both agree in setting off women, children, the aged, the blind, cripples, and the insane as classes of persons who should be spared killing or mutilation in war, the Islamic juristic tradition limits only the degree of harm that may be done to them, while the Western tradition extends a more general immunity from harm to such persons. Both traditions define a conception of noncombatancy as dependent on function and hence variable, while the core of Islamic tradition on noncombatant immunity is the authoritative command of the Prophet, and Western tradition has also produced various understandings of noncombatancy as an absolute right. From the functional perspective in the West, noncombatants are essentially to be left alone so far as possible, while from the absolutist perspective they are never, under any circumstances to be made the subjects of direct, intentional harm, whether attack, imprisonment, or seizure of property. Classical Islamic tradition as exemplified by Shaybani, however, allows enslavement of those noncombatants who are judged to be of possible use to the Muslim community, namely women and children, as well as seizure of property. The same reasoning on both sides extends to men of fighting age who have been taken prisoner and thus transformed into noncombatants.

Comparison between these traditions can be misleading, since the two traditions developed for quite different purposes and with quite different contexts in mind. The Western consensus aimed at limiting the ravages of war within Christendom among Christians; except for those restraints that followed from considerations of knightly virtue and Christian charity, they did not directly bear on warfare outside of Christendom or against a non-Christian foe. Thus they did not apply, notably, in the Crusades. The classical Islamic juristic doctrine developed for a quite different reason and assumed a different context: it was designed to explain how a Muslim army should conduct itself while on jihad within the *dar al-harb*, outside the bounds of the territory of Islam and with enemies who were not Muslims. This kind of question was never explicitly addressed in the medieval formation of the Christian tradition on restraining war, though it is addressed implicitly in (later) absolutist conceptions of noncombatant immunity and is explicitly embraced in the formation of modern naturalist theory on the *jus in bello* and in the development of positive international law. These, however, assume an environment in which war for religious difference has no place.

Neither tradition, in its classical form, anticipated the development of an international order of independent states within which religious affiliation is treated as structurally meaningless. Western tradition adapted by becoming secular, not Christian; Islamic tradition adapted by accepting the *de facto* division of the *dar al-islam* and by effectively giving up much of the ideology that was included in the distinction between the *dar al-islam* and the *dar al-harb*. So far as these two forms of adaptation hold, there is no open space for holy war. Yet the classical theory remains as an ideology that retains much power to inflame conflict and undermine modern conceptions of noncombatancy and noncombatant immunity.

A closer comparison can be drawn between the Islamic juristic tradition, as represented above by Abu Hanifa via Shaybani, and the perceptions of Western practices from classical antiquity as summarized by Hugo Grotius in his *De Jure Belli ac Pacis*. Referring somewhat unsystematically to a variety of ancient sources representing diverse cultural contexts, Grotius argues that collectively they represent the consensus of antiquity. That consensus allowed all inhabitants of the enemy country to be treated as enemies and killed anywhere they are found. This right extended to women and children and applied against prisoners as well as in the heat of battle. Enslavement was allowed as an alternative; Grotius remarks that this represents a step in the direction of moderation, since it is a less severe form of harm than killing. Such moderation is not the enemy's right but a result of mercy on the part of the warrior, and it allows the captor to draw benefit from the captive, just as the victor in battle may take for his own the property of the vanquished. (See Grotius 1949, bk. 3, chaps. 4–7 and 11–14.)

Grotius notes that moderation of such extreme permission to harm the enemy began even in antiquity, and he argues that Christian charity has influenced the law of nations to adopt even more stringent restraints — namely, those received through just war tradition. At the same time, he lived and wrote in a historical context in which Christian religion was being used as a justification for the sort of unrestrained warfare that was waged in antiquity. His purpose is to urge greater restraint; yet his catalog of what was allowed by the law of nature, as evinced by the practices of antiquity, closely matched the practice of holy war in his own time.

The similarity between these practices of warfare in antiquity as represented by Grotius and the practices allowed in jihad according to Shaybani
highlights the difficulty of finding common ground between the classical
Islamic and Western Christian traditions on the conduct of war for religion.
For even if the conduct of such war as Grotius knew it from the beginning
stages of the Thirty Years War closely corresponded to what was allowed in
antiquity, these very practices created the sense of revulsion found in the
cultural rejection of war for religion in the West. Yet these same sorts of
practice are accepted in classical Islamic juristic tradition on jihad as
represented by Shaybani, and this tradition still has normative force within
the Islamic community. These are considerably less stringent and universal
than normative Western tradition today holds. Despite some points of
contact, then, this question of what sort of conduct is to be allowed in war
constitutes a deeply problematical difference between the Western and
Islamic traditions.

6

HOLY WAR AND THE
PRACTICE OF STATECRAFT

The concept of holy war hides a paradox: while such war depends on a divinely given rationale, its actual form and its results are deeply this-worldly. Holy war is justified by appeal to divinely given obligations and purposes, and its authorization depends ultimately on divine sanction. Extreme means in its conduct are likewise measured against transcendent ends and sometimes even represented to be in response to specific divine commands. Yet holy war itself is enacted and experienced by the belligerents in the here and now. Though the cultural approval for holy war comes by means of religion, the war itself is carried on by means of the power of the state or other politically defined communities. Though holy war promises to achieve results that will further ultimate divine purposes, the actual results impact on the world of the present—the state, which will find its territory increased or reduced by it; the political and military authorities, who will find their prestige and power enhanced or diminished by it; ordinary individuals, who may lose their lives, health, or property by it or may gain riches and social advancement from it; and families, who must gamble their male members and their treasure to finance it and may lose or gain when the fighting is done.

A further element of the paradox is that while those who undertake holy war conceive it as the noblest of causes, indeed, nothing short of service to God, those against whom holy war is waged experience it entirely differ-ently. Unless both sides think of their undertaking as holy war—in which case each side may represent the other as the agent of the Devil—the objects

of holy war experience it as an ungodly, this-worldly threat undertaken
to dominate and perhaps enslave them, to take away their goods, their
freedoms, their lives, and the social and political structures—including
religion—they have made for themselves according to their own ideals.

Nor does the nobility of the cause of holy war insulate it from being
employed for purely secular ends. Within the culture that is waging holy war,
its high motivations, authorization, and tendency toward unlimited prosecution can make appeal to such warfare extraordinarily useful as a means to
serve the purposes of the state, so long as the state is careful to honor the
religious orientation that makes the holy war possible. Conversely, however,
the state may be endangered by holy war: if the state is perceived as
dishonoring religion or governing by standards at odds with those given
through religious faith, then appeals to ultimate standards may give rise to
holy war in the form of a rebellion to set the state right. Historical and
contemporary examples of both sorts of phenomena abound.

The paradox inherent in holy war, then, requires that it be assessed not
only in terms of its appeal to the ultimate as defined by religion but also from
the perspective of the temporal world—as an element in the practice of
statecraft within the world of political communities.

The Context: Worldly Authority
and the Success of God's Plan

Religious Theory and Temporal Government
in the Two Traditions

In both Christian and Islamic tradition the idea of holy war follows from
fundamental assumptions about the nature of history, the divine plan, and
human responsibility relative to that plan. Both religions understand history
as a linear process that embodies God's intentions for the world; living in
history, humans have a responsibility to assist the realization of those
intentions through their beliefs and their behavior.

For both religious traditions God has intervened numerous times by
means of prophets, beginning with Abraham, to guide human belief and
behavior. For both, the revelation given in this way is now complete: for
Christians, through the actual presence of God in Jesus Christ as well as
through his teachings; for Muslims, through the word of God as revealed to

the Prophet Muhammad and preserved in the Qur'an. The present stage of history is thus special for both traditions: it is the stage in which God's will for humankind has been made fully manifest, and right believers are called to live according to that will and to spread its knowledge and rule throughout the world. Holy war in both traditions is at once a metaphor for the struggle between God's will and the forces of resistance and a moral obligation to assist actively in establishing that rule concretely, protecting it where it exists, and spreading it into areas as yet untransformed.

Because of their understanding of history as part of the divine plan, for both traditions the political character of the world is of profound importance. It must be in accord with the will of God for the ordering of human affairs within history, or if it is not, it must be made so. Islam and Christianity agree that true religion knows what good politics should be. And thus for both these religious traditions the existence of governments that ignore the divine plan or openly flaunt it challenge faith's understanding of the course of history and ultimately God's will itself.

As we noted earlier when discussing the problem of authority for holy war, however, Christianity and Islam differ significantly in their conception of normative public order.

The Development of Christian Ideas of Religious Supremacy and Temporal Autonomy

As we observed in Chapter 3 when discussing the problem of authority for holy war, the Christian religion originated apart from and in opposition to the existing political and social order. The early Christians believed that the end of history was at hand and that the worldly order would perish with it. Gradually, though, the fact that history had not ended and the increasing role of Christians in worldly affairs had to be taken into account. By the second century C.E. Christianity had largely made its peace with the worldly order and with the idea that the ongoing existence of history is also a part of God's plan. Yet the distinction between church and world remained central, and accordingly normative Christian thought on the relationship of the divine plan for salvation to the governance of human affairs in history developed around an acceptance of two spheres, a temporal and a spiritual, not a single reality combining the two. Putting these into a common historical framework and explaining how they relate in the process of divine salvation was the work of Augustine's magisterial work of consolidation,

The City of God, at the beginning of the fifth century. Augustine's concept of the two "cities," one ordered by the concerns of earth and one ordered by the concerns of heaven, permeated medieval thinking about war for religion and provided the basis for the normative medieval understanding of state-craft.

While Augustine regarded the *civitas terrenae* as gradually and inexorably giving way to the *civitas dei*, he understood the two to be distinct realities so long as history may last. Until that time the state, as the manifestation of the *civitas terrenae*, though never able to achieve completely the goals of good politics—defined as temporal order, justice, and peace—is nevertheless to seek to serve those ends as fully as possible, guided by the vision of the church, the contemporary though incomplete presence of the *civitas dei*.

Augustine's medieval heirs forgot or disregarded the importance of his conception of the incompleteness of both the earthly and the heavenly cities. Emphasizing the idea of the ultimate superiority of the heavenly over the earthly, papal triumphalists treated the church as already having power over the state. This argument produced the claim for papal authority to initiate war for religion examined earlier. The medieval holy wars or Crusades were thus rationalized by this conception of the church's dominion over history. Nonetheless, the identification of military power with temporal rule, not spiritual, meant that actual warfare for religion had to be waged in partner-ship with temporal princes. Nor did the triumphalist view translate into theocratic control over Christendom. Whatever the theory of the pope's supremacy in spiritual affairs as head of the church, the temporal rulers of Europe were supreme in their own domains. Both in church circles and in the larger Christian community, moreover, the church's right to be involved in any way at all in political governance and in the authorization of war was put in question. (See further Russell 1975, 112–26, 180–212, and Walters 1973.)

The doctrinal battleground was the same Augustinian theory which, when developed in one direction, could be made to produce arguments for papal supremacy and theocratic government. Taken in another direction by the medieval opponents of papal triumphalism in the temporal sphere, Augus-tinian theory led to something much more fundamental for the long run. This line of theoretical recasting produced a Christian conception providing a theoretical justification of autonomy for temporal government relative to religion as long as history may last. This autonomy is something that neither the papal triumphalist nor the Islamic normative model allows. The medi-eval opponents of papal power developed this side of the inherited Augustinian model, stressing the separateness of the sacred and temporal realms, but moving beyond Augustine to use natural-law theory to provide a norm whereby rulers could govern according to the divine plan independently of guidance from the church.

Augustine had regarded the *civitas terrenae* as incapable of achieving fully the goals of politics—order, justice, and peace. Full realization of these goals would be reached, he expected, only in the *civitas dei*. This followed, on his reasoning, from the inherent imperfection of the *civitas terrenae* due to sin. Late medieval theorists, thinking in terms of the theological assumptions of Thomas Aquinas rather than those of Augustine but still working within the context of a fundamentally Augustinian conception of politics, accepted the idea that the temporal order is less nearly perfect than the heavenly, but interpreted this as meaning that the state is capable of reaching its own proper perfection, that appropriate to the temporal realm as defined in natural law. Within the parameters of this law of nature, set in place by God for the governance of the world, there can be a politics of genuine order, justice, and peace. (On this conception see further the discussion of Dante's *De Monarchia* and Marsilius of Padua's *Defensor Pacis* in Johnson 1987, 113–27.)

The modern period marks the development of this conception of temporal government into the secular state, a political unit capable of good government on its own terms, without need for revelatory guidance from the sphere of religion. After one last cathartic spasm of holy war, the religious wars of the Reformation era which ended by the middle of the seventeenth century, Western culture decisively rejected any role for holy war in the practice of statecraft. Indeed, the balance has, if anything, shifted in the opposite direction. Rather than providing justification and authorization for war, contemporary Christianity is more likely to criticize the use of military force by the state. In the West, then, holy war has become an object of suspicion from both the secular and Christian perspectives.

The Islamic Ideal of Religio-Political Unity

The case of Islam is somewhat more complicated. In the classical Islamic understanding, as we have seen, the Muslim community is at one and the same time religious and political; the *dar al-islam* is a specific territory and it is ruled by an authority who is at once the community's religious and political leader. This ordering, according to the tradition, corresponds to the actual nature of the original Islamic community under Muhammad. The two main branches of Islam, the Sunni and Shi'ite, differ not over this classically defined norm, but over whether subsequent governments of the Islamic community have honored it and over whether any government according to this norm is possible in the world as it now is.

The classical ideal was, in both cases, framed in explicitly religious terms and images. Unlike the philosophers, whose writings were influenced by Greco-Roman political thought, the jurists, both Sunni and Shi'ite, took the Qur'an and the example of the Prophet as their lodestones. Because they understood the Qur'an to be the word of God, they regarded its wisdom as having a timeless quality; similarly, because Muhammad was the final prophet of God, they regarded the example of his life as manifesting right guidance by God, thus carrying timeless implications for rightly guided rule by subsequent leaders. Present-day Muslim fundamentalists insist on the same timelessness.

Yet the actual theoretical constructs of the jurists inevitably introduced a contingent element: the words of the Qur'an and the example of the Prophet needed to be understood, interpreted so that their meaning was clear, and placed in relation to each other so that their implications for ongoing life could be fully grasped and appreciated. To resolve seemingly contradictory passages in the Qur'an, a method of interpretation was needed. Revising the text of the Qur'an itself was out of the question; it was, for them, divine revelation, and the form of the text had been established since the time of the second caliph, 'Uthman (Holt, Lambton, and Lewis 1970, 1:32, 73–74). The jurists resolved the problem before them by understanding the divine revelation in the Qur'an as having been progressively given to Muhammad as he gained ability to receive it. The textual sequence of the Qur'an, however, did not correspond to the sequence of revelation, and so it became necessary to connect particular passages or sections of the Qur'an to events or stages in the life and experience of the Prophet. This in turn required decisions about the nature, authenticity, sequence, and context of the traditions associated with his life. Differences in dealing with these traditions and in making these connections became distinguishing marks of the juristic schools (Holt, Lambton, and Lewis 1970, 1:74; Goldhizer 1981, 31–66). Moreover, even when the jurists agreed on the sources to be taken as authoritative and the modes of reasoning or interpretation to be applied to them, they still left room for disagreement on the judgments to be reached concerning questions of practice. So despite the assumption of timelessness in the wisdom contained in the sources of juristic reasoning, the actual product of that reasoning introduced contingent elements, elements that reflected the social, political, and intellectual contexts of the jurists themselves. The work of the classical jurists on statecraft can thus be read as providing a window on the ideal of statecraft for the historical context in which they wrote; the degree to which it provided a blueprint for the actual conduct of statecraft in that age or subsequent ones must be judged by comparing this ideal construct with the actual conduct of statecraft in those times.

The governance of the caliphate was never religiously pure enough to satisfy the desires of the Shi'ites and other religiously dissident groups, such as the Kharijites; yet Muslim society under the caliphs was governed by Islamic law, and the purposes of state were defined in terms provided by Islamic tradition. Structurally this society was dependent on religion not only for moral and spiritual guidance but also for the goals of political life and the rules by which the society should conduct itself. The development of Sunni Islamic jurisprudence beginning early in the eighth century, reflecting the consolidation of caliphal rule in the period after the defeat of the Shi'ite forces at Karbala in 680, shows the importance within the Muslim community of a settled religious foundation for the governance of the state. Somewhat ironically, the corresponding development of Shi'ite juristic thought makes the same assumption about the structural relation between religion and the state, though the Shi'ite jurists differed sharply with their Sunni counterparts on the matter of caliphal rule.

How juristic theory on statecraft evolved was important for the development of the state for three major reasons.

First, the juristic schools substantially agreed in the matters essential to the religious foundation of the state and most matters of everyday law and governance; their differences were on matters that from the political standpoint were of less moment, however important they might be religiously.

Second, among the Sunnis the differences that existed among the jurists concerning the accepted interpretions of the Qur'an and the traditions associated with the Prophet made them less of a rival to state power than they would have been if united. Rather than the jurists as a group being ranged against the caliphs as a source of religious authority, thus diminishing caliphal power, the divisions among the juristic schools tended to augment caliphal power by placing the caliphs in a position to choose among the opinions of the various schools as suited state purposes or to cite the differences as a rationale for taking an independent path. The important exception was the difference represented by the Shi'ite jurists, who hated the caliphate with an implacable hatred; yet rather than diminishing caliphal power, this stance of opposition made it easy for the rulers to ignore the Shi'ite teachings in favor of those of the Sunni schools.

Third, for the 'Abbasid caliphs, who reigned during the classical period of Islamic juristic thought, the religious foundation provided by the jurists suited the political purposes of the society very well. Internally, it provided sanction for the pyramid of authority at the head of which was the caliph, by contrast with the diffused leadership of various sorts that obtained in the areas over which Islamic society spread. Also internally, this religious foundation provided a rule for the conduct of every member of society whatever his or her station, as well as sanctions against the breaking of rules. On the juristic view, the law of Islam was not understood as simply an arbitrary imposition by the political authorities; it was promulgated both as the law of God and as the most fulfilling way of behavior for individuals. In the latter sense Islamic law took the place of natural law within the culture of Western Christendom, removing the need for a separate set of rules for life in the temporal world. Understood this way, Islamic law put the political authorities in a positive position, whether they were understood as acting on behalf of God to enforce his will or as enforcing that behavior most beneficial both to individuals and to society as a whole. The result was thus to enhance the power of the authorities and of the state itself. (Cf. Goldhizer 1981, 44–47.)

Externally, the most important effect of the religious foundation for the state defined by the jurists was that it not only sanctioned a distinct Muslim political entity but defined it as the norm. Islam, as understood by the jurists, was not destined to be a purely spiritual religion, dwelling within the hearts of individuals and indifferent to the governance of the world. Its goal for life was not contemplation and withdrawal from the affairs of history but action and involvement in shaping the course of those affairs. Thus Islamic law, as understood by the jurists, required a robust state. It is important to note again that this was a matter on which Sunnis and Shi'ites strongly agreed; the crux of their disagreement was the nature of the ruling authority within that state and succession to that authority. Nor was this ideal diminished even as the actual character of the state became more diffuse and rival centers of rule emerged.

In both Christian and Islamic theory, then, an ideal rationale can be found for linking religious authority and religiously defined ends and ideas to the practice of statecraft, including the waging of war. This is not, however, the whole story. Conflicting themes in both traditions have diminished the authoritativeness of this ideal pattern, and in historical practice both Christian and Islamic communities have developed in the form of multiple political entities independent of one another and with the exercise of statecraft functionally independent of religious rule.

All this is important for understanding holy war as a phenomenon simultaneously religious and secular. From the standpoint of the state holy war has functioned as a factor to be taken into account within the practice of statecraft, but one whose character is rooted outside the state. Thus while it can be the manifestation of an actually or potentially powerful ideology that might advance the cause of the state, holy war may also interfere with that cause and redirect the state's resources to serve ends other than those defined as worthy by the state, or even pose an outright challenge to the political authorities and the interests of the state. It is the ideological power of holy war that makes it of interest from the perspective of statecraft, just as it is the temporal power of the state that makes it of interest for achieving the historical goals of religion.

The Islamic Juristic Ideal and the Historical Practice of Statecraft

The Tension Between Ideal and Reality

Theory postulating the religious and political unity of all Muslims diverged from reality in Islamic statecraft very early. Even with Muslim unity held up as the ideal on the religious level, disagreements over doctrine and succession to the Prophet's authority repeatedly led to conflict and often divided Muslims into competing groups, each claiming to represent the true unity of the faith. The first major split, that of the Shi'ites, is described in Muslim tradition as beginning in a conflict between the Caliph 'Ali and his rival Mu'awiyya over leadership of the Muslim community, only fifteen years after the death of the Prophet and within the lifetime of persons who had known him. The withdrawal of another major group, the Kharijites, came soon after. Throughout the period of the Umayyad caliphate, begun by Mu'awiyya, religious disputes simmered continuously, and conflict erupted over the succession almost every time a caliph died. At the same time, growth of the territory under Muslim rule to incorporate non-Arab peoples intro-duced social heterogeneity into what had been originally a purely Arab movement. (On the early history of Islam see further Holt, Lambton, and Lewis 1970, vol. 1, part 1, chaps. 2–4.)

Systematic juristic attention to the doctrines of Islam did not begin until after the pattern of such disputes had already been well established. The earliest schools of Islamic law began to take shape only toward the end of the Umayyad period, with most of the major legal schools being established during the 'Abbasid dynasty (Goldhizer 1981, 46–47; Piscatori 1986, 151). Classical juristic works of statecraft were in turn the product of these schools; Shaybani's *Siyar*, one of the earliest and most important of these, was written more than a full century after the Shi'ite and Kharijite splits took place (Khadduri 1966, 41–43; Piscatori 1986, 151). Indeed, within the Sunni realm the development of such works, with their introduction of the distinction between the *dar al-islam* and the *dar al-harb* and their emphasis on the unity of the *dar al-islam* under a single religio-political leadership, can easily be read as serving the purposes of the 'Abbasid caliphs, having an apologetic edge directed against the Shi'ites and other challengers to caliphal rule. Many of the most prominent jurists, including Shaybani, were closely linked to the caliphal regime, often holding official positions within it and sometimes providing legal advice directly to the caliph himself.

Shi'ite jurisprudence too, as it developed, put forward the ideal of a single Muslim realm headed by a just ruler. The Shi'ite jurists, though, gave their doctrine exactly the opposite apologetic edge from that of the Sunnis, directing their doctrine against the empire of the caliphs, whose rule the Shi'ites regarded as unjust and illegitimate (Sachedina 1988; cf. Johnson and Kelsay 1990, 44–46).

Classical juristic theories of statecraft, then, as they developed, despite their close reliance on the Qur'an and the traditions of the Prophet, were not simply statements of a transcendently defined ideal any more than they were descriptions of the reality of the Islamic state. Rather, they were doctrines that emerged in particular historical contexts and served specific historical purposes, either to support the caliphal system in one or another of its forms or to seek to undermine it.

Another dimension of the tension between the juristic ideal and the reality was that the *dar al-islam* itself, in its empirical form, was not the single universal entity described in the ideal. Along with religious differences and disputes over rule, territorial and other divisions within an ostensibly unitary Muslim state developed comparatively early, leading to plural centers of rule even as the theorists were setting forth the concept of a single Islamic empire. Indeed, *de facto* or *de jure* independent Muslim states have been a fact

through the great majority of the history of Islam. Such divisions characterized even the classical age of Islamic jurisprudence, so that the juristic theory
of the ideal never actually matched the reality of statecraft in the world in
which the jurists lived (Holt, Lambton, and Lewis 1970, vol. 1, part 1,
chaps. 3 and 4). At the center of the Islamic world disputes over succession
often led to armed conflicts at the end of each caliph's reign, sometimes
creating *de facto* divisions in the *dar al-islam* and from time to time
producing rivals each of whom simultaneously took the title caliph. On the
periphery autonomous Islamic states came into being which rejected central
caliphal authority and defied the ideal of a unified religio-political *dar
al-islam*. 'Abd al-Rahman, an Umayyad *amir*, became the independent ruler
of Cordova, Spain, in 756, rejecting the rule of the new 'Abbasid caliph;
another rival dynasty, the Idrisid, began in Morocco in 788, followed by the
establishment of the Aghlabid dynasty in Tunisia in 799. In 910 the Fatimid
caliphate began in North Africa, and in 929 'Abd al-Rahman III, governor of
Cordova, adopted the title of caliph for himself. Three years later the
Buwayhid dynasty was established in Persia. This list might go on right up to
the secularly governed Muslim states of the present day (Piscatori 1986, 151;
Holt, Lambton, and Lewis 1970, vol. 1, part 1, chap. 4).

The point of these examples, though, is that even in the early years of
Islam and throughout the classical age of Islamic jurisprudence, the ideal of
statecraft by which the *dar al-islam* was understood as a single religio-
political entity under unitary rule, opposed only by the non-Muslim *dar
al-harb*, did not correspond to the actual political shape or governance of the
Islamic world. As these examples show, religious differences and challenges
to the rule of particular caliphs arose early, and over time the Islamic world
fragmented into independent states. Each ruler of his own fragment of the
dar al-islam might claim, on the basis of appeal to the jurists and the example
of the Prophet, to exercise supreme religious as well as political authority
and might even adopt for himself the title of caliph to associate his rule more
directly with the legitimacy of a connection with the Prophet. As a result the
concept of a unified Islamic religio-political order under a single head and
internally at peace—by contrast with the picture the jurists painted of a
fragmented and conflict-prone *dar al-harb*—was already at odds with
reality even while the juristic schools were developing theories of statecraft
with this concept as the ideal.

Empirically also, within historical Muslim states, alongside claims to be
faithful to the religion of the Prophet a broad spectrum of relationships
developed between the temporal authorities and the representatives of

religion, paralleled by a spectrum of popular adjustment between temporal life and the requirements of religion. The philosopher al-Farabi recognized this as early as the tenth century, despite what the juristic theory claimed, when he described the qualities that should be found in a "king" (*malik*, not caliph), that is, an independent Muslim temporal ruler. The possibility that the king might also personally possess religious authority is only one of four alternatives Farabi identified: the other three define various degrees of separation between political and religious leadership (al-Farabi 1961, 50–51 [secs. 54–55]). Along with the possibility that a Muslim king might not himself be the religious leader Farabi gave him a set of duties and responsibilities largely temporal in nature (40–42 [secs. 27–29]). In this philosopher's thought political authority had no necessary tie to religious, whether in the person of the king or in the conduct of his office.

Another issue in the classical juristic ideal, that the caliph was also the *imam* for all Islam, was also empirically unclear in the early centuries. Certainly the Prophet had been *imam* for all Muslims; his immediate successors also exercised this role. By contrast the Umayyads, who ruled from 661 to 750, behaved in effect as temporal rulers, not religious leaders; their lack of religious authority was one of the core elements of the Shiʻite and Kharijite opposition to their rule. The ʻAbbasids moved back toward incorporating religion into the caliph's role, seeking religious as well as political sanction for their rule by stressing their descent from Muhammad's family and adopting throne names suggesting divine support; yet none of them before al-Maʼmun (813–33) took the title *imam* as well as caliph (Holt, Lambton, and Lewis 1970, 1:104, 120).

We have noted earlier how in practical usage the term *imam* for the Sunnis over time became more and more the title for a local religious leader, as it is today, and not one of the titles of the politico-religious leader of the *dar al-islam*, as it was in classical juristic theory. For the Shiʻites the term *imam* became a title attached specifically to the figure of the *sultan al-ʻadil*, the just ruler, a religiously authoritative figure who also would, in Shiʻite theory, exercise political rule. After the occultation of the twelfth Shiʻite Imam in the tenth century, the term was reserved for him alone, not passed down to lesser religious leaders and certainly not accepted as applying to the increasingly political rule of the caliphs and other Muslim rulers.

All this suggests that the state of affairs today, in which the Islamic world is divided into numerous independent states whose rulers, with only limited exceptions, make no claims to religious authority and govern on secular terms, is not an anomaly in Islamic practice but simply the present-day embodiment of trends that appeared early in the history of Islamic society. The fundamentalist and traditionalist opponents of the secular governments of contemporary states like Egypt and Algeria, who criticize them as examples of a Western style of government unlike the ideal of the classical *dar al-islam*, as well as those voices in the Muslim world who denounce the entire international system as un-Islamic, rest too much on an ideal that was never a picture of reality and simply do not take the history of empirical Islamic states into account. While over time Islamic culture has spread to become dominant in a band extending across the northern portion of Africa, through the Middle East, up into Central Asia, down into northern India, and reaching to Indonesia and parts of the Philippines, this region is not and has never been empirically a single *dar al-islam* under a unified religio-political leadership. Rather, as Islam spread, indigenous rule developed apace—not as the exception, which the early independent caliphates in Spain and North Africa were when they came into being, but as the normal course of affairs.

To be sure, the juristic ideal of the unitary *dar al-islam* with leadership at once religious and political has deeply impressed itself on historical Muslim polities. Both major imperial states, like those of the Ottomans and the Safavids, as well as minor regional sultanates depended on the continuing popular expression of belief in this ideal for their position and power. Yet these cases are also interesting for their departures from the classical juristic ideal. One example is provided by Douglas Porch's description of the fealty of the population of the Tuat oasis complex in the Western Sahara to the sultan of Morocco around 1900. Porch writes as follows:

> Islamic notions of polity differed from European ones. Moslems drew no distinctions between spiritual and temporal power—as far as they were concerned, the two were inseparable. As a descendant of the Prophet, the sultan was regarded as a holy personage. They sent him gifts of fealty and mentioned him in their Friday prayers. For the Tuatans, there was no contradiction in acknowledging the sultan as lord and then refusing to pay his taxes. The important thing was to be included in the Dar al Islam—the House of Islam—of which, in the northwest corner of Africa, he was head. (Porch 1984, 212)

There is no reason to think this description of the Tuatans's position inaccurate. Yet while depending on claims to the traditional ideas of the universal *dar al-islam* under a unified religio-political leadership, the conception given here is different in important ways from that developed by the classical Islamic jurists. Despite the allusion to the conception of spiritual and temporal power as "inseparable," clearly in this case they were in fact quite separate. The *dar al-islam* here had become identified with the religion of Islam, with fealty to the "holy personage" of the Moroccan sultan, and with cultic observances—the Friday prayers. As for temporal power in the Tuat, the sultan had none; as Porch comments earlier in the same context, he "could neither garrison the Tuat nor collect taxes there." And it is notable that despite the implicit universality of the *dar al-islam* here, its empirical fragmentation was assumed; the sultan was its head only "in the northwest corner of Africa."

A second example is provided by the case of the Ottoman empire in its heyday—different from the case of the Tuatans in virtually every respect, yet still a departure from the juristic ideal. The early emperors sought consciously to connect their rule with that of the classical conception of the caliphate and to incorporate the *shari'a*, Islamic law, into the governance of the empire. Yet they proceeded from first establishing political control through the exercise of power, and their religious claims functioned to bolster their right to rule. The Ottoman sultans were not "holy personages" by blood; their claim to religious leadership was actually derived from their exercise of ruling power through the *ghaza* or holy war. To govern the empire they set in place two separate sets of laws and their associated administrations, one based on the *shari'a* and one entirely temporal, so that in practice the ostensibly unitary religio-political nature of the government of the empire actually proceeded through separate channels for the religious and the political or temporal. (See further Holt, Lambton, and Lewis 1970, vol. 1, part 3, 300–306, 320–22.)

The point is that while the historical development of indigenous Muslim states has continued to reflect the classical juristic conception of the *dar al-islam*, that conception has translated into polities quite different from the ideal formed by the jurists, and the traditional ideal has been honored at least as much in the breach as in the observance.

As an extension of the pattern of development of autonomous local states, today the Muslim portion of the world is, structurally, much like the non-Muslim part: divided into independent states whose forms of government are, for the most part, secular. In this context the case of Iran, prominent though it is, stands out as an exception, not a new norm. Indeed, even leaving aside the very problematic question of how faithful the actual government of Iran is to the traditional ideal, Shi'ite Iran is in many ways a difficult model for putative "Islamic" governments in Sunni countries. While Iran today is the source of much support for the overthrow of secular governments in Muslim states, Shi'ite doctrine from the beginning has regarded all non-Shi'ite governments as insufficiently religiously pure, and even the government of some of the earliest caliphs, the only Muslim rulers with any historical claim (though somewhat tenuous because of rebellions and conflict over the caliphal succession) to have exercised combined religio-political authority over a unified *dar al-islam*, was regarded as unjust by the Shi'ites. Shi'ite doctrine and history provide no reason to think that a contemporary Sunni "Islamic" government would receive better treatment.

The Classical Juristic Ideal and the "Universal" Islamic State

For Western readers the most accessible statement of the classical juristic ideal of statecraft is the *Siyar* (Law of Nations) of the Hanafite jurist Shaybani, written during the reign of the 'Abbasid caliph Harun al-Rashid around 800. This work is also one of the most important of its kind, drawing previous juristic treatments of statecraft together in a single work with a focus on the context of international affairs.

Shaybani lived early in what Khadduri (1966, 20) calls the "universal" period of the caliphal state, a period ushered in with the establishment of the 'Abbasid dynasty. Prior to this, Khadduri observes, during the rule of the Umayyads, Islamic society had largely retained an Arabian character and bias, dependent on the Arab tribes for its power and biased ethnically toward Arabs in such matters as taxation and service to the state. Nonetheless, the population balance was increasingly changing in favor of non-Arab Muslims, whose numbers grew along with the expansion of territory under Muslim control. The 'Abbasids, backed by elements within the religiously oriented Islamic community who stressed the universal religious character of Islam, reshaped policy and governance in this direction, recognizing the importance of the non-Arab Muslims alongside the Arabs. The 'Abbasid policy was important both internally and externally, contributing to controlling the disputes over authority and leadership that had ultimately led to the downfall of the Umayyads and establishing the idea of a universal Islamic community in which all races, linguistic groups, and cultures could in principle be brought as equal participants under a single tent (Khadduri 1966, 19–20).

Normative juristic theory developed under the 'Abbasids provided a religiously defended rationale and justification that complemented and supported the 'Abbasid approach to statecraft. The jurists attached this concept of the Islamic community to the Qur'anic ideal of Islam as a universal religion, representing the destiny of the Islamic state as they knew it to be that of the Islamic community itself, ultimately to include all of humankind. The actual increase of peace, order, and justice brought about by 'Abbasid rule was interpreted as manifesting the ideal state of affairs described by the Qur'an as characteristic of the Islamic community, the community where life is governed by submission to the will of God. The place of this community in history the jurists expressed theoretically through the division between the *dar al-islam*, the territory of peace, order, and justice, and the *dar al-harb*, the territory of conflict not yet in submission to the will of God for humanity. This conception was important, in context, as providing an alternative description of the Islamic community that was inclusive of Arabs and non-Arabs alike, not one based on tribal, ethnic, linguistic, or cultural differences. The inferiority of communities defined by these latter differences was underscored by their being associated with the plurality of communities in the *dar al-harb*, and the peace of the Muslim community was thus contrasted to the mutual hostility endemic to communities defined in these latter ways. In this conception only the Islamic state was recognized as truly legitimate, since only it was ordered according to God's law; other political entities, those of the *dar al-harb*, were considered illegitimate or even as not properly communities at all, since their nature was marked by failure to order themselves according to this law.

Yet in practice the Islamic state had to find ways to deal with other political entities outside its borders, however they were defined, whether to trade or otherwise coexist peacefully with them or to make war against them. A tension thus existed between juristic theory and the actual practice. Some jurists, especially within the school of Shafi'i, introduced a third category, that of the *dar al-sulh* or *dar al-'ahd* (the territory of peaceful arrangement or covenant), intermediate between the *dar al-islam* and the *dar al-harb*, as a way of resolving this tension theoretically. Shaybani's *Siyar* too reflects the need to work out a theoretical framework for dealing with non-Muslim political entities, whatever their ultimate legitimacy in Islam's understanding of God's will for the world. In his thought, though, which is typical of the Hanafi school and corresponds in fundamental matters to that of most other jurists of the period, those entities which had entered into agreements with the Muslim state and paid tribute to it were understood as assimilated to the *dar al-islam*. Entities that did not enter into such agreements and did not pay tribute as a sign of submission to Islamic authority were enemies to be dealt with however might be expedient by the *dar al-islam*. Both the Shafi'i and the Hanafi schools, then, agreed on the essentials: implacable enmity between the *dar al-harb* and the *dar al-islam* and identification of the caliphal state under the 'Abbasids as the empirical expression of the latter, unified under a single religio-political rule according to divine law and universal in its makeup and its destiny. (See further Khadduri 1966, 10–14, 23ff.)

The roots of the concept of *siyar* developed by Shaybani can be found in the works of earlier jurists, who treated relations with non-Islamic entities under the general heading of jihad; in these early conceptions the *siyar* is essentially limited to the law of war (Khadduri 1966, 39). Shaybani in effect turns the priorities around, developing his thoughts on the jihad of the sword within the context of an idea of *siyar* expanded to take into account the broader range of relations with non-Muslim polities.

Shaybani's reordering reflects the actual nature of the Islamic state during his lifetime—late in the eighth century and into the beginning of the ninth—as viewed from near the center of caliphal government: a widely spread but still highly unified empire whose relations with its neighbors ranged from peaceful and productive interaction to hostility and war. In the time of Shaybani jihad in the sense of war against the enemies of the faith was no longer propelled by the existential needs and fears of the early Islamic community, which knew genuine and almost universal hostility on its borders, and accordingly such jihad had moved away from being a life-and-death matter in the affairs of the Islamic state. In this historical context it is better understood as one among the tools available to the ruler for the purposes of statecraft. Indeed, jihad in the sense of war was a very useful tool for the ruler's purposes: since by religious tradition he was to wage jihad once a year unless prevented by circumstances (Lambton 1981, 208–9), the idea of jihad offered religious sanction to any war the ruler might determine to wage against an entity in the *dar al-harb*. With a wide variety of neighbors on the extended borders of the *dar al-islam*, the caliph could choose his target of opportunity from among a range of options, then initiate war against it within the framework of the idea of jihad and with the religiously sanctioned goal of bringing more of the *dar al-harb* into the *dar al-islam*. Alternatively, he could invoke defensive jihad against an aggressor neighbor, adding religious sanction to the political justification of self-defense. The goals of religion thus provided enhancement to the ends of the state, and religious motivations added to other reasons why a man might join the Islamic army.

Early Islamic Statecraft, the Juristic Ideal, and the Practice of Jihad

Turning now specifically to the relationship between Islamic statecraft and the practice of jihad against the non-Muslim world, the robust Islamic state honored in both theory and practice existed, for the jurists, both to defend the Muslim community and to spread the rule of divine law over new territories. It is important to take notice of the defensive aspect of the state. The significance of the state's defensive purpose for the jurists is clear from the extensive juristic discussion of such matters as the implications of peace treaties with non-Muslim states and the regulation of behavior of non-Muslims inside Muslim territory: rules covering "people of the Book" dwelling in the *dar al-islam* (who are required to pay the poll tax and to conduct themselves by their own laws, except where these contradict Islamic law), specifying terms for the granting of safe-conduct (*aman*) to inhabitants of the *dar al-harb* to permit their entering the *dar al-islam*, and governing the conduct of such *musta'min* while in the territory of Islam. Also defensive in nature are the discussions of the rights of the state in suppressing internal rebellion, whether civil or religious in nature. (In Shaybani's *Siyar*, for example, more than twice as much space is given to these subjects as to the subject of offensive war; see Khadduri 1966.)

If Islam had been conceived by the jurists as a religion of individuals who might live indifferently under various temporal rulers and not a religiously defined temporal community, the state would not loom so important in their thought. The same would be true if the classical tradition had conceived Islam as a religion of inwardness alone and not one of right behavior along with right attitude and belief. Functionally the jurists' definition of the Muslim community simultaneously in political and religious terms served to underscore the importance of religion as the defining ideology of the state. Once established, this linkage gave religion an implicit authority over affairs of state; yet at the same time, it also gave a political character to activities that otherwise might have developed as affairs of personal religious behavior alone. The understanding of jihad provides a case in point. As noted earlier, the root meaning of this word is "striving" (in the path of God), and the jihad of the sword is the lesser one by comparison with those forms of jihad carried on internally within the believer's own life. Yet nonetheless, in the context of the juristic understanding of statecraft, jihad as the warfare of the Islamic state became the preeminent vehicle by which Islam dealt with the sphere of unbelief, identified as the *dar al-harb*, the sphere of war. Whether defensive, to protect the Muslim community from threats to its well-being, or offensive, to extend the borders of the state or to amplify its resources, jihad was understood as serving political as well as religious ends. The usefulness of this idea of jihad for political undertakings, whether in the jurists' own time or subsequently, is undeniable.

As we have seen earlier, the authority to wage jihad according to classical Islamic tradition is lodged in the *imam*, the religious leader; he is to wage jihad against the territory of unbelievers once a year unless circumstances prohibit this. As we have also emphasized, the juristic model of government was a single, united religious-political rule over the entire Muslim community. On this model, historically the *umma* would have risen in offensive jihad yearly, led by its religio-political leader, for the purpose of spreading Islam into new territories until all the earth was eventually brought into the sphere of Islam. It is important to keep in mind that this was an ideal model, never quite matched by reality, though the expansion of territory governed by Muslim rulers, often through war or the threat of war, brought immense areas under their rule. From the time of the first successors to Muhammad their opponents argued that these caliphs were using the religious authority they had usurped to justify employing the military force of the Muslim community not to extend the faith but to consolidate their own position and to serve their own goals. In other words, they had co-opted the concept of jihad for their own ends, not the service of God.

Nor is this line of argument limited to Islamic critics of the caliphs and the caliphal system. Western scholarship too has often interpreted the consolidation and expansion of the territory under Islamic rule as preeminently political under the ideological cover of religion. For example, Rudolph Peters writes flatly, "Historical research . . . has proved that the wars of the Islamic states were fought for purely secular reasons" (Peters 1979, 4). A similar but somewhat less extreme judgment is expressed by Laura Veccia Vaglieri, in "The Patriarchal and Umayyad Caliphates" in *The Cambridge History of Islam*, where she argues that from within the perspective of Western scholarship the growth and expansion of the Islamic empire is first of all to be understood in political and economic terms, with religion playing a supportive role, though a role of great importance. Providing historical examples to back up this judgment, Vaglieri comments that while the initial rebellion against the first caliph, Abu Bakr, "acquired a certain religious character, . . . it was in reality mainly political," with the clear inference that the same judgment should be made about his use of military force to suppress the rebels (Holt, Lambton, and Lewis 1970, 1:58). Again, referring to the involvement of the bedouin tribes on the side of the caliph in the warfare against the settled communities of Iraq, this author writes that Islam "was the co-ordinating element behind the efforts of the bedouin and instilled into the hearts of the warriors the belief that a war against the followers of another faith was a holy war, and that the booty was the recompense offered by God to his soldiers" (1:60). The fundamental structure of bedouin warfare remained, however, that of raiding to collect booty.

Whatever the relationship of religion and politics here, this last passage cited by Vaglieri introduces another element in the normative understanding of jihad as religiously sanctioned war within Islamic tradition, the influence of the pattern of warfare engaged in not only by the bedouin but by settled Arabs as well: the *ghaza*, "razzia or raid." According to tradition, this was the character of the warfare between the Prophet and his enemies (Holt, Lambton, and Lewis 1970, vol. 1, part 1, chap. 2). Incorporation of the desert tribes into the purposes of statecraft by the Umayyads honored this pattern and further reinforced it as the normative understanding of warfare for the Muslim community. Thus the standard form of desert warfare, periodic raids by the nomadic tribes against one another and the settled areas, was transformed into a centrally directed military movement and given an ideological rationale. The conduct of this warfare, which provided a pattern for the later jurists' conception of how jihad should be conducted, was that of the bedouin raid institutionalized. This suggests why the extension of government to the conquered territories is ignored in Shaybani's *Siyar* and other juristic works, though detailed attention is given to the capture, repatriation, and disposition of slaves and other booty among the warriors. Of course, the caliphs' government was in fact regularly extended over the conquered territories, which were thereby added to the *dar al-islam*. But the bedouin tribes raided to collect slaves and booty, not to settle and govern, and the former is the picture of jihad known by Shaybani and other jurists of the classical era.

Fragmentation of the Islamic World and Opposition to the Crusades: The Idea of Defensive Jihad as a Tool of Statecraft

Despite the theoretical importance of the idea of jihad in classical Islamic juristic thought, this concept in fact did not occupy a controlling place in the actual statecraft of the 'Abbasid caliphs and their successors in their dealing with lands on the borders of their domains. In considerable part this correlates with the fact that they were increasingly occupied with challenges from Muslim rivals for leadership, particularly the Fatimids in Egypt, the Buwayhids in Persia, and the Seljuks, who came from Central Asia and established their own state in Anatolia, as well as other invaders such as the Mongols from the steppes. Political and economic control, not religious conversion, were also the major factors also through most of this period in the long-running conflict with the Byzantine empire, the major non-Muslim rival for control of the Middle East and Anatolia, whichever Muslim state was involved. Another principle laid down in Muslim tradition and system-atized in classical juristic thought governed the treatment of Christian and Jewish inhabitants of conquered Byzantine lands: as "people of the Book," they were not required to convert to Islam and were to be allowed to live according to their own religious practices under Islamic rule, so long as they paid the *jizya*, or poll tax, and in some cases the *kharaj*, or property tax. (Cf. Shaybani, secs. 1701–9, in Khadduri 1966, 275–78.)

Even the Crusades, which loom large as exemplifying holy war in Western tradition, were long assimilated by the Muslims to the pattern of warfare ongoing with the Byzantines. Bernard Lewis comments,

> It is noteworthy that in the vast Arabic literature of the period of the Crusades, the terms Crusade and Crusader are missing, and indeed seem to have no Arabic equivalents. For the Muslim historians, the Crusaders are always "the Franks," who at first came as barbarian auxiliaries of the Byzantines, and then branched out on their own. . . . [T]he new invaders, like the Turcomans and Seljuks from the East, seemed to be settling down in their new principalities, and to be ready to join in the complex and multipartite game of Syrian politics. (Holt, Lambton, and Lewis 1970, 1:197)

This attitude toward the Crusaders changed with the rise of Nur al-Din and Saladin, who fostered "a new mood of Holy War against the Christian invaders" (1:201) as a means of raising and sustaining the forces needed to drive them out. Both these Muslim leaders, however, had their own purposes for rule within the Islamic lands as well, and their wars against the Crusaders in Syria and Palestine can also be read in terms of those purposes. In particular, Nur al-Din's defeat of the Crusaders in the struggle for Damascus during the Second Crusade (1148) also succeeded in cementing his authority over Syria (1:200–201), and Saladin's conquest of Jerusalem and large portions of the Crusader kingdom in Palestine (1187–92) also served to open a line of communication between his base of power in Egypt and his new domain of Syria, taken over after the death of Nur al-Din (1:203–5).

The jihad against the Crusaders, then, was not the religiously motivated and authorized offensive warfare that the classical jurists had had in mind. As pursued under the leadership of Nur al-Din and Saladin this jihad defined a different normative model. It was, in first place, defensive in character, aimed at retaking lands once part of the core of the *dar al-islam*, rather than expansionist; thus it violated the classical assumption that the function of jihad would be always to extend the boundaries of the *dar al-islam* to new territory with the ultimate end of occupying all the earth. In second place, the jihad as waged by Nur al-Din and Saladin was closely tied up with their purposes as regional Muslim rulers; their campaigns were not warfare of the entire *dar al-islam* against the forces of unbelief. That Saladin's war in Palestine ended not with capitulation of the Crusaders but a treaty between the Muslim and Christian sides (Holt, Lambton, and Lewis 1970, 1:204) fits with the character of a war for limited territorial and political goals but not with the classical juristic concept of jihad by the Muslim community, which envisions an inevitable total victory by the Muslims and rules out the possibility of permanent treaties with non-Muslims (Shaybani, secs. 602ff., in Khadduri 1966, 154–57 and passim). And in third place, Nur al-Din and Saladin were temporal rulers who, though personally pious, had no credentials as the *imam* of which the classical jurists spoke. Their authority to lead such a jihad had to come from a different source. That source was the individual duty of every Muslim to defend Muslim religion and territory against unbelievers.

While not fitting the juristic conception of the offensive jihad, the warfare of Nur al-Din and Saladin against the Crusaders of the Second and Third Crusades established an alternative model for subsequent Muslim statecraft, that of the collective defensive war for the faith under the command of a local ruler but authorized by the individual duty of all Muslims. This model utilized the standard juristic position on defensive jihad but went beyond it in important ways. The jurists had recognized defense of the *dar al-islam* as an individual duty (*fard 'ayn*), so that anyone should respond to an attack on the *dar al-islam* even in the absence of a formal call to jihad by the *imam*, that is, the caliph. The kind of case the jurists clearly had in mind was that of an attack in progress, presumably on the borders of Islamic territory, which would need to be opposed immediately by whatever Muslims were at hand. While their fighting in such cases would be on their own authority, the individual Muslims involved should be assured that their action was a religious duty and exemplified jihad as fully as any formally declared by the caliph.

On the new conception of jihad associated in particular with Saladin the idea of the individual duty of defense of the *dar al-islam* is extended beyond reactions to attacks in progress. Rather, on the conception employed here, lands once Islamic are always properly part of the *dar al-islam* and Muslims are justified in retaking them as part of the individual duty of defense. Specific authorization by the supreme religious leader, the *imam* of the *dar al-islam*, is not needed for such jihad, for the authority to wage this war lies in the personal obligation of each and every Muslim to defend Islam against invaders. Thus secular rulers may take a leading role in organizing Muslim forces to take part in such conflict, but religious authorization for each soldier to fight comes from within his own faith. In this way the individual responsibility of all Muslims is made the basis of a collective undertaking organized and led by a chief. Thus the authority of such a leader is not the same as that of the *imam* of the *dar al-islam* as described by the classical jurists; nor is it derived from the delegated authority a regional *amir* (commander) possesses as a result of his appointment by the caliph. Rather than coming in such a manner from above, the authority to lead a jihad defined by the individual duty to defend the religion and territory of Islam wells up from below, from the common exercise of the individual duty of the leader himself and all his followers to defend Islam. This is a significant change in the concept of the justification and authority for jihad in the sense of war, a change which had an important effect in adapting the idea of such jihad to the realities of a fragmented and sometimes beleaguered Islamic world. The model thus defined is of particular significance for understanding many contemporary appeals to jihad as calls for violence in the defense of Islam.

Ghaza—War for the Faith—and the Origins of the Ottoman State

The original idea of jihad in the context of statecraft as developed by the classical jurists, offensive war to expand the borders of the *dar al-islam* as one form of the "striving in the path of God" required of all Muslims, is exemplified in the postclassical period not by the defensive wars to turn back the Crusaders but by the offensive practice of *ghaza* in the frontier wars of the Turcoman principalities of the thirteenth century (Osman Turan, in Holt,

Lambton, and Lewis 1970, 1:251–52; Halil Inalcik, *ibid.*, 263–64) and the rise of the Ottoman state (Holt, Lambton, and Lewis 1970, vol. 1, part 2, chap. 4). Of the culture of these principalities and the place of *ghaza* in them Halil Inalcik writes: "This culture was dominated by the Islamic conception of Holy War or *ghaza*. By God's command the *ghaza* had to be fought against the infidels' dominions, *dar al-harb* (the abode of war), ceaselessly and relentlessly until they submitted. . . . The actions of the *ghazis* [warriors for Islam] were regulated by the *Shari'a* to which they paid heed" (1:269).

Increasingly important among the Turcoman principalities were the Ottomans, led by figures such as 'Osman Ghazi, whose title indicates the nature of his leadership. "In 1354," writes Inalcik (1:270), "they told Gregory Palamas that the constant expansion westward of Muslim power was a predestined event reflecting the will of God. They considered themselves the sword of God."

The infidels in this case were Christian subjects of the Byzantine empire, and the practice of *ghaza* as offensive war for the faith of Islam against these infidels led to the expansion and consolidation of Turkish power not only in Anatolia but in the Balkans as well. The Ottomans also extended the *ghaza* to military control of the seas and of commerce (1:271). Their success against the Byzantines, joined to their sense of commitment to the spread of Islam, also served as the basis for a claim to leadership of the *dar al-islam* itself, thus establishing the foundation for the development of the Ottoman empire not only over the territory of the Byzantines but also over the lands ruled by the various caliphal dynasties: "The Holy War or *ghaza* was the foundation stone of the Ottoman state. . . . The Ottomans took in all seriousness the duty of protecting and extending Islam, and even tried to justify their claim to sovereignty over the whole Islamic world, by the argument that they alone were carrying out that duty" (1:283).

The climax of the Ottoman *ghaza* against the Byzantine empire, though warfare against Christian Europe went on for centuries longer, was the capture of Constantinople by the Sultan Mehmed II (The Conqueror) in 1453. This gave the Ottoman sultan the right to claim to be heir to all that the Byzantine emperors had claimed—lordship throughout the entire region over which the Roman empire had once extended. He understood this to include not only the regions already under his dominion but also those portions of the Islamic world once belonging to Imperial Rome and all of the Christian world as well (1:296–97). Thus his claim to authority included several complementary elements: his role as *ghazi*, the Islamic leader who above all others was engaged in carrying out the expansion of Islam by the jihad of the sword; the destiny of the *dar al-islam* eventually to cover all the earth; the title of caliph for all the Ottoman realm, which all the sultans had borne since Murad I in the late fourteenth century (1:320); and his assumption of the title of caesar and with it domain over all that Rome had ruled.

Mehmed the Conqueror, like the earlier Ottoman leaders, in practice identified the sultan's religious role with leadership of Muslim forces in war against non-Muslims, stressing the importance of holy war (*ghaza*, war for the faith) against the Christian forces of Byzantium and the West and styling themselves and their followers as *ghazis*, warriors for the faith (1:251, 263, 269–70, 283–86, 295). Particularly prominent leaders, such as 'Osman Ghazi and Mehmed II himself, bore the term *ghazi* as a personal title. But alongside their authority the *'ulema'*, the Islamic clergy, had their own role.

Within the Ottoman state as organized by Mehmed the Conqueror, two lines of responsibility extended downward from the person of the sultan through his grand *vezir*: that of the *defterdar*, responsible for the financial side of the administration, and that of the *qadi 'asker*, responsible for the administration of justice (1:302). Since the position of *qadi* was limited to Islamic clergy trained as jurists, this amounted to a structural incorporation of religion into the imperial rule and the assumption of religious authority by the sultan himself. At the same time, Mehmed did not establish a theocracy, a state over which the interpreters of the *shari'a* had absolute authority, or adopt the *shari'a* as the only law of his domains. Rather he and his successors claimed "the absolute right to promulgate state law without the intervention of the *Shari'a* jurists" (1:303). In fact, with respect to state law, the finances of the empire, and most relations with the outside world Mehmed the Conqueror and his successors conducted the affairs of the empire on an essentially secular basis.

Mehmed the Conqueror, his successors, and their apologists claimed for the Ottoman empire, as an ideology to support the sultans' rule and its expansion, the classical idea of the unified *dar al-islam* and its destiny to conquer the *dar al-harb*. The sultans' use of the title of caliph implied religious authority alongside that of secular leadership in their realms. Yet they sought broader recognition as preeminent in the entire Muslim world. Their method in securing such recognition was to tie Ottoman military and political successes to important Islamic traditions and religious functions. Most basic was their association with the *ghazi* tradition: through it the sultans "claimed to succeed the Prophet and the Patriarchal Caliphs as 'the best of *ghazis* and of fighters in the Holy War'" (Holt, Lambton, and Lewis

1970, 1:320, quoting Mehmed Ata's *Tarikh*, written in 1291). This was a powerful claim. On the one hand it associated the sultans with the *baraka* of the Prophet and his immediate successors, suggesting that the sultans too had been specially chosen by God for blessing. At the same time it tied the rule of the Ottomans, relative newcomers, to the very earliest period in the rise of Islam, thus setting in place an implicit challenge to the authority of the 'Abbasid caliphs, who though much in decline by this period could still root their claim to authority in descent from the Quraysh, the tribe of the Prophet.

A serious practical problem for Mehmed and his immediate successors was posed by the rival Mamluk sultans, who ruled Egypt, Palestine, the Hijaz, and Syria, had physical custody of the 'Abbasid caliphs, and bore the important title "Servitor of the Two Holy Sanctuaries." Some sixty years after Mehmed I, his successor Selim I (sultan 1512–20) solved this problem by overthrowing the Mamluk sultanate and extending Ottoman rule to the areas formerly under Mamluk control. To associate himself with the 'Abbasid tradition, Selim transported the Caliph al-Mutawakkil and the relics associated with the Prophet from Egypt to Istanbul. A late tradition, not confirmed by contemporary sources, has al-Mutawakkil transferring the supreme caliphate to Selim and his successors at this time. In fact Selim needed no such confirmation from the heir to the 'Abbasid caliphate. It was sufficient for his purposes to neutralize al-Mutawakkil as a rival focus of power; putting al-Mutawakkil in his capital city, directly under his control, ensured this. Functionally more important were other factors: Selim's association with the *ghazi* tradition, the power available to him and the vast extent of the lands under his rule, and his formal proclamation of himself as the protector of Mecca, Medina, and the pilgrimage routes. On this basis he claimed the obedience of all the other rulers of Islam, referring to his rule as the "Exalted Caliphate" (Holt, Lambton, and Lewis 1970, 1:320–21). Thus he passed on to his successor, Süleyman the Magnificent, a consolidated position as supreme ruler of Islam, possessing both political and religious authority.

In this way Selim wedded the *ghazi* tradition and the empire won by it to the classical juristic conception of the *dar al-islam* and the caliphs' right to rule over it as heirs to the Prophet. Yet the claim to authority based in the concept of the *ghazi* remained significantly different from that based in juristic tradition. This difference centered on the way the two traditions derived authority to rule over the *dar al-islam* from the Prophet: by line of succession through the recognized caliphs, according to the concept of legitimacy defined by the jurists; by demonstrably possessing the Prophet's *baraka*, according to the concept of legitimacy defined by the *ghazi* tradition.

The Ottoman practice of *ghaza* thus provides a third model of war for the faith and its place in statecraft alongside the jihad of classical juristic tradition and the jihad of Saladin. Like the model of war for the faith and authority to undertake such war derived from the example of Saladin, the model of such war and authority to undertake it derived from the *ghazi* tradition has considerable influence in contemporary Islamic understandings of statecraft.

Jihad, Authority, and Statecraft: Three Historical Conceptions

The above discussions identify three importantly different conceptions of the relation between religio-political authority in the Islamic world and the practice of jihad in the sense of warfare for the sake of religion by those possessing this authority.

First, there is the ideal description of caliphal authority and the unitary Muslim state found in the classical jurists, who themselves thought of this conception as deriving directly from the Qur'an and the traditions associated with the Prophet. On this conception the *dar al-islam* is ruled over by a single leader, the legitimate successor to Muhammad, who as *imam* of all Islam possesses the authority to lead the *dar al-islam* in offensive jihad against the *dar al-harb* and the responsibility to do so once a year, circumstances permitting. Also included in the classical conception of the ruler of the *dar al-islam* was the authority, acknowledged but not explored above, to wage jihad against internal troublers of the peace of Islam: bandits, heretics, apostates, and dissenters. Sunni thought developed the concept of the caliph, literally the "successor" of the Prophet, as the only rightful possessor of such unified religio-political authority within the Muslim world. Shi'ite juristic theory accepted the fundamental terms of a single *dar al-islam* with a single religio-political ruler at its head, but rejected the caliphate as illegitimate, putting in its place the concept of the Imam as alone the rightly guided successor of the Prophet. Like the Sunni conception of caliphal rule, the Shi'ite concept of rule by the rightly guided imams was defined in terms of a line of succession. Persons outside these respective lines of succession could not, by definition, assume the authority to lead all Islam. Both lines of succession have now been broken or suspended. For Sunnis this has led to alternative conceptions of the authority to rule and to engage in jihad, conceptions embodying the Saladin and *ghazi* models in various ways. The case of Shi'ism is theoretically stricter: with the occultation of the Twelfth Imam, no earthly ruler, according to Shi'ite doctrine, possesses the authority to wage offensive jihad, so that the only remaining option for jihad is defensive.

The second conception of jihad and the authority to lead jihad also derives from the classical jurists, both Sunni and Shi'ite, but took new form in the wars to turn back the Crusaders. This conception is associated historically with the heroic figures of Nur al-Din and Saladin, but actually the authority they possessed to wage jihad arose from the authority and responsibility of all Muslims, incumbent on every one as an individual duty, to defend the religion and territory of Islam against aggressors. The concept of such individual responsibility and the accompanying authority is defined in classical juristic thought. What was different in the conception of the leader's authority in the struggle against the Crusaders, and particularly in Saladin's war against the Latin Kingdom of Jerusalem, was that this Muslim leader put himself at the head of a jihad legitimized not by the authority of the caliph or *imam* of the Muslim community, but by the individual responsibility and authority of Muslims to oppose the Crusaders as aggressors against the *dar al-islam*. Their authority as leaders of jihad, that is, did not flow downward from the juridically correct authority of caliph or *imam* but upward from the religious and moral authority implied by the individual obligations of every Muslim. A second significant difference between the model of jihad defined here and that defined by the classical jurists was in the concept of the defense of the *dar al-islam*: this defensive concept of jihad aimed to recover territory once part of the core of the *dar al-islam* but lost to another power, while the jurists, not anticipating such an eventuality, conceived defense in terms of resistance to attacks in progress from the *dar al-harb* against the borders of the *dar al-islam*.

The third concept of jihad in relation to authority in the Islamic community, as identified above, is that of the *ghaza* tradition exemplified by the Ottoman sultans. Here the waging of *ghaza* itself confers authority on the *ghazi*, the warrior for the faith. Success in the *ghaza* implies the presence of the *baraka*, or blessing, of God and establishes the *ghazi* as a direct heir of the tradition that began with the Prophet and his immediate successors. This conception was at the core of the claim to religio-political authority by the Ottoman sultanate. As late as the eighteenth century, when the Ottoman state was in serious decline and apologists sought to bolster the sultan's authority by claiming that the 'Abbasid Caliph al-Mutawakkil had transferred all rights of the classical caliphate to the Sultan Selim I and his successors, a former *deftardar* of the empire penned a *Book of Counsel for Vezirs and Governors* in which he appealed to the importance of war for the faith: "Let not the preachers and [religious] advisers who are in the imperial army hold back from . . . proclaiming the benefits of the Holy War and inciting to *ghazza*" (Wright 1971, 127).

It is useful to highlight the most important similarities and divergences among these three models. Like the offensive jihad, which for the jurists could be declared only by the *imam* of the *dar al-islam*, but unlike the defensive jihad engaged in by Nur al-Din and Saladin against the Crusaders, *ghaza* was offensive warfare intended to spread Islamic rule. The concept of the authority possessed by the leader is different in all three cases: conferred by line of succession through the caliphs, according to the model of classical juristic tradition; conferred by the collective practice of the individual religious duty to defend the territory of Islam, according to the model of Saladin's war against the Crusaders; conferred by the *baraka* of the Prophet, as verified by the sultans' victories over unbelievers, according to the model of the *ghaza* tradition. Thus the two later models of jihad also provide important alternatives to the classical juristic tradition for understanding how legitimate rule might be understood within the framework of Islam after the break in the caliphal line and after the occultation of the Twelfth Imam.

Appropriating the Models for Jihad in the Modern Context

Applying the Idea of Jihad in Islamic Opposition to Colonialism

The classical juristic ideal of unified religio-political rule over a unitary Muslim state was never embodied even during the age when the jurists were composing their definitions of it. Still less is such a concept embodied in the political structures of the modern age. There is no supreme caliph; there is no *imam* for all Islam. The *dar al-islam*, whatever this term may mean as a symbol of the spiritual unity of all Muslims, is not in the contemporary world a single territory but is broken into many states, most of them avowedly secular. Shi'ite doctrine on the occultation of the last Shi'ite Imam implies that there has been no authority for offensive jihad in the world from the tenth century onward, and that there is none today (Sachedina, in Johnson and Kelsay 1990, 45). A Sunni, relying on classical juristic doctrines like that exemplified by Shaybani's *Siyar*, could easily argue the same way: there is no caliph to authorize offensive jihad, so there can be none. Indeed, Sunni modernists argue exactly this (Peters 1979, 127–30).

Yet claims for the right to wage jihad continue to be made, and they continue to have the power to call forth a response among persons who consider themselves faithful Muslims. Are these claims simply unwarranted? Are those persons who issue calls to jihad misguided, ignorant, or worse— opportunists or charlatans seeking personal advantage by cloaking their own cause in the aura of jihad?

No doubt some of this latter exists, but by the standard of the classical juristic ideal, it is not necessary to examine the motives of those who call for jihad today. By the classical standard, all calls for offensive jihad are wrong, since there is no *imam* of all Islam to authorize such a call. Only the possibility of defensive jihad remains, for the authority to wage such war is found in the duty of every individual Muslim to protect the religion and territory of Islam from attacks by aggressors from the *dar al-harb*. On this understanding collective defensive jihad is closely analogous to the Western concept of the *levée en masse*: a spontaneous uprising without leadership or organization.

As the above discussion shows, however, the classical juristic standard is not the only one to be found in Islamic tradition. There is also the concept of defensive jihad under Islamic leadership together with the expanded notion of the defense of Islam associated with Saladin's warfare against the Crusaders, and there is the argument that the successful waging of jihad implies the presence of divine *baraka*, which gives the leader of such warfare the authority to do so. Both themes are to be found in the jihad-warfare of the modern period, from the colonial era and the present day.

Bruce Lawrence, commenting on the appeal to jihad in colonial warfare, cites Douglas Porch's description of the Moroccan rebel leader (and pretender to the throne) el Hiba, who in July 1912 raised an armed challenge to the French Protectorate established in that country three months earlier:

> Tall, bearded, swathed in the blue cloth of the Sahara nomads, el Hiba's credentials as a resistance leader were impeccable. His father, Ma el Ainin, had achieved legendary status among his people for opposing the French in Mauretania. When Ma el Ainin died . . . , el Hiba had succeeded to his father's *baraka*. Once again it seemed that

the duty of the people of the trans-Atlas was to purify Dar el-Islam—to expel corrupt functionaries, annul taxes not sanctioned by the Qur'an and drive out the infidel. . . . [El Hiba's followers] trusted to the sanctity of their cause and the *baraka* of their chief. (Lawrence, in Kelsay and Johnson 1991, 148, quoting from Porch 1983, 258)

This description is interesting for several reasons. Lawrence comments, "His followers could . . . accept el Hiba as an initiator of jihad because he was, for them, the sultan" (Kelsay and Johnson 1991, 148). But this is a bit misleading. In a context in which the right of leadership did not automatically flow from father to son by right of primogeniture, el Hiba's authority to assume the mantle of sultan was a direct result of his being perceived as having inherited his father's *baraka*, a blessing conferred only by God. This authority was strengthened by his leadership of his people in war for the faith against corruption within Islam and against the invading infidels, the French. Not to do so, or to do so unsuccessfully, could undermine the assumption of a leader's *baraka*, as another example from Porch's history of the Moroccan conquest makes clear (Porch 1983, 70) and as el Hiba's own defeat in the face of superior French firepower illustrates (266–67). At the same time the jihad against the French, for el Hiba and his followers equally, was justified and authorized as a religious duty, a duty of all the people of the trans-Atlas as individual Muslims, and this duty gave them the right to rise up against the French whatever the results.

There is thus in Porch's description of el Hiba an evocation of both the postclassical traditions of jihad and authority to rule the Muslim community, the tradition of Saladin and that of the Ottoman *ghazis*. El Hiba led by virtue of his *baraka* but also by virtue of his doing what duty required: to oppose the infidel French and the implicit aggression against part of the territory of Islam. His followers followed him not only because of the *baraka* they believed he possessed but also because it was their own duty as Muslims.

The case of el Hiba is of course one of resistance in the name of Islam against colonial encroachment into Islamic lands. Rudolph Peters, examining Islamic resistance against colonialism in a variety of contexts, notes that these struggles produced a sizable popular literature on jihad that was aimed at mobilizing the Muslim populations to support the resistance efforts (Peters 1979, 105). Carrying the same argument a step further, Ann Mayer holds that the "Third World context" of much of Islam has generated an institutionalized anticolonial conception of jihad. "Contemporary discussions of jihad," Mayer writes, "now often assert that wars are justified in Islamic law when they are conducted to end exploitation and oppression by the superpowers or to achieve liberation from the forces of imperialism" (Kelsay and Johnson 1991, 205). The rationale for this line of argument is well stated by Peters, summarizing the position he associates with contemporary Muslim fundamentalists:

> The offensive aspect [of jihad] is that all states and governments will be resisted as long as they are based on principles contradictory to Islam. . . . The defensive aspects are, firstly, the self-evident fact that the present territory of Islam must be protected as a basis for expansion and, secondly, the fact that the Islamic movement protects Man against all factors that hinder his freedom and emancipation. (Peters 1979, 133)

Embedded in this reasoning is the concept of the authorization for jihad exemplified by the historical struggle of Saladin against the Crusaders—a coincidence magnified by the frequent pejorative references to "Crusaders" by contemporary radical Muslim advocates of revolutionary jihad, who associate any kind of Western influence with the Crusades. Fundamentally, though, the rationale is that the duty to protect Islam and the territory of Islam is every Muslim's, and that this universal duty is what gives particular spokespersons for revolutionary action the right to call for jihad. In doing so they are not claiming authority to declare offensive jihad, for this would be a usurpation of a right the classical tradition reserves to the *imam* of all the *dar al-islam*; rather, they are simply calling all Muslims to do their duty to defend Islam against attack.

Individual Duty and the Right to Wage Jihad

One of the characteristics of an ethics of duty is that the consequences for the actor are not factored into deciding what action should be taken and whether to take it. Though the consequences that follow from particular acts of duty may at times appear heroic and at other times tragic, the duty itself and not such possible results is what matters for the moral decision. The duty for individual Muslims to resist attacks against the religion and territory of Islam as spelled out in classical juristic tradition thus defines an approach to moral decision-making in which other sorts of moral norms may be abrogated and in which the actor's own temporal welfare becomes of no account. At the same time, if the duty is defined as reflecting a universal moral order, so that acting in accord with that duty will serve the universal order regardless of its effect on the actor or others in the immediate context of the act, then the actor may undertake the performance of the act in question with great confidence that any sacrifice by him or others affected by the act will be more than offset by the service of universal moral order. The overall structure of Islamic ethics is that of an ethics of duty in which each individual Muslim by submitting to God takes on the duty of acting according to God's will as revealed to the Prophet and through his life. More specifically, the ethics of duty as defined in Islamic juristic tradition has the form of an ethic based in divine commands, where the human duty is to act in accord with those commands (cf. Kelsay 1994). Such a concept of the source of ethical duty tends to intensify the responsibility to act ethically: the duties the moral agent seeks to serve are not abstract but intensely personal responsibilities, put in place by the relationship between God and the individual when that individual affirms Islam.

Juristic tradition in Islam serves to identify the actual duties implied by the state of *islam*, submission to God, and to set these duties in relation to one another so that in any given context the potential for conflict among duties is removed. *Ijtihad*, "interpretation," historically provided the vehicle for doing this, and differences in interpretation defined the various juristic schools. The coming into being of the schools and their restriction of the right to engage in *ijtihad* to interpreters qualified by knowledge and standing in the Islamic community meant that *ijtihad* was not an activity in which ordinary Muslims were to engage. Classical juristic theory limited the right to engage in *ijtihad* to the *'ulama* or community of clergy and prescribed rules for this activity. But the tendency was to close down the possibilities for innovation even among those qualified to perform *ijtihad*. For the magisterial jurist al-Shafi'i *ijtihad* was "not a right but a privilege, even among the *'ulama*" (Piscatori 1986, 6). Beginning by the tenth century the possibilities of innovation were sharply limited (7). For practical purposes, then, in the arena of individual behavior the matter of the duties incumbent on each Muslim was settled by this time, and in hard cases the individual was not to decide alone but to seek a ruling from someone qualified to give it, ideally a *qadi* (judge) or *mufti* (specialist in giving legal opinions). In remote areas the local *'alim* (member of the *'ulama*) would often fulfill this role, but would be limited by the established standards.

The above paragraph greatly compresses and simplifies the historical

debates and developments surrounding how to understand the nature of
Islamic revelation in the form of law, rules for behavior, and the proper scope
for interpretation of such law. (For fuller discussion, see Piscatori 1986,
1–21.) My purpose here, though, is not to provide a full discussion of these
topics but to indicate how the development of juristic tradition affected the
scope of individual ethical reflection and moral decision-making. In this
context Islamic ethics, though founded on a concept of individual duties, did
not imply freedom for each individual to determine how, when, and in what
way to carry out those duties.

Because of the limits on the scope of individual initiative the model of
jihad associated with Saladin did not in historical context translate into a
justification for individuals or groups of individuals, on their own account,
to initiate jihad of the sword against enemies they determined to be aggressors against Islam. Rather that model applied only to actions such as el
Hiba's rebellion, justified by the *fard 'ayn* of el Hiba himself and each of his
followers but necessarily headed by someone already recognized to occupy a
leadership role in the Muslim community. Individual Muslims had no right
to interpret the scope of their own duty to defend Islam in such a way.

For various reasons, however, the historical limitations on the right of the
individual Muslim to interpret the requirements of divinely imposed duty for
personal action have loosened in the contemporary context. Piscatori expresses this in terms of change in the concept of who may engage in *ijtihad*:

> The [contemporary] proponents of *ijtihad* have had one purpose in
> mind: to make Islam relevant to the demands of the modern world
> and, in this way, to defend it against the West. In doing so, they have
> been less concerned with procedure than with results. In conse-
> quence, it is not clear at all who can exercise *ijtihad*, when, or by what
> rules, even as important modifications of the law have taken place in
> its name. We are left to conclude that this "neo-*ijtihad*" is more
> amorphous than the old one, but . . . infinitely more permissive
> and available for use. In effect, what was seen as a privilege is now
> seen as a right. (Piscatori 1986, 8–9)

The examples Piscatori cites as results of this change are in personal ethics,
specifically the laws of marriage. Yet I suggest that the change in understanding the role of the individual in interpreting the requirements of Islamic
ethics also bears on the development of revolutionary groups and activities
in the name of jihad. Let me provide two examples, one illustrating the

traditionally acceptable appropriation of the Saladin model of jihad, the other illustrating an appropriation of this model based on individual reasoning.

The first is the case of the Iranian government's use of suicide units of volunteers against the Iraqi army in the Iran-Iraq war. Lightly armed or bearing no arms or personal defenses at all, such units were sent out against heavily armed Iraqi positions, often defended by minefields. Authorized and called into being by the religious and political authorities in postrevolutionary Iran, these units depended on the willingness of the volunteers to act on their individual duty to oppose the Iraqi forces, which they understood (as did the religious leadership) as engaged in a secular attack against the Islamic Republic of Iran, the immediate presence of the *dar al-islam*. That following this duty might lead to individual martyrdom was not to be feared; indeed, death was to be embraced if it resulted from participation in the jihad this duty required against the Iraqi aggressor. Conforming to the model of defensive jihad described by Sachedina as the only form of jihad allowable in the contemporary world according to Shi'ite doctrine, this type of action also conformed to the model of collective, yet individually duty-based, jihad associated with the historical warfare of Saladin against the Crusaders.

Consider by contrast the argument posed in *The Neglected Duty* (*Al-Faridah al-Gha'ibah*, also known as "the creed of Sadat's assassins"), and the revolutionary movement it justifies (Jansen 1986, Appendix). Though the perceived threat to Islam against which this argument sets the duty to wage jihad is domestic—rulers of Islamic states themselves judged to be unfaithful to Islam—rather than foreign, the argument is a straightforward one from individual duty to jihad (secs. 50, 65ff.; Jansen 1986, 183, 190ff.). In order of priority, the jihad is first to set right the government of Islamic states ("the enemy who is near") even before the liberation of Jerusalem. The author's description of how this is known provides a clear example of the reasoning that runs throughout *The Neglected Duty*: individual Muslims know it immediately in themselves by virtue of being Muslims.

> It is said that the battlefield of *jihad* today is the liberation of Jerusalem, since it is (part of) the Holy Land. It is true that the liberation of the Holy Land is a religious command, obligatory for all Muslims, but the Apostle of God—May God's peace be upon Him—described the believer as "sagacious and prudent" (*kayyis fatin*), and this means that a Muslim knows what is useful and what is harmful,

and gives priority to radical definitive solutions. (Sec. 68; Jansen 1986, 192)

By this reasoning each Muslim has not only the individual duty to wage jihad against threats to Islam but also the individual competence to choose which of many threats he or she is to direct such jihad against. It is not necessary to wait for the leadership of the Muslim community to determine which threats are to be opposed by violence and to raise the call to fight against such threats—all the more important since some of those leaders are themselves the source of some of the threats. Identifying the threats, prioritizing them in order of the danger posed, determining the response, and carrying it through are, for the author of *The Neglected Duty*, all within the power of the individual true Muslim as "sagacious and prudent."

In this the model of jihad associated historically with Saladin is utilized but importantly transformed. The argument of *The Neglected Duty* begins in the same place as that of this historical model: with an expanded conception of the defense of Islam that concentrates on recovering what once was Islamic and has been lost to unbelievers. Yet whereas the model associated with Saladin focused on the duty to recover lost Islamic lands, the argument of *The Neglected Duty* does not put even the recovery of Jerusalem in first order of priority for its jihad; rather that first priority is to recover the government of Islamic states from leaders who are perceived as having themselves taken those states out of the *dar al-islam*. "There is no doubt that the first battlefield for jihad is the extermination of these infidel leaders and to replace them by a complete Islamic Order" (sec. 70; Jansen 1986, 193). And simultaneously the authority to lead such jihad is transferred from the leadership of the Muslim community to the individual Muslim. Thus both the justification and the authority for jihad are changed importantly, though the basic model remains. We should remember that the origin of the model of jihad associated with Saladin arose as a way of providing for jihad in the absence of leadership by the caliph. In the contemporary world there is no longer any caliph, and the leadership of Muslim states may be itself suspect. In this context the argument of *The Neglected Duty* may be understood as a radicalization of the idea of jihad in defense of Islam on the basis of individual duty, a radicalized conception by which individuals acting alone or in groups providing mutual support themselves take on the role of initiating and conducting the jihad of the sword, so that each *mujahid* is in effect his own Saladin.

The Incorporation of the *Ghazi* Model:
Dealing with the Problem of Legitimacy

The two examples sketched above, the Iranian use of unarmed or lightly armed volunteers as martyr brigades in the war against Iraq and the so-called "creed of Sadat's assassins," illustrate the broad range of contemporary Islamic appropriation into political action of the model of jihad associated with the historical figure of Saladin. The latter also raises the considerable problem of legitimacy confronting the leaders of present-day Islamic states and, indeed, those states themselves. For this reason the Saladin model often does not stand alone (as it does in the two examples just treated) but alongside that of the *ghazi*, the warrior who gains legitimacy by proving his *baraka* through success in jihad.

The Saladin and *ghazi* models are, in terms of the ethics they embody, diametrical opposites. While the Saladin model is based on individual duty, the *ghazi* model depends on reasoning from consequences. In other words, *ghaza* is shown to have been justified only if the *ghazi* is victorious. El Hiba and other anticolonial leaders of the nineteenth century, such as 'Abd al-Qadir in Algeria and Muhammad Akhmad, self-proclaimed to be the Mahdi, in Sudan, fit the *ghazi* model better than contemporary leaders of Islamic jihad movements, if only perhaps because they had rather more success in establishing political entities under their rule. The obvious problem with this conception of the relation between jihad and authority is that it is wholly dependent on results: if one proclaims jihad and fails, one obviously did not possess the requisite *baraka*. Yet the only way to find out is to try.

By contrast, the tradition associated with Saladin rests on a common duty, one that must be observed whatever the short-term results. But either approach to the relation of jihad and authority within the Muslim community offers a corrective to the dead-end contemporary implications of the classical juristic ideal of jihad. How does one know today, when there is no caliph, no *imam*, and no universal Muslim state, whether or when there is legitimate authority in the world for leadership in the waging of jihad by faithful Muslims? The tradition built on the example of the Ottoman *ghazis* relies on a pragmatic test. It says, try it and see; if it works, then divine *baraka* was present and the leader's rule is approved by God. The tradition built on the example of Saladin relies instead on an individual and collective consciousness of duty. It does not matter whether success flows in the short term; God will triumph in the end.

Linking these two postclassical models of jihad makes for a somewhat uneasy conception of ethics, but such a link can be most useful for political purposes. If a leader goes to war under the cover of jihad, he can claim that success proves his possession of *baraka* and thus the legitimacy of his leadership, while if he loses he can claim that he was only fulfilling the general duty of all Muslims even in the face of superior power and thus bolster the image of his piety.

In recent history the case of Saddam Hussein's call for jihad against the coalition forces gathering to drive his occupying army out of Kuwait provides perhaps the most interesting effort to tap simultaneously into both these streams of historical Muslim tradition on jihad and authority to rule. This was, in the tradition of Saladin, a call to fight against the presence in Islamic territory of the Western military forces which made up the backbone of the coalition. That this very presence constituted aggression against Islam was Saddam's message, and though through Western eyes this appeared no more than a cynical appeal to religion for his own purposes, in the context of Muslim history and culture in the Middle East it had a different symbolic value. As John Kelsay comments, "Once [Saddam Hussein] spoke of Iraq's confrontation with coalition forces as a jihad, the Gulf War came to involve prestige, moral authority—even religion. . . . Saddam Hussein did not have to be religious, or even a particularly moral man, to make effective use of symbols that suggest the highest ideals and motivations of people in the Middle East" (Kelsay 1993, 12–13).

At the same time, it was important as well that the same people who were swayed by the appeal to the idea of defensive jihad perceived Saddam as having succeeded in this fight against the superior military forces of the West. Hence even after losing decisively on the battlefield he went out of his way to depict himself in terms of what he and his forces had accomplished: attacking Israel directly, maintaining power, and retaining strong military forces, so that the loss could be claimed to be temporary only. Thus the *ghazi* tradition regarding jihad and political authority was honored, though stretched well beyond anything the eminently successful Selim or 'Osman Ghazi might have recognized.

The Idea of War for Religion as a Response to the Problems of Contemporary Statecraft

As the these examples show, the historical models of jihad and political authority associated with Saladin's resistance to the Crusaders and the Ottoman *ghazis'* extension of the borders of Islam by force bear importantly on contemporary Islamic political debate and decision-making. At the same time, the formal framework for Islamic statecraft continues to be that erected by the classical juristic schools, according to which there is a single *dar al-islam*, simultaneously religious and political in nature, so that right leadership must satisfy criteria both of true religion and of political effectiveness. In the face of this still-powerful traditional conception there is a tendency for each individual Muslim state to identify itself and its government with the jurists' *dar al-islam*. Thus, for example, in describing how the state of Pakistan and its government should be constituted, Masudul Hasan, working out of the theory of Maulana Mawdudi, postulates that because "the basic political principle of Islam is Tauhid," that is, unity, "this means that an Islamic State must be a unity" (Hasan 1988, 156). Its leader may not bear the title of caliph, but his function is the same as that of the historical caliphs, and the qualifications for the head of an Islamic state are the very same ones, mingling religious and political elements, laid down by Ibn Khaldun in the Middle Ages (137–42). At the same time, as James Piscatori notes, the Islamic world has embraced territorial pluralism within the *dar al-islam* (Piscatori 1986, chap. 3); indeed, as has been observed above, such pluralism has characterized Islamic politics from very early in the history of Islam.

This pluralism complicates the problem of jihad in its relation to statecraft. Rather than there being a single religio-political leadership able to authorize a collective jihad on the part of the entire community of the *dar al-islam*, there are multiple leaders embodying different relationships between the religious and the secular, and there are multiple entities instead of one unitary *dar al-islam*. The historical models of jihad associated with Saladin and the Ottoman *ghazis* originally appeared as earlier responses to a disjunction between the official theory of the jurists and the reality of the political life of Muslim states. That they remain relevant to Islamic statecraft in the present day suggests the perennial nature of this disjunction.

While from the perspective of the West the idea of jihad as an element in statecraft is deeply problematical, threatening, and even offensive, from within the framework of traditional Islam it provides a way of linking the problems of contemporary statecraft—notably, the plurality of states, the need for a way to demonstrate political legitimacy, and the perceived threat posed by the West—to the classical conception of the *dar al-islam*, its leadership, and its relationship with the *dar al-harb*.

CONCLUSION

To carry on a conversation across different cultural traditions it is necessary to find ideas, concerns, and other points of commonality close enough and substantial enough to support the building of bridges of mutual understanding between them. For conversation between normative Western and Islamic cultures on war for religion, this requires beginning in the past, with the roots and sources of the two traditions and classical forms of historical expression attaching to the idea of war for religion in each of the traditions. I have attempted to do this by focusing on three shared issues: when is war for religion justified, what is the location of authority for such warfare, and what limits, if any, are to be observed in its conduct. In discussing these issues I have sought to show the implications the idea of holy war has had for the conduct of statecraft. Some additional comments are in order on the implications of these traditions of holy war for statecraft as it is conducted under the system of modern international law.

The regulation of war as an element in relations between and among nations has in the modern period become a major element in international law. Within this framework offensive warfare as a means of settling disputes between states is outlawed, and no place is allowed for the propagation of religion by force. By the standard of contemporary statecraft established in positive international law, the only justification for force between states is self-defense. The Western rejection of war for religion fits well into this legal framework, but so, indeed, does the classical Islamic juristic model of jihad of the sword, for today, according to that model, only war in defense of Islam is allowed. The *ghazi* model of jihad, which is offensive in character, does not. The claim to be fighting in defense, however, is also subject to the test of proximity of the threat. Both the classical Sunni and Shi'ite positions pass this test, since they envision defensive jihad as response to an immediate threat. The broader conception of defense at the root of the model of jihad associated with Saladin is, however, problematical: if possession of a territory at one time in the past justifies retaking it under the name of defense when circumstances allow, then there is no spot on earth free of the possibility of a grievance. Contemporary Muslim evocations of this rationale for jihad of the sword thus fail the test of immediacy of the threat, an important requirement of the concept of defense in contemporary international law on war.

Another issue raised for the practice of statecraft by contemporary international law on war is that of the proper conduct of war. This is a particularly sensitive issue between the West and Islam, since calls for jihad have often been associated with acts of terrorism (much of the war against Israel and the West's support of Israel), seemingly senseless self-sacrifice (suicide bombings, Iran's martyr brigades), and violent revolution (the assassination of Sadat, violent fundamentalist Islamic revolutionary movements in Egypt, Sudan, Algeria, and even Saudi Arabia). Yet the idea of jihad in Islamic tradition cannot be reduced to such acts, and many Muslims would condemn them in terms of Islamic tradition as having nothing to do with the broader requirements of jihad, struggle in the path of God. There should be space within the dialogue between the West and the Muslim world to find common ground in rejecting such forms of violence while still recognizing the centrality of the jihad idea to Muslim religious identity.

The remaining issue is that of the authority for war. International law resolves this question by reference to the modern doctrine of the state, but the question of the legitimacy of rule over the state is left up to the states themselves. As we have seen, the *ghazi* model of jihad was historically the expression of a quest for legitimacy, and it poses a temptation for contemporary Muslim rulers whose right to rule on other grounds is slim to nonexistent. The rejection of the *ghazi* model implicit in international law's outlawing of offensive war restrains this way of seeking to prove legitimacy, but it is for Muslim political communities themselves to solve the problem of legitimate political authority.

While Western tradition has rejected war for religion, it continues to be shaped by influences framed in the debate over the place of such war in the moral understanding of statecraft. The secular form of modern Western culture incorporates a great deal of this presence. For Islamic tradition on war for religion and the conduct of statecraft, the terms are essentially reversed: the importance of the classical conception of the *dar al-islam* from which comes the idea of the state, legitimate political authority, jihad in the sense of war, and relations with other political entities tends to overshadow the actualities of Islamic history. For both, there is need to move toward a better balance: for the West, to recognize and come to terms with the importance of religion in the shaping of attitudes and behaviors in the framework of the political community; for Islam, to recognize and come to terms with the possibilities already realized throughout much of Islamic culture through most of its history, a statecraft able to find its own way, working with the principles and concerns of Islamic religion but not bound by a particular dogmatic conception of them. In such greater balance lies the possibility of fruitful dialogue.

NOTES

Chapter 1: Two Cultures, Two Traditions

1. Franciscus de Victoria is the Latinized version of this author's name as used in the reference cited. Victoria is also often cited by the Spanish version of his name, Francisco de Vitoria. Cf. James Brown Scott's classic study, *The Spanish Origin of International Law* (1934), which has the subtitle *Francisco de Vitoria and His Law of Nations* but in the text alternates between the Latin "Victoria" and the Spanish "Francisco de Vitoria."

2. On this development in Western thought on the *jus in bello* from the medieval to the modern period see Johnson 1981.

3. The rejection of war for religion by Western culture early in the modern period did not in fact eradicate totalistic forms of warfare from Western practice. While a century and a half of limited warfare followed the end of the Thirty Years War, the French Revolution ushered in a new form of justification for total war, one based on appeal to secular rather than religious ideologies, and new styles of war which in principle involved all the citizens of a belligerent nation. The Swiss military historian and theorist from the age of Napoleon, Baron Antoine de Jomini, linked "wars of opinion," that is, "wars originating in religious or political dogmas," together with "national wars," describing them as follows: "They enlist the worst passions, and become vindictive, cruel, and terrible" (Jomini 1862, 22). What Jomini meant by "national wars" was a new form of unlimited warfare: partisan warfare by an entire people against an invading army, exemplified for him by the Spanish popular campaign—also called "guerilla" or "little war"—against Napoleon's army during the Peninsular War. Such warfare was especially dangerous (Jomini calls it "the most formidable of all") because it raised passions and eroded the combatant-noncombatant distinction and because the partisans could not be counted on to observe conventions of restraint established between regular armies (Jomini 1862, 22–29). Not long after Jomini another conception of "national war," also reflecting the wars of Napoleon, appeared in Carl von Clausewitz's *On War* (Clausewitz 1976). For Clausewitz "national war" was the kind of warfare that Napoleon waged, war that brought to bear the entire resources of the nation. Napoleon, in Clausewitz's opinion, understood far better than anyone else of his time both the stakes of war and the means necessary to realize them. The result, as Clausewitz described it, was a practice of war that brought to bear on the enemy the utmost force of which the nation was capable to carry on the war "without respite until the enemy succumbed" (Clausewitz 1976, 580). Such warfare closely approached, for Clausewitz, his theoretical ideal

of "absolute war." (For further discussion of Jomini, Clausewitz, and the rise of totalistic war in the Napoleonic period see Johnson 1981, 237–56.)

The issues identified here have continued to arise in later wars. While the Hague Convention of 1907 (Roberts and Guelff 1989, 48) provided a set of rules that sought to regularize partisans, irregular warfare of various sorts has continued to challenge and erode the legal and moral restraints on the practice of war. What Jomini called "wars of opinion" have been reconfigured in terms of appeal to nationalistic and transnationalistic ideologies (e.g., Nazism, Communism, and even liberal democracy) (cf. Johnson 1981, 256–67). The American Civil War and the two world wars can fairly be described by the same terms Clausewitz used for Napoleon's practice of war.

The upshot is that the Western rejection of warfare for religion strikes only at one part of the problem of totalistic warfare, one of the possible sources of justification and authority for total war. Western culture has dealt with this by defining the efforts to limit the resort to war and the practices allowable in war in secular terms that are intended to be universal in scope. By definition and history, war for religion is prominent among the totalistic forms of war thus outlawed, and any invocation of religious justification or authority for a conflict sets off a warning: this opens the door to total war.

4. This is the period during which the effective breakup of the 'Abbasid empire accelerated. Essentially independent rule over certain regions of the empire distant from Baghdad began much earlier, however: 756 for 'Abd al-Rahman in Cordova, 788 for the Idrisids in Morocco, 799 for the Aghlabids in Tunisia.

5. It may be argued that Byzantium, also a Christian culture, bore the brunt of conflict with Islam far longer and more directly than Western Europe. Nonetheless, this experience has nothing to do with the present comparative inquiry. Byzantine Christian culture never developed a tradition on war for religion either in the sense of the Islamic idea of jihad or in the sense of the holy war idea which developed in the West (cf. Oikonomides 1995, 62–67). Further, this Western tradition developed independent of influence from Byzantium. Furthermore, the conflict between the West and Islam has been importantly shaped by the historical experience of the interaction of these two cultures during the modern period, and by the response of each of the two cultures to modernity itself. This book is not about the historical interaction between Christian and Islamic cultures in general, but rather a thematic comparative study of two traditions on religion, statecraft, and war—traditions with deep implications for the interrelation between the two cultures involved in the present. In the actual inquiry on which this book is focused the experience of Byzantium has no place.

Chapter 3: Holy War and the Question of Justification

1. Walters (1973) summarizes the official rationale for the Crusades as directly comparable to the rationale for just wars for nonreligious reasons, as in the following comparison of just causes for the two kinds of war (Walters 1973, 590):

Nonreligious just wars	Religious just wars (Crusades)
Defense of the fatherland	Defense of the Holy Land
Aid to allies	Aid to the Eastern church
Defending the right of innocent passage	Defending the right of missionaries to preach freely
Defense of the innocent	Defense of Christian converts
Punishment of wrongs done to society	Punishment of wrongs done to the church or to God

For a view that, by contrast, focuses on motivational factors in the early Crusades, linking them to various changes in medieval European society, see H.E.J. Cowdrey in Murphy 1976, 9–32.

2. I have elsewhere (Johnson 1975, chap. 2) examined more broadly the Continental influences on the development of English holy war thought. These influences differed at different periods. Bullinger and Allen reflect an early stage in the English debate, where the focus was clearly doctrinal; Bullinger's contribution reflected not only his own Continental experience but his Reformed theology. While theological and doctrinal influences continued, later in the English debate other kinds of influence were added, notably the direct experience of Englishmen who participated in the Continental religious wars and publication in England (and in English) of books about the wars by both English and Continental authors.

3. The concept of the *levée en masse*, though based in the individual's private right of self-defense, was differentiated from spontaneous popular uprisings in that the *levée en masse* had to be ordered by the governing authority of the political community in response to invasion (cf. Jomini 1862, 26, and Lieber 1862, 15). Similarly, in discussions of the right of the Islamic state to wage *jihad* in the absence of the conditions for offensive *jihad* (that is, for Shi'ites after the occultation of the twelfth Imam and for Sunnis after the end of the unitary *dar al-islam* marked by the caliphate), the juristic tradition placed authority for such war at the level of individual obligation, though the jurists clearly thought of defensive *jihad* as fought not by individuals acting alone but under the leadership of the Islamic state.

Chapter 4: Authority to Make Holy War

1. This account is a greatly compressed summary of a far more complex reality, though it is accurate as a general account reflecting what has for some time been the standard view. The reality was considerably messier. First, there were real geographical differences among regions: feudalism was not the same, for example, in Germany or England as in France, and Italy was different from all three. Second, the degree to which regional nobles actually honored their theoretical obligations to their feudal overlords varied greatly, even in highly feudalized areas. To take a prominent example, one of the contributing factors to the origin of the Peace of God movement in France (discussed further in the following chapter) was the inability of the French king to prevent regional nobles from fighting among themselves for various kinds of advantage. Third, conflicting obligations to different feudal lords were not uncommon; through titles and property ownership received from different sources a single individual might be the vassal of two rival lords, owing fealty to both despite their rivalry. Fourth, the situation changed over time, gradually becoming more orderly as feudal superiors were able to bring their vassals into line and as the central authority of kings increased. For a variety of perspectives on the temporal social structure, its relation to the practice of war, and its relation to the ecclesiastical structure see Contamine 1984; Delbrück 1982, bks. 2 and 3; Nicholas 1992, parts 3 and 4; and Reynolds 1994.

Chapter 5: The Conduct of Holy War

1. This paragraph summarizes four centuries of quite complicated development in Western moral doctrine on war, which include contributions from canon law, theology, the rediscovered idea of *jus gentium*, chivalric ideals and practices, and evolving customs and practices of statecraft. This section as a whole focuses on one segment of that process, the churchly, as it relates to the conduct of war for religion, but is still a summary treatment suitable to the context of the present book. I have elsewhere examined this process of development in Western moral doctrine in fuller detail: see Johnson 1975, chap. 1, and 1981, chap. 5; and cf. Russell 1975, chaps. 3–5.

2. Whether and to what degree the Crusades were an element in the church's effort to reduce the level of violence within Europe has been the subject of considerable debate among medieval historians. For an overview of this debate and references to some of the principal arguments see Bull 1993, 21–23; cf. Bull's own perspective on the relation between the Peace of God and the First Crusade in Bull 1993, 56–69.

3. A general Truce of God was promulgated for all Christendom by the Third Lateran Council in 1179, but the Decretalists, in various ways, explained it away or limited it severely. See Russell 1975, 183–86.

WORKS CITED

Abou El Fadl, Khaled. 1990. "*Ahkam al-Bughat*: Irregular Warfare and the Law of Rebellion in Islam." In Johnson and Kelsay 1990, 149–76.

Abraham, A. J., and George Haddad. 1989. *The Warriors of God*. Bristol, Ind.: Wyndham Hall Press.

Ahmad, Hazrat Mirza Tahir. 1990. *Murder in the Name of Allah*. Rev. Ed. Cambridge: Lutterworth Press.

Ali, Moulavi Cherágh. 1977. *A Critical Exposition of the Popular "Jihad."* Karachi, Pakistan: Karimsons.

Allen, William Cardinal. 1583. *A True, Sincere, and Modest Defence of English Catholiques*. London.

Bainton, Roland. 1960. *Christian Attitudes toward War and Peace*. Nashville, Tenn., and New York: Abingdon Press.

Barber, Richard. 1970. *The Knight and Chivalry*. New York: Charles Scribner's Sons.

Barnes, Thomas. 1626. *Vox Belli, or An Alarme to Warre*. London.

Best, Geoffrey. 1980. *Humanity in Warfare*. New York: Columbia University Press.

Blankinship, Kjalid Yahya. 1994. *The End of the Jihad State*. Albany: State University of New York Press.

Bull, Marcus. 1993. *Knightly Piety and the Lay Response to the First Crusade*. New York: Oxford University Press.

Bullinger, Henry. 1849. *The Decades*. Ed. Thomas Harding. Cambridge: Cambridge University Press.

Butterworth, Charles E. 1986. *Philosophy, Ethics, and Virtuous Rule*. Cairo: The American University in Cairo Press.

———. 1990. "Al-Farabi's Statecraft: War and the Well-Ordered Regime." In Johnson and Kelsay 1990, 79–100.

Cadoux, C. John. 1982. *The Early Christian Attitude to War*. New York: Seabury Press.

Clark, Sir George. 1958. *War and Society in the Seventeenth Century*. Cambridge: Cambridge University Press.

Clausewitz, Carl von. 1976. *On War*. Princeton: Princeton University Press.

Contamine, Philippe. 1984. *War in the Middle Ages*. Oxford: Basil Blackwell.

Delbrück, Hans. 1982. *History of the Art of War within the Framework of Political History*. Vol. 3, *The Middle Ages*. Westport, Conn.: Greenwood Press.

Denny, Frederick Mathewson. 1985. *An Introduction to Islam*. New York: Macmillan; London: Collier Macmillan.

Donner, Fred M. 1991. "The Sources of Islamic Conceptions of War." In Kelsay and Johnson 1991, 31–69.

Al-Farabi. 1961. *Fusul al-Madani: Aphorisms of the Statesman*. Ed. and trans. D. M. Dunlop. Cambridge: Cambridge University Press.

Galston, Miriam. 1990. *Politics and Excellence: The Political Philosophy of Al-farabi*. Princeton: Princeton University Press.

Goldhizer, Ignaz. 1981. *Introduction to Islamic Theology and Law*. Princeton: Princeton University Press.

Gouge, William. 1631. *Gods Three Arrowes: Plague, Famine, Sword*. London.

Grotius, Hugo. 1949. *The Law of War and Peace (De Jure Belli ac Pacis)*. Trans. Louise R. Loomis. Roslyn, N.Y.: Walter J. Black.

Hasan, Masadul. 1988. *Reconstruction of Political Thought in Islam*. Lahore, Pakistan: Islamic Publications.

Hindley, Geoffrey. 1971. *Medieval Warfare*. London: Wayland Publishers.

Holt, P. M., Ann K. S. Lambton, and Bernard Lewis, eds. 1970. *The Cambridge History of Islam*. 2 vols. Cambridge: Cambridge University Press.

Huntington, Samuel P. 1993. "The Clash of Civilizations?" *Foreign Affairs* 72 (Summer): 22–49.

Huntington, Samuel P., et al. 1993. *The Clash of Civilizations? The Debate*. New York: Council on Foreign Relations.

Ibn Khaldun. 1967. *An Introduction to History: The Muqaddimah*. Trans. Franz Rosenthal. London: Routledge and Kegan Paul.

Jansen, Johannes J.G. 1986. *The Neglected Duty: The Creed of Sadat's Assassins and Islamic Resurgence in the Middle East*. New York: Macmillan; London: Collier Macmillan.

Johnson, James Turner. 1975. *Ideology, Reason, and the Limitation of War*. Princeton: Princeton University Press.

———. 1981. *Just War Tradition and the Restraint of War*. Princeton: Princeton University Press.

———. 1987. *The Quest for Peace: Three Moral Traditions in Western Cultural History*. Princeton: Princeton University Press.

Johnson, James Turner, and John Kelsay, eds. 1990. *Cross, Crescent, and Sword: The Justification and Limitation of War in Western and Islamic Tradition*. Westport, Conn.: Greenwood Press.

Johnston, Douglas, and Cynthia Sampson, eds. 1994. *Religion: The Missing Dimension in Statecraft*. New York: Oxford University Press.

Jomini, Antoine Henri Baron de. 1862. *The Art of War*. Philadelphia: J. B. Lippincott. Reprint. Westport, Conn.: Greenwood Press, n.d.

Kelsay, John. 1990. "Islam and the Distinction between Combatants and Noncombatants." In Johnson and Kelsay 1990, 197–220.

———. 1993. *Islam and War: A Study in Comparative Ethics*. Louisville, Ky.: Westminster/John Knox Press.

Kelsay, John, and James Turner Johnson, eds. 1991. *Just War and Jihad: Historical and Theoretical Perspectives on War and Peace in Western and Islamic Traditions*. Westport, Conn.: Greenwood Press.

Khadduri, Majid. 1955. *War and Peace in the Law of Islam*. Baltimore: Johns Hopkins University Press.

———. 1966. *The Islamic Law of Nations: Shaybani's Siyar*. Baltimore: Johns Hopkins University Press.

Lambton, Ann K. S. 1981. *State and Government in Medieval Islam*. Oxford: Oxford University Press.

La Noue, François, Sieur de. 1587. *The Politicke and Militarie Discourses of the Lord de la Noue*. London.

Lawrence, Bruce. 1991. "Holy War (*Jihad*) in Islamic Religion and Nation-State Ideologies." In Kelsay and Johnson 1991, 141–60.

Leighton, Alexander. 1624. *Speculum Belli Sacri: or the Looking Glass of the Holy War*. N.p.

Lieber, Francis. 1862. *Guerilla Parties, Considered with Reference to the Laws and Usages of War*. New York: D. van Nostrand.

MacIntyre, Alasdair. 1981. *After Virtue*. Notre Dame, Ind.: University of Notre Dame Press.

———. 1988. *Whose Justice? Which Rationality?* Notre Dame, Ind.: University of Notre Dame Press.

McDonough, Sheila. 1985. *Muslim Ethics and Modernity*. Waterloo, Ont.: Wilfrid Laurier University Press.

Mehmed, Sari Pasha. 1971. *Ottoman Statecraft: The Book of Counsel for Vezirs and Governors*. Trans. Walter Livingston Wright, Jr. Westport, Conn.: Greenwood Press.

Mosse, George L. 1957. *The Holy Pretence*. Oxford: Blackwell.

Murphy, Thomas Patrick, ed. 1976. *The Holy War*. Columbus: Ohio State University Press.

Nicholas, David. 1992. *The Evolution of the Medieval World*. London and New York: Longman.

Noth, Albrecht. 1966. *Heiliger Krieg und Heiliger Kampf in Islam und Christentum*. Bonn: Ludwig Röhrscheid Verlag.

Oikonomides, Nicholas. 1995. "The Concept of 'Holy War' and Two Tenth-Century Byzantine Ivories." In Timothy S. Miller and John Nesbitt, eds., *Peace and War in Byzantium*. Washington, D.C.: The Catholic University of America Press. Pp. 62–86.

Oman, Charles. 1924. *A History of the Art of War in the Middle Ages*. 2 vols. Boston: Houghton Mifflin.

Painter, Sidney. 1940. *French Chivalry: Chivalric Ideas and Practices in Medieval France*. Baltimore: Johns Hopkins University Press.

Peters, Rudolph. 1979. *Islam and Colonialism: The Doctrine of Jihad in Modern History*. The Hague: Mouton.

Piscatori, James P. 1986. *Islam in a World of Nation-States*. Cambridge: Cambridge University Press.

Porch, Douglas. 1983. *The Conquest of Morocco*. New York: Alfred A. Knopf.

Previté-Orton, C. W. 1952. *The Shorter Cambridge Medieval History*. 2 vols. Cambridge: Cambridge University Press.

von Rad, Gerhard. 1991. *Holy War in Ancient Israel*. Grand Rapids, Mich.: William B. Eerdmans. Originally published as *Der Heilige Krieg im alten Israel*. Göttingen: Vandenhoek & Ruprecht, 1958.

Rahman, Fazlur. 1966. *Islam*. Second Edition. Chicago: University of Chicago Press.

Reynolds, Susan. 1994. *Fiefs and Vassals: The Medieval Experience Reinterpreted*. New York: Oxford University Press.

Roberts, Adam, and Richard Guelff, eds. 1989. *Documents on the Laws of War*. 2d ed. Oxford: Clarendon Press.

Russell, Frederick H. 1975. *The Just War in the Middle Ages*. Cambridge: Cambridge University Press.

Sachedina, Abdulaziz A. 1988. *The Just Ruler (al-sultan al-'adil) in Shi'ite Islam*. New York: Oxford University Press.

Salmon, J.H.M. 1959. *The French Religious Wars in English Political Thought*. Oxford: Clarendon Press.

Schaff, Philip, and Henry Wace, eds. 1896. *A Select Library of the Nicene and Post-Nicene Fathers*. Second series, vol. 10. New York: Christian Literature; Oxford: Parker.

Schwarzenberger, Georg. 1967. *A Manual of International Law*. 5th ed. London: Stevens and Sons.

Scott, James Brown. 1934. *The Spanish Origin of International Law*. Oxford: Clarendon Press; London: Humphrey Milford.

Sivan, Emmanuel. 1985. *Radical Islam: Medieval Theology and Modern Politics*. New Haven: Yale University Press.

Sonn, Tamara. 1990. "Irregular Warfare and Terrorism in Islam." In Johnson and Kelsay 1990, 129–47.

Swift, Louis J. 1970. "St. Ambrose on Violence and War." *Transactions and Proceedings of the American Philological Association* 101:533–43.

———. 1973. "Augustine on War and Killing." *Harvard Theological Review* 66:369–83.

Vaglieri, Laura Veccia. 1970. "The Patriarchal and Umayyad Caliphates." In Holt, Lambton, and Lewis 1970, 57–103.

Vanderpol, Alfred. 1919. *La Doctrine scolastique du droit de guerre*. Paris: A. Pedone.

Verkamp, Bernard J. 1988. "Moral Treatment of Returning Warriors in the Early Middle Ages." *The Journal of Religious Ethics* 16:223–49.

Victoria, Franciscus de. 1917. *De Indis et De Jure Belli Relectiones*. Ed. Ernest Nys. Washington, D.C.: Carnegie Institute.

Walker, Williston. 1959. *A History of the Christian Church*. Rev. ed. New York: Charles Scribner's Sons.

Walters, LeRoy B. 1973. "The Just War and the Crusade: Antitheses or Analogies?" *The Monist* 57 (October): 584–94.

Walzer, Michael. 1965. *The Revolution of the Saints*. Cambridge: Harvard University Press.

———. 1985. *Exodus and Revolution*. New York: Basic Books.

Weeks, Albert L. 1993. "Do Civilizations Hold?" *Foreign Affairs* 72 (September/October): 24–25.

Wright, Robin. 1985. *Sacred Rage: The Crusade of Modern Islam*. New York: Linden Press/Simon & Schuster.

Wright, Walter Livingston, Jr. 1971. *Ottoman Statecraft: The Book of Counsel for Vezirs and Governors of Sari Mehmed Pasha, the Defterdar*. Princeton: Princeton University Press, 1935. Reprint. Westport, Conn.: Greenwood Press.

INDEX

'Abbasid caliphate, 18, 48, 98, 135, 138, 143–45, 148, 154, 156, 174 n. 4
Abou El Fadl, Khaled, 37, 177
Abu Bakr, 115, 147
Abu Hanifa, 68–69, 70, 115, 116, 122, 124, 126, 145
akham al-bughat, 38, 64
Ali, Moulavi Cherágh, 20, 36, 51, 61, 178
Allen, William Cardinal, 57–58, 175 n. 2
Ambrose, Saint, 79, 80, 86
Aquinas, Thomas, Saint, 52, 53, 133
Augustine, Saint, 48–52, 54–56, 73, 79, 80, 86, 110, 132, 133
authority for war, idea of, 22–23, 25, 26, 37–42, 43, 44, 55, 71, 77–99, 129, 130–37, 147–57, 170–71, 175. See also *imam*, Imam, *jus ad bellum*

baghi, 64, 67
Bainton, Roland, 33, 34, 45, 101
baraka, 42, 155, 156, 158–59, 165–66
Barber, Richard, 35, 101, 107, 177
Best, Geoffrey, 14
Blankinship, Kjalid Yahya, 20, 178
Bull, Marcus, 104–5, 176 n. 2, 177
Bullinger, Heinrich, 57–58, 175 n. 2
Butterworth, Charles, 73–74

caliph, caliphate, 93–99, 115, 135–40, 143, 147, 148, 153, 155, 157, 158, 175. *See also* 'Abbasid caliphate, *imam*
Cambridge History of Islam, 20, 90, 94, 98,

134, 138, 139, 140, 142, 147–48, 149, 150, 151–52, 153–54, 178
canon law, 81, 82, 86–87, 105, 107, 108, 110, 176 n. 3
chivalry, 109, 110–11
City of God. See Augustine
civilizations, importance of, 2, 4–9
civitas dei, 48–52, 68, 81, 132–33
civitas terrenae, 48–52, 68, 132–33
colonialism, 24, 157–60
community, idea of, 1, 16, 17, 26, 47, 74, 91. See also *umma*
compétence de guerre, 14, 113
conduct of war, idea of, 26–27, 43, 45–46, 71, 101–27, 129, 175. See also *jus in bello*
Contamine, Philippe, 104, 107, 178
Crusades, crusaders, 16, 20, 23, 33, 34, 37, 38, 50, 52–56, 79–82, 101, 102, 103, 105, 107, 109, 111, 125, 148–50, 156, 158, 160, 167, 174–75 n. 1, 176 n. 2; idea of, 30, 31, 33, 35, 45
"Cuius regio, ejus religio," 12
culture: as influencing normative traditions, 6–25, 18–25; Islamic, 15–25; Western, 10–15, 2–25

Dante Alighieri, 55, 133
dar al-harb, 39, 48–52, 60–75, 90, 92, 97, 98, 116, 121, 122, 123, 124, 125, 126, 139, 144–45, 146, 152, 153, 155, 158, 168

dar al-islam, 24, 39, 40, 48–52, 60–75, 90, 92, 112, 121, 122, 123, 124, 126, 133, 138, 139, 140, 141, 142, 143, 144–45, 146, 150–51, 153, 154, 155, 156, 157, 160, 163, 167, 168, 171, 174
da'wa, 36, 70–71, 116
Donner, Fred, 90

El Hiba, 158–59, 162
Enlightenment, 1–4, 7

al-Farabi, 72–75, 140
fard 'ayn, 63, 92, 150–51, 160–64
fard kifaya, 62, 92
feudalism, 85–86, 103–12, 175

ghaza, 151–55, 156, 157
ghazi, 152, 153, 154, 155, 156, 159, 165–66, 167, 169, 170
ghazw, 90
Goldhizer, Ignaz, 134, 136, 138, 178
Gouge, William, 58
Gratian, canonist, 52, 53, 86, 105, 108
Grotius, Hugo, 13–14, 45, 55, 63, 69, 114, 126–27

hadith, 22, 23, 24, 35, 117, 135. *See also* Muhammad, Prophet
Hanafi school. *See* Abu Hanifa
Harnack, Adolf, 40
Hundred Years War, 107
Huntington, Samuel P., 2, 4–6, 7, 8, 18

Ibn Rushd (Averroes), 119
Ibn Tamiyya, 17
ijtihad, 161–62
imam, 40, 62, 64, 65, 71, 91, 92, 93, 96, 122, 123, 140, 147, 150, 151, 155, 156, 157, 158, 160
Imam, in Shi'ism, 36, 66, 94–95, 98, 155, 156, 157, 175 n. 3
international law, 23, 169–71, 174 n. 3
Iran-Iraq war, 163

Jesus, 25
jihad, vii, viii, 18, 19–20, 25, 29, 30, 31, 35–39, 60–75, 90–93, 101, 115, 116, 122, 123, 124, 125, 127, 145, 146–68, 169–71, 174 n. 5, 175 n. 3
Johnston, Douglas, 3

juristic tradition, Islamic, 23, 24, 25, 38, 48–52, 60–75, 89–99, 101, 115–27, 133–51, 160–62, 175
jus ad bellum, viii, 13, 14, 43, 103, 105
jus in bello, viii, 14, 43, 102, 104, 110, 111, 112, 113, 114, 116, 173 n. 2
just war, vii, 11, 13, 23, 25, 42–46, 51, 52–54, 73, 102
justification of war, idea of, 26, 37–42, 43, 44, 48–75, 77, 129, 169–70, 174. *See also jus ad bellum*

Kelsay, John, ix, 15, 33, 37, 39, 44, 59, 116, 119, 138, 158, 159, 160, 161, 165
Khadduri, Majid, 20, 39, 48, 51, 52, 62, 63, 64, 67, 68–72, 115, 116, 118, 138, 179
khalifa. See caliph
khariji, Kharijites, 67, 135, 137

Lambton, Ann K. S., 62, 63, 64, 65, 91, 145
Lawrence, Bruce, ix, 158–59
laws of war, 14
levée en masse, 63, 158, 175 n. 3
Lewis, Bernard, 18, 149
Luttwak, Edward, 3

MacIntyre, Alasdair, 2, 6–9
mahdi, mahdism, 41, 95, 98
al-Malik, 115
Marsilius of Padua, 55, 133
al-Mawardi, 64
Mayer, Ann E., 15, 159–60
Muhammad, Prophet, 22, 24, 25, 35, 67, 71, 89, 90, 91, 93, 94, 95, 116, 117, 118, 119, 122, 125, 133, 135, 137, 138, 139, 141, 148, 154, 155, 156
mujahid, and derivatives, 64, 70, 74. *See also ghazi*

Neglected Duty, The, 163–64, 178
New Testament, 53, 56, 103
noncombatancy, noncombatant immunity, 117–25. *See also* Peace of God
Nur al-Din, 149–50, 157

Old Testament, 33, 34, 37, 38, 39, 40, 41–42, 56, 57–59, 86
Orientalism, 21–22
Ottomans, 23, 27, 98, 141, 142, 151–55, 156, 167

pacifism, 23, 25, 78
Peace of God, 103–7, 108, 109, 176 n. 2
"people of the Book," 51, 66, 67, 118, 146, 149
Peters, Rudolph, 20, 36, 39, 40, 41, 52, 62, 91, 98, 147, 158, 159, 160, 180
Piscatori, James, 138, 139, 161, 162, 167, 180
political community. *See* community, idea of
political realism. *See* realism, political
politics, sphere of, 1–4, 10, 15, 16, 23, 47
Porch, Douglas, 20, 41, 141, 158–59, 180
Previté-Orton, C. W., 37
Puritans, Purtianism, 31, 37–38, 39, 46, 57–60, 101, 114

qital and derivatives, 35–36, 61–62, 70, 90
Qur'an, 22, 23, 24, 35, 36, 61–64, 70, 89, 90, 93, 95, 97, 116–17, 119, 133, 135, 138, 144

von Rad, Gerhard, 34, 37, 39, 40, 41–42, 180
Rahman, Fazlur, 89, 90
realism, political, 2–4
Reformation, Protestant, 12, 31, 33, 38, 56, 57–60, 98, 101, 102, 112–15, 133
regalian episcopacy, 84–85, 86
religion, Christian, 10, 11–15, 18–25, 48–60, 77, 78–89, 103–15, 130–32, 136
religion, Islamic, 15–25, 48–52, 60–75, 77, 89–99, 115–27, 132–37
religion, sphere of, 1–4, 10, 15, 16, 23, 47
ridda, 64, 67
Rubin, Barry, 3
Russell, Frederick H., 79, 81, 82, 86, 87, 107, 108

Sachedina, Abdulaziz A., 20, 36, 39–40, 63–64, 65–66, 94, 96, 97, 138, 158, 163, 180
Saddam Hussein, 166
Saladin (Salah al-Din), 149–51, 155, 156, 157, 158, 159, 160, 161, 163, 164, 165, 166, 167, 170

Sampson, Cynthia, 3
Schwarzenberger, Georg, 14
secular state, idea of, 16, 24, 65, 91, 170
siyar, 68–72, 116, 117, 122, 143
al-Shafi'i, 72, 115, 144, 145, 161
shari'a, 142, 152, 153. *See also* juristic tradition, Islamic
al-Shaybani, 39, 52, 66, 67, 68–72, 116–19, 121, 122–24, 125, 126, 127, 138, 143–45, 146, 148, 149, 150
Shi'ism, 18, 35, 36, 37–38, 63–64, 66, 94–99, 133, 135, 136, 138, 143, 155, 157, 163, 170, 175 n. 3
Sivan, Emmanuel, 17, 20, 180
Sonn, Tamara, 16–17
state, 1, 4, 5, 10, 12, 13, 16
statecraft, viii, 1, 10, 23, 75, 77, 129–68, 169–71
sultan, 141–42, 152–54, 156, 157, 158
Sunni tradition, 18, 36, 37–38, 64–65, 66, 72, 95–99, 133, 138, 140, 143, 155, 158, 170, 175 n. 3

Thirty Years War, 13, 31, 55, 88, 101, 113, 127, 173 n. 3
traditions, importance of, 6–25
Truce of God, 103–4, 107–8, 109, 176 n. 3
"two-worlds" concept, 48–52, 54–56, 65–68, 69–70, 130–37. See also *civitas dei*, *civitas terrenae*, *dar al-harb*, *dar al-islam*

umma, 91, 92, 147

Victoria, Franciscus de, 11–12, 45, 58, 69, 173 n. 1
Vitoria, Francisco de. *See* Victoria

Walker, Williston, 37, 54, 79, 82, 181
Walters, LeRoy B., 34–35, 43, 53, 174 n. 1, 181
warrant, idea of. *See* justification
weapons, limits on, 104, 108–9, 124
Weeks, Albert L., 5, 181
Wright, Robin, 20, 30–31, 35, 181